SCIENCE AND METAPHYSICS

International Library of Philosophy and Scientific Method

EDITOR: TED HONDERICH

A Catalogue of books already published in the
International Library of Philosophy and Scientific Method
will be found at the end of this volume.

SCIENCE
and
METAPHYSICS

Variations on Kantian Themes

---

by

WILFRID SELLARS

ROUTLEDGE & KEGAN PAUL: London
HUMANITIES PRESS INC.: New Jersey

First published 1968
Reprinted in 1982 in the
United States of America by
Humanities Press Inc. and in England by
Routledge and Kegan Paul Ltd.

England ISBN: 0 7100 3501 2
U.S.A. ISBN: 0 391 02621 6

Manufactured in the United States of America

CONTENTS

PREFACE

The invitation to give the John Locke Lectures provided the challenge, and the award of a Reflective Year Fellowship by the Carnegie Corporation the opportunity, to present in systematic form the views I have developed and modified in paper after paper over the past twenty years.[1] The result of this challenge and this opportunity is the present book. It is my hope that in addition to standing on its own feet as a piece of sustained argument, it will provide a framework within which the above mentioned papers will gain in intelligibility and show their family resemblance.

Six lectures have become seven chapters by the addition, as Chapter V, of a study of the specific traits of empirical truth which, taking its point of departure from an earlier essay on the correspondence theory of truth,[2] was presented in schematic form at a meeting of the British Association for the Philosophy of Science on May 23, 1966. This chapter, the third in a series on the conceptual and the real, adds, in my opinion, a decisive step to the series of attempts I have made over the past ten years to evaluate the comparative claims to reality of the 'manifest' and 'scientific' images of what there is. Unless I am very much mistaken, the argument of this chapter also provides that missing ingredient, the absence of which from Peirce's account of truth leaves the 'would-be' of the acceptance 'in the long run' of propositions by the scientific community without an intelligible foundation; a fact which has obscured the extent to which this gifted composer of variations on Kantian themes succeeded in giving metaphysics a truly scientific turn.

[1] A representative selection of these papers was published in this series under the title *Science, Perception and Reality*, London, 1963.
[2] 'Truth and "Correspondence",' *Journal of Philosophy*, 59, 1962; reprinted with minor alterations in *Science, Perception and Reality*.

vii

Preface

In a sense this book is a sequel to my essay on 'Empiricism and the Philosophy of Mind'[1] which was originally presented at the University of London in 1956 under the title 'The Myth of the Given: Three Lectures on Empiricism and the Philosophy of Mind'. In preparing the present book for publication, I have deliberately avoided extensive revision of the spoken text, limiting myself to the stylistic changes required by transposition to the printed page. It has been my repeated experience that when I write directly for a reading public a different 'control' takes over, resulting, I am told, in an involution of ideas which parallels the flower in the crannied wall. In the case of the London lectures the strategy of keeping textual changes to a minimum proved successful. If it works half as well on the present occasion I will be more than satisfied.

The argument of the book can be described as follows:

Chapter I combines a sympathetic but critical account of Kant's attempt to disentangle the respective roles in experience of sensibility and understanding, intuitions and concepts, with an independent discussion of the issues involved. I argue that many of the confusions of his treatment of Space and Time can be traced to a failure to do justice to the complexities of the distinctions required, but that when they are more adequately drawn they maintain their Kantian flavour, and that when his views are correspondingly reformulated they are substantially correct. The heart of the chapter is a clarification and defence of the Kantian concept of a 'manifold of sense'.

In Chapter II I explore Kant's distinction between 'appearances' and 'things in themselves' and argue that it is so basic a feature of his philosophy that if it is ignored or misinterpreted little remains but a fancy-dress costume for quite unKantian, if fashionable, ideas. In the course of the argument I defend, with reservations, the thesis that the world of 'ordinary experience' (the 'manifest' image) is, in the Kantian sense, phenomenal. This theme is picked up again in Chapter V after a closer look at the theory of mental acts or representations which underlies Kant's distinction between existence as appearance and existence in itself.

---

[1] *Minnesota Studies in the Philosophy of Science*, Volume I, edited by Herbert Feigl and Michael Scriven, Minneapolis, 1956, pp. 253–329; reprinted as Chapter 5, in *Science, Perception and Reality*.

Preface

In the third chapter I develop in detail the account of 'intentionality' which was sketched in 'Empiricism and the Philosophy of Mind' and defended in a lengthy correspondence with Roderick Chisholm.[1] Among other things, this chapter provides, as I see it, the cash for a long standing promissory note concerning the non-relational character of 'meaning' and 'aboutness', a thesis I have long felt to be the key to a correct understanding of the place of mind in nature. It also offers an analysis of the sense in which overt behaviour can provide 'logically adequate criteria' for mental episodes, which avoids the Scylla of logical behaviourism and the Charybdis of the synthetic a priori. The concepts of 'semantical rule' and 'semantical uniformity' are examined, and it is argued that the temptation to construe all linguistic 'acts' as *actions* has played a destructive role in attempts to interpret the relation of language to thought.

The fourth chapter is devoted to an analysis of the concept of truth which, in my opinion, integrates the formal results of Tarski and Carnap with the richer account which must be given of the role of 'meaning' and 'truth' as categories in the philosophy of mind. I attempt to show, in the spirit of the latter Brentano, that the appearances discriminated by careful phenomenology in the Platonic tradition can be saved without too much affront to 'extensionalistic', 'nominalistic' and 'naturalistic' sensibilities.

The fifth chapter is, as already indicated, the heart of the enterprise. In it I attempt to spell out the specific differences of matter-of-factual truth. Levels of 'factual' discourse are distinguished and shown to presuppose a basic level in which conceptual items as items *in rerum natura* 'represent' or 'picture' (in a sense carefully to be distinguished from the semantical concepts of reference and prediction) the way things are. The distinctions drawn enable a definition of 'reality' and '(ideal) truth' in terms of *adequate representation*. It is argued, that although in no simple sense does truth admit of degrees, there is more to the Idealistic conception of 'degrees, of truth and reality' than has been thought possible in recent years.

In the sixth chapter some of the implications of Scientific Realism for the philosophy of mind developed in Chapter III are

[1] This correspondence, with an introductory essay by Chisholm, was printed as an appendix to Volume II of the *Minnesota Studies in the Philosophy of Science*, Minneapolis, 1957.

explored. The discussion prepares the way for the final chapter by concluding that unless and until the 'scientific realist' can give an adequate explication of concepts pertaining to the recognition of norms and standards by rational beings his philosophy of mind must remain radically unfinished business.

Chapter VII[1] on objectivity and intersubjectivity in ethics is, consequently, the keystone of the argument, for the lectures have stressed at every turn the normative aspects of the concepts of meaning, existence and truth. Yet this chapter can be read separately as an attempt to exhibit the, to me at least, astonishing extent to which in ethics as well as in epistemology and metaphysics the fundamental themes of Kant's philosophy contain the truth of the variations we now hear on every side.

---

[1] A substantial part of this chapter originally appeared as the 1967 Lindley Lecture (*Form and Content in Ethical Theory*), © by The Department of Philosophy University of Kansas, and is reprinted by permission.

I

SENSIBILITY AND
UNDERSTANDING[1]

1. The history of philosophy is the *lingua franca* which makes
communication between philosophers, at least of different points
of view, possible. Philosophy without the history of philosophy,
if not empty or blind, is at least dumb. Thus, if I build my discussion of contemporary issues on a foundation of Kant exegesis
and commentary it is because, as I see it, there are enough close
parallels between the problems confronting him and the steps he
took to solve them, on the one hand, and the current situation
and its demands, on the other, for it to be helpful to use him as a
means of communication, though not, of course, as a means only.
In their most general aspect both his problems and our per-
plexities spring from the attempt to take both man and science
seriously.

2. Although my aim in these lectures is ambitious, to discuss in
a systematic way issues in the philosophy of nature and the philosophy of mind in its practical as well as theoretical aspects (can
they be separated?), this discussion in the nature of the case must
be a *Prolegomenon* rather than a *Critique*, let alone a series of *Criti-
ques*. The initial steps must, as always, be humble, concerned with
basic concepts and distinctions, which, since they do not have
the authority of the natural light of reason, are to be tested or
'proved' by the illumination they provide, and the coherence of
the story they make possible.

[1] Quotations from the *Critique of Pure Reason* are taken from Norman Kemp
Smith's translation, and references to the text are given in parentheses with the
customary 'A' and 'B' for the first and second editions.

I

3. One of the most striking features of Kant's epistemology is his insistence on the need for a sharp distinction between sensibility and understanding. 'Our knowledge,' he tells us (A50; B74), 'springs from two fundamental sources of mind; the first is the capacity of receiving representations (receptivity for impressions), the second is the power of knowing an object through these representations (spontaneity [in the production of] concepts). Intuitions and concepts constitute, therefore, the elements of all our knowledge . . .' In spite of this radical difference in role, both sensibility and understanding are construed as, in a broad and ill-defined sense, faculties of representation. It is this, perhaps, which leads him to suggest (A15; B29) that they may 'spring from a common, but to us unknown, root'.

4. It is tempting to think that Kant's distinction between the representations of the understanding and the representations of sensibility is essentially the same as that which many philosophers have drawn between conceptual and non-conceptual representations; and therefore to construe his distinction as a clear-cut advance on the notorious tendency of his predecessors on both sides of the Channel, to run these together.

5. Yet an examination of the use to which Kant puts his distinction soon makes it evident that while there is *something* to this interpretation, there is little which is 'clear cut' about the way in which the distinction is drawn. One is tempted to say that here, as in so many aspects of his argument, Kant is fighting his way towards a clarity of structure which he never achieves, and which is in his thinking only as the oak is in the acorn. A strong indication of this is found in the close relationship which exists in Kant's mind between the two dichotomies: sensibility, understanding; intuition, concept. The first item on each pair is introduced under the heading of 'receptivity', the second under that of 'spontaneity'. Alas! this neatness soon falls victim to the exigencies of argument. 'Intuition' turns out to be Janus-faced, and the understanding to have its own mode of receptivity.

6. Indeed, the moment we note that Kant's *primary* use of the

term 'concept' is to refer to general concepts, whether sortal or attributive, a priori or empirical, it is bound to occur to us that what he speaks of as 'intuitions', at least in certain contexts, might well be, in a broader but legitimate sense, *conceptual*. And since it is clear that Kant thinks of intuitions as representations of individuals, this would mean that they are conceptual representations of individuals rather than conceptual representations of attributes or kinds. Indeed Kant refers in the *Aesthetic* to the individuals Space and Time as concepts (A24; B38: A32; B48).

7. On the other hand, since it is clear that not all conceptual representations of individuals can plausibly be construed as Kantian intuitions, additional restrictions must be placed on this interpretation before it can be seriously entertained. A plausible suggestion is that 'intuitions' differ from other conceptual representations of individuals by not being mediated by general concepts in the way in which, for example,

the individual which is perfectly round

is mediated by the general concept of being perfectly round. A more positive clue is provided by Kant's reference to intuitions as 'in immediate relation to an object' (A68; B93). Unfortunately, this clue, though it reinforces the above suggestion, is not without ambiguity. It might be interpreted along causal lines, telling us that intuitions are generated by the immediate impact of things in themselves on our receptivity. An intuition is *caused* by its 'object'. I think that there is *something* to this suggestion, and I shall return to it later. On the other hand, 'immediate relation' can be construed on the model of the demonstrative 'this'. On this model, which I take to be, on the whole, the correct interpretation, intuitions would be representations of *thises* and would be conceptual in that peculiar way in which to represent something as a *this* is conceptual.

8. Another consideration which should make us wary about the supposed clarity with which Kant is distinguishing conceptual from non-conceptual representations is the fact that he allows for 'intuitions' which belong to the 'intellect' (and hence spontaneity), rather than to sensibility (and hence receptivity), though he emphasizes that 'intellectual intuitions' are not enjoyed by human minds nor, presumably, finite minds generally.

3

9. Our intuitions, unlike God's, essentially involve receptivity. I say 'involve' because, as begins to emerge, the connection of *intuition* with *receptivity* is not as simple as Kant's initial formulations imply. It would, for example, be puzzling in the extreme to assert that the representation of Space is in *no* sense intellectual. Furthermore, Kant clearly commits himself to the view that some representations of individuals are intuitions and *yet* involve a 'synthesis' which, if not a function of the understanding in its role of subsuming representations under general concepts, is certainly no matter of sheer receptivity, but rather of that interesting meeting ground of receptivity with spontaneity which is the 'productive imagination'.

10. We seem, therefore, to be led to a distinction between intuitions which do and intuitions which do not involve something over and above sheer receptivity. It is the former, Kant tells us in the metaphysical deduction (A78; B104), which the understanding subsumes under general concepts. And since he tells us shortly afterwards that it is 'the same function which gives unity to the various representations *in a judgment*' which 'also gives unity to the mere synthesis of various representations *in one intuition*' (A79; B104-5), we are not surprised when, after vaguely characterizing 'synthesis' as 'the mere result of the power of imagination, a blind but indispensible function of the soul' (A78; B103), it turns out, most clearly in the second edition (B151-3), that this imagination, under the name 'productive imagination', is the understanding functioning in a special way. Since what we typically speak of as 'imagined' are individual states of affairs, the use of this phrase to refer to the understanding *qua* engaged in that representing of individuals which involves receptivity, and is basic to experience, is not inappropriate. The idea that the understanding *qua* productive imagination works 'unconsciously' should undoubtedly be interpreted by contrast with the understanding *qua* engaged in the question-answering activities of classifying and relating intuitively represented objects of experience, which Kant refers to in this passage as 'analysis'.

11. We are now in a position to elaborate the earlier suggestion that to 'intuit' is to represent a *this*. For of intuitions those, at least, which are synthesized by the productive imagination would seem to have a form illustrated by

4

this-cube

which, though not a judgment, is obviously closely connected with the judgment

This is a cube

If this suggestion is correct, we are at once struck by the kinship of Kant's view that the basic *general* concepts which we apply to the objects of experience are derived (by the analytic activity of the understanding) from the intuitions synthesized by the productive imagination, with classical Aristotelian abstractionism. The two positions have in common the idea that we move from representations of the form

this-cube

which is a representation of a *this-such* nexus, specifically of *this as a cube*, though it is not a judgment and does not involve 'cube' in a predicative position, to representations in which the same nexus and the same content occur in explicitly propositional form

This is a cube[1]

12. A key difference would be that for Kant (unlike the Aristotelian) the nexus is 'in' the intuitive representation because it has, so to speak, been put there, not being present in the representations of *sheer* receptivity on which, in some sense, the synthesized intuition is founded.

13. The view that before we can have representations of the form

x is a cube

we must have representations of the form

this-cube

is a puzzling one. The different ways in which the representations *cube* and *white* occur in

This cube is a die. This white thing is a man.

---

[1] I have explored this feature of Aristotelian theories of concept formation in Chapter IV ('Aristotle's Metaphysics: An Interpretation') of *Philosophical Perspectives*, published by Charles G. Thomas (Springfield, Illinois, 1967).

on the one hand, and

This is a cube. This is white.

on the other, once as part of the subject, once as predicate, should, indeed, be taken seriously. But they should not be interpreted in terms of genetic priority. For, surely, the representations

this cube
this white thing

are essentially *incomplete* in that while they can occur in a mental listing, they would be unable to play even this role unless one knew how to complete them to form such representations as

This cube is a die
This white thing is a man

14. The point stands out even more clearly with respect to our representations of Space and Time. These representations are representations of 'individuals' in that sense of this term according to which anything referred to by a singular term of whatever logical level is an individual. I shall shortly be calling attention to key ambiguities in Kant's treatment of Space and Time. What concerns me now is the implausibility of the idea that general concepts pertaining to Space, e.g. the concepts of line, intersection, surface, etc., are genetically posterior to such representations as

this-line
this-intersection
this-surface
etc.

15. Notice that what I am attacking is not the idea that the occurrence of *universal* representations within the subject terms of actual or possible judgments is genetically prior to their occurrence in a predicative position, though this idea certainly merits attack. The *this-ness* is essential. For the traditional claim was that in the representation

this-cube

cube is not occurring as a *general* at all. The hyphenated phrase 'this-

6

cube' expresses a representing of something *as a cube* in a way which is conceptually prior to *cube* as a general or universal representation; that is, in a way which is conceptually prior to prediction or judgment. The strength of the position lies in the fact that the individual represented in perception is never represented as a mere *this*, but always, to use the classical schema, a *this-such*.

16. On the other hand, it is clear that in mature experience the 'this-*suches*' which typically get expressed in language are conceptually rich, even 'theory laden', and presuppose the predicative use of general representations. Kant's thesis, like the Aristotelian, clearly requires the existence of perceptual *this-suches* which are limited in their content to what is 'perceptible' in a very tough sense of this term (the 'proper sensibles'). It requires the existence of completely determinate 'basic' perceptual this-suches.

17. All this suggests that Kant's use of the term 'intuition', in connection with human knowledge, blurs the distinction between a special sub-class of *conceptual* representations of individuals which, though in some sense a function of receptivity, belong to a framework which is in no sense prior to but essentially includes general concepts, and a radically different kind of representation of an individual which belongs to sheer receptivity and is in no sense conceptual.

18. In any event, it is clear that Kant applies the term 'intuition' to both the representations which are formed by the synthesizing activity of the productive imagination and the purely passive representations of receptivity which are the 'matter' (A86; B108) which the productive imagination takes into account. Yet if he is not unaware that he is using the term 'intuition' somewhat ambiguously, he does not seem to be aware of the radical nature of the ambiguity.

19. It is implicit in the preceding remark, but needs to be emphasized, that Kant attributes to the representations of sensibility as such, which, following the tradition, he calls impressions (A86), the character of not being 'of' anything complex. Thus (A99 ff.) we find a principle to the effect that receptivity provides

us with a *manifold of representations*, but not with a *representation of a manifold*, which latter he proceeds to equate with *representation of a manifold as a manifold*. Other passages in both editions make essentially the same point. It is, indeed, the opening theme of the second edition *Deduction*. It might be thought that Kant is simply denying that the representations of sheer receptivity represent anything as having what might be called a *categorial* structure or complexity. Certainly the distinction between categorial structure and, say, spatio-temporal structure is essential to his argument, but it does not operate in this way. It might also be thought, in view of his thesis that Space is the form of outer sense, that he would admit that sheer receptivity can provide us with a representation of a spatial structure. I am convinced, however, and shall argue that this is not the case. He is committed to the stronger claim that what the representations of sheer receptivity are *of* is in no sense complex, and hence that the representations of outer sense as such are not representations of spatial complexes. If I am right, the idea that Space is the form of outer sense is incoherent. Space can scarcely be the form of the represent*ings* of outer sense; and if it is not the form of its represent*eds*, i.e. if nothing represented by outer sense as such is a spatial complex, the idea that Space is the form of outer sense threatens to disappear. The explanation of this incoherence, as we shall see, is the fact that his treatment of the 'form' of outer sense shares the ambiguity of his treatment of 'outer intuition'.

20. Thus, the above considerations would not count against the idea that Space is the form of outer *intuition*, i.e. of outer intuit*eds*, if we attribute *all* 'outer intuition' to the 'figurative synthesis' (B151) of the productive imagination. But, then, Space would seem to disappear altogether from receptivity as such. To reconcile the insights contained in Kant's treatment of 'sensibility' and 'intuition', the distinction we have been drawing between the impressions of sheer receptivity and the intuitions of the productive imagination must be paralleled by a corresponding distinction between two radically different senses of spatial terms, in one of which we can speak of *impressions* as having a spatial form, while in the other we can speak of *the objects of intuition* as having a spatial form.

8

II

21. I have been arguing that of the items Kant calls 'intuitions', those which are representations of a manifold *as a manifold* constitute a special class of representations of the understanding. They belong, as such, to spontaneity. Their 'receptivity' is a matter of the understanding having to cope with a manifold of representations characterized by 'receptivity' in a more radical sense, as providing the 'brute fact' or constraining element of perceptual experience.

22. The latter manifold has the interesting feature that its existence is postulated on general epistemological or, as Kant would say, transcendental grounds, after reflection on the concept of human knowledge as based on, though not constituted by, the impact of independent reality. It is postulated rather than 'found' by careful and discriminating attention. The concept of such a manifold is, in contemporary terms, a theoretical construct. Let us, following Kant (and a long tradition which goes back at least to Aristotle), call the items which make up such a manifold 'sense impressions', and let us explore independently the idea that it is reasonable to postulate the existence of sense impressions. As usual the case will be argued in terms of visual perception, but the conclusions reached can readily be extended to all modes of perception.

23. Among the themes which can be distinguished in the classical treatment of sense impressions the following three can be shown, I believe, to be fundamental, however entangled they became with other lines of thought. I shall assume, as a working hypothesis, that the standard form of expressions referring to sense impressions is that illustrated by

an impression of a red rectangle

In terms of this example, the three themes can be formulated as follows:

(*a*) Impressions of a red rectangle are states of consciousness.

(*b*) Impressions of a red rectangle are brought about in normal circumstances by physical objects which are red and rectangular on the facing side.[1]

[1] In the following I shall abbreviate 'physical object which is red and rectangular on the facing side' by 'red and rectangular physical object'.

(*c*) Impressions of a red rectangle *represent*, in a sense to be analysed, red and rectangular physical objects.

24. The phrase 'state of consciousness' is both ambiguous and obscure. The obscurity, I believe, is an honest one, the result of the coming together of many ideas at different levels of description and explanation. The conception of visual impressions as states of consciousness can be clarified to some extent by pointing out that they were assimilated to bodily sensations and feelings. The ambiguity I have in mind is manifold. There is, in the first place, the distinction between conceptual and non-conceptual states of consciousness, which it is the purpose of this chapter to explore. Sense impressions are non-conceptual states of consciousness. Then there is the distinction between 'states' and 'objects' of consciousness. The phrase 'object of consciousness' is itself highly ambiguous but for the moment, at least, I shall use it as roughly equivalent to 'noticed'. Like bodily sensations, visual impressions were construed as not only *states* but as, at least on occasion, *objects* of consciousness. Whatever Descartes himself may have thought, there is nothing absurd in the idea that states of consciousness occur which are not apperceived, a fact which was appreciated by Leibnitz.[1] More startling, and to many absurd, is the idea that there are broad classes of states of consciousness *none* of the members of which are apperceived. Startling or absurd, the idea is at least not obviously self-contradictory. (This *may* be due to its obscurity.) In any case, I shall push it to the hilt.

25. I must hasten to add that, according to the position I shall defend, even if visual sense impressions are never apperceived, they are so intimately related to certain *other* inner episodes which *are* apperceived that the temptation, for one who grants their existence, to say that they are themselves apperceived is difficult

---

[1] Though Leibnitz appreciated the fact of unapperceived representings, his account of the distinction between apperceived and unapperceived representings is by no means unambiguous. He fails to nail down the point that the apperception of a representing involves a numerically distinct representing, i.e. a distinction between an apperceptive representing and the representing it apperceives. At times the distinction between apperceived and unapperceived representings seem to coincide with a 'qualitative' distinction between *grandes* and *petites* representings. He may, however, have intended it to be a synthetic proposition that *petites* representings are (usually?) unapperceived.

indeed to resist, particularly when all of the relevant distinctions have not been drawn.

26. To avoid saying that there are visual sense impressions but that they are never apperceived, one might be tempted to take a familiar weapon from the Cartesian arsenal and put it to a new use. Appealing to the fact that (Cartesian confusions aside) the apperception of a representing always involves a conceptual act which, however intimately related to the apperceived representing, is numerically distinct from the latter, one might suggest that visual impressions *are* apperceived, but 'inadequately' in that the conceptual framework of the apperceptive act does not 'adequately' represent the state of which it is the apperception.

27. Thus philosophers have been known to claim that we perceive the world inadequately *sub specie Strawsonii*, but would perceive it adequately *sub specie Smartii* as whirls of atoms in the Void. It might, therefore, be claimed that there are states of consciousness which are inadequately apperceived *sub specie Warnockii* ('it seems to me as if I were seeing an orange'[1]) but which we might some day apperceive under a more adequate *ratio*. And, indeed, in spite of modern reinterpretations of the contrast between scientific reason and common sense, the Cartesian view that concepts which are subtly adapted to the demands of everyday living might yet be 'inadequate' retains its vitality.

28. Since, however, the respect in which apperception *sub specie Warnockii* is 'inadequate' turns out to be exactly what the postulation of sense impressions is designed to correct, I shall drop this theme of 'inadequate conceptual frameworks' (at least for the present) and concentrate on the original task of exploring the idea that it might be reasonable to postulate the existence of states of consciousness which are not apperceived at all. I have already indicated that this was, in essence, the Kantian position, though he tends to restrict the term 'consciousness' to apperceiving and to the apperceived as such. I shall argue that Kant was right to postulate the existence of a manifold of outer sense on epistemological ('transcendental') grounds—even if the details of his argument are open to serious objection.

29. There are, of course, many who would say that it is the

[1] G. J. Warnock, *Berkeley*, London, 1953, p. 188.

business of science to introduce hypothetical entities, and *therefore* not the business of philosophers to do so. The pragmatically useful division of intellectual labour, reflected in the proliferation of academic departments and disciplines, has been responsible for many necessary evils, but none more pernicious than this idea. Philosophy may perhaps be the chaste muse of clarity, but it is also the mother of hypotheses. Clarity is not to be confused with insight. It is the latter which is the true final cause of philosophy, and the insight which philosophy seeks and which always eludes its grasp is total insight. If the maxim *hypotheses non fingo* had captured classical and medieval philosophy there would have been abundance of clarity but no science, and, in particular, no theoretical science as we know it today.

30. Unless a purely instrumentalist account of the language game of hypothetical entities is to be taken for granted, philosophers must concern themselves with the ways in which these entities are related to the more familiar objects of everyday life. It is clear that if a scientific psychology untrammelled by philosophical traditions were to postulate non-Warnockian states of consciousness in their explanation of certain features of perception, philosophers would regard this step as an eminently suitable topic for philosophical reflection. That 'behaviouristics' as a separate discipline was precluded from moving in this direction when behaviourism was substantive rather than methodological is, of course, no guarantee that it will not do so, now that its conceptual strait-jacket has been loosened.

31. In any event, the time for philosophers to cease looking for explanatory hypotheses will come when the puzzles which demand them are adequately taken care of under another professional tag. No doubt the *distinctive* talent of philosophers today, as in the late middle-ages, is concept-chopping, but there just may be the same need today as there was then for hardy souls to dig up new concepts to chop, as did the great proto-scientists of the medieval schools.

III

32. It is, I suppose, as non-controversial as anything philosophical can be that visual perception involves conceptual representations. And if one accepts the idea that candid overt speech is the expres-

12

sion, in a broadly causal sense, of non-Rylean conceptual episodes it is reasonable to take the considered verbal reports of one who is scrutinizing his environment in a 'what do we have here?' frame of mind, to be the expression of conceptual episodes which are a function of (*a*) his perceptual capacities and set; (*b*) the impingement of the environment on his visual apparatus.

33. We have already noted that the vocabulary of these verbal reports is far richer than classical philosophers would admit into the proper philosophical description of sense impressions. Thus, people report that they see a red book on a brown table, but while it is appropriate to say of a third party that he is under the (visual) impression that there is (in front of him) a red book on a brown table (i.e. that he visually takes this to be the case), and that he has the (visual) impression of there being (in front of him) a red book on a brown table, philosophers have been notoriously reluctant to speak of sense impressions of a book on a table. If we think of sense impressions as belonging to the category of conceptual episodes expressed by perceptual reports, this fact is rather a puzzle. According to the tradition, sense impressions are present in all perception, however sophisticated, and it is surely odd to suppose that such rich conceptual episodes as that expressed by 'here is a red book on a brown table' are invariably accompanied by such thin conceptual episodes as that expressed by 'here is a red rectangle standing out from a brown background'.

34. In certain circumstances of perception, however, as has often been pointed out, even the verbal expression tends to become minimal, thus, as the speaker becomes more cautious or puzzled. There are, however, two ways in which reports may be minimized, which must be carefully distinguished, though they may both be present in any given situation. Compare the following:

Tom: See that red book over there.
Dick: [I don't see a book over there but] there is a red and rectangular physical object over there.
Harry: [I don't see a red book over there, though I grant that] it looks to me as though there were a red book over there.

Dick's report is a minimal *objective* report, minimized with respect to the physical state of affairs it claims to obtain. Harry's report repeats the content of Tom's assertion but places it in the rubric 'it looks (to me) . . .'. A still more cautious report might be made by Jones, thus

> Jones: [I grant that] it looks to me as though there were a red and rectangular physical object over there.

Dick made an objective assertion which is extremely limited in its content. Jones suspends even this limited claim by his use of the 'looks (to me) . . .' rubric.

35. There are interesting differences between the statements made by Dick and Jones, and, correspondingly, between the conceptual representation they express. For our purposes the most interesting is that Jones' statement is on a higher level, much as belief statements, e.g.

> Mary believes that it is raining

are on a higher level than the statements they in some sense contain, in this case

> It is raining

Jones is saying of himself what we might say of Dick if we thought that his statement was considered but false. And it seems clear that if we were to say

> It looks to Dick as though there were a red and rectangular physical object over there

part of what we would be expressing would be *our* conceptual representation that *Dick* is conceptually representing that there is, in front of him, a red and rectangular physical object. Presumably, therefore, Jones' statement expresses a conceptual representation, part of which consists in attributing to *himself* a conceptual representation that there is (in front of him) a red and rectangular physical object. And if we ask what kind of representation this is, the answer must surely be 'that kind of conceptual representation which is being under the visual impression that (visually taking it to be the case that) there is (or of there being) a red and rectangular physical object in front of one'.

36. But if it were not for the recurring puzzles of sense percep-

tion there would be no reason to think that even when candid reports, and, therefore, the conceptual representations they express, are unguarded and conceptually rich, they are accompanied by unverbalized minimal conceptual representations of either the objective or 'looks (to me)' variety. Yet many philosophers have been strongly inclined to say that visual perception always involves representations which are appropriately described in objectively minimal terms, and are appropriately called impressions, as being, in some sense, functions of 'receptivity'. I think that these philosophers are right, and that the point is of great importance. I also think, however, that most influential accounts mistakenly assimilate impressions, thus understood, to minimal conceptual representations, minimal both with respect to the physical content in terms of which they are described, and in being bracketed by *looks* or *seems*.

37. That the idea that visual perception always involves minimal conceptual representations is false does not, I believe, need to be argued. On the other hand, the idea that visual perception always involves sense impressions properly described by a special use of a minimal physical vocabulary does seem to me eminently capable of defence, once the confusion of sense impressions with the minimal conceptual representations which do occur in extremely guarded perception has been overcome.

38. Before taking steps in this direction, let me note that even on the hypothesis, contrary to fact, that visual perception as such involves minimal conceptual episodes, reflection on the nature of perceptual experience would lead us to the idea that the receptivity or secondness (Peirce) involved in visual perception has three distinguishable aspects:

(1) a purely physical aspect which could, in principle, be described in terms of physical theory—though it can also be described (as by Aristotle) in common-sense terms;

this physical aspect would bring about:

(2) the primary mental aspect, contributed by this account as a minimal conceptual episode, which latter in turn would bring about, given the set of the perceiver, and in a way which is no matter of sheer receptivity;

Sensibility and Understanding

(3) a rich conceptual episode involving such concepts as those of cabbages and kings and pigs in barnyards.

39. My objection to this analysis is not to the idea that some such trichotomy is involved, nor to the contrast between the 'receptivity' of sense impression and the *guidedness*, to use a relevant concept from the *Investigations*,[1] of the flow of conceptual representations proper involved in normal perceptual activity. Indeed, I think that the latter distinction is exactly what Kant needs to make his theory work. Thus, when he speaks of the productive imagination as 'taking up' (A120) the manifold of outer sense into its activity (the synthesis of apprehension) the metaphor implies, of course, that the manifold is an independent factor which has a strong voice in the outcome. On the other hand, it is only if the manifold is mistakenly construed as belonging to the conceptual order that it *makes sense* to suppose that it, so to speak, bodily or literally becomes a part of the resulting intuitive representation. If it is, as I take it to be, non-conceptual, it can only guide 'from without' the unique conceptual activity which is representing of *this-suches* as subjects of perceptual judgment.

40. Indeed, it is only if Kant distinguishes the radically non-conceptual character of sense from the conceptual character of the synthesis of apprehension in intuition [which is, of course, to be distinguished from the conceptual synthesis of recognition in a concept, in which the concept occupies a predicative position] and, accordingly, the *receptivity* of sense from the *guidedness* of intuition that he can avoid the dialectic which leads from Hegel's *Phenomenology* to nineteenth-century idealism.

IV

41. But is it genuinely necessary to interpose non-conceptual representations *as states of consciousness* between the 'physical' impact of the sensory stimulus and the conceptual representations (guarded or daring) which find verbal expression, actually or potentially, in perceptual statements? Can we not interpret the receptivity involved in terms of 'purely physical' states, and attribute to these the role of guiding conceptualization? Why should

[1] Ludwig Wittgenstein, *Philosophical Investigations*, Oxford, 1953, §§ 169 ff.

16

we suppose that receptivity culminates in a state which is neither 'purely physical' *nor* conceptual? Yet to do just this is, I shall argue, of the greatest importance for the philosophy of mind and, in particular, for an understanding of how the framework of physical science is to be integrated with the framework of common sense.

42. If what might be called the 'sense impression inference'[1] is an inference to an explanation, what specifically is it designed to explain? Clearly not, at least in the first instance, facts of the form 'it seemed to Jones that O was red, when it wasn't', for we can do this without invoking sense impressions, appealing instead to the specific abnormalities of either Jones or his circumstances. Nor, at least primarily, is it designed to explain 'discrimination behaviour' of the type which can be acquired by flatworms and encouraged in white rats; 'consecutiveness' which in Leibnitz' phrase 'apes reason'. Rather its primary purpose is to explain the occurrence of certain *conceptual* representations in perceptual activity. The representations I have in mind are those which are characteristic of what we have called 'minimal conceptual representations'.

43. If we construe physical objects, for the moment, in Strawsonian terms we can say that the aim is to explain the correlation of the conceptual representations in question with those features of the objects of perception which, on occasion, both make them true and are responsible for bringing them about.

44. Thus, the sense impression inference is an attempt to account for the fact that normal perceivers have *conceptual* representations of a red and rectangular object both

   (*a*) when they are being affected in normal circumstances by a red and rectangular object; and
   (*b*) when they are being affected in abnormal circumstances by objects which have other, but systematically related characteristics.

---

[1] As contrasted with the 'sense-datum inference' described by Roderick Chisholm in his essay 'The Theory of Appearing', in *Philosophical Analysis*, Max Black (ed.), Ithaca, 1950, p. 107. Unlike the latter, the 'sense impression inference' is not a matter of explaining the fact that an object looks red (or that there looks to be a red object) in terms of the idea that there is something, a sense-datum, which actually *is* red; for a sense impression of a red rectangle is neither red nor rectangular.

It is essential to note that the *explanandum* concerns *conceptualization* rather than behavioural discrimination as such. It is also essential to note that the correlation of the correct conceptual response with objects perceived in normal circumstances by normal perceivers is as much in need of explanation as the correlations of conceptual responses with abnormal perceptual situations. It is not enough, for reasons which I shall give in a moment, to explain the latter by saying that the proximate physical stimulus caused, e.g., by a black object in normal circumstances, is the same as that caused by a red object in abnormal circumstances. For even in normal cases there is the genuine question, 'Why does the perceiver *conceptually represent* a red (blue, etc.) rectangular (circular, etc.) object in the presence of an object having these qualities?' The answer would seem to require that all the possible ways in which *conceptual representations* of colour and shape can resemble and differ correspond to ways in which their *immediate non-conceptual occasions*, which must surely be construed as states of the perceiver, can resemble and differ.

45. Thus, these non-conceptual states must have characteristics which, *without being colours*, are sufficiently analogous to colour to enable these states to play this guiding role. If the notion of one family of characteristics being *analogous* to another family of characteristics is obscure and difficult it is nevertheless as essential to the philosophy of science as it has been to theology and, it would seem, somewhat more fruitful. That it is a powerful tool for resolving perennial problems in epistemology and metaphysics is a central theme of this book.

46. If the *explanandum* formulated above is a genuine one there are, it would seem, other possible accounts than the one I am recommending. Thus either of the following lines might be taken:

    (a) The tendency to have conceptual representations of a red (blue, etc.) and rectangular (circular, etc.) physical object under certain stimulus conditions, even though, as Aristotle pointed out, the eye does not assume a red and rectangular state, and no red and rectangular object may be present, is innate.

    (b) One is taught by one's linguistic peers, who already have the relevant concepts and propensities, to play the colour-shape language game and, by so doing, acquire these concepts and propensities.

47. I shall ignore the former suggestion. As for the latter, I do not wish to deny the insights it contains. Nevertheless, the ability to teach a child the colour-shape language game seems to imply the existence of cues which systematically correspond, in the manner adumbrated above, to the colour and shape attribute families, and are also causally connected with combinations of variously coloured and shaped objects in various circumstances of perception. If so, the account in terms of the *transmission* of the colour-shape language game from generation to generation supplements, but does not replace, the original suggestion. If we adopt this suggestion, however, we are faced with the task of explicating the idea that physical objects bring about states of perceivers which have attributes systematically analogous to perceptible colour and shape, without literally *having* perceptible colour and shape.

48. I have, it will be remembered, taken as my paradigm of a sense impression

an impression of a red rectangle

where this locution is carefully distinguished from one which says, for example, of Jones that he has

an impression of a man lurking in the corner

The latter clearly attributes to Jones a conceptual state. Thus the above paradigm should not be taken as a truncated form of

an impression of a red rectangle being (for example) over there

49. Since the sense impression of which we are speaking is clearly described in terms of its standard cause, one might be inclined to think that we should refer to it as

an impression of a physical object which is red and rect-angular on the facing side

But although this would have been in the spirit of what might be called the Aristotelian phase of the concept, reflection on the nature of the proper remote cause of impressions resulted in a tendency increasingly to *minimize* their description. It is this minimizing tendency, inspired by what I referred to (in paragraph 23 above) as the causal theme, which, combined with empiricist abstractionism, led directly to Hume. The description of impressions loses those features which made it plausible to think that a Jack Horner intellect could pluck from them the categories of physical object discourse.

50. Thus, since only the surface of an opaque object is relevant to the description of the corresponding sense impression, the latter tends to become an

impression of a facing red and rectangular expanse

Again, since the causal powers of an object are not themselves causes, the description of impressions tends to be purged of all expressions which logically imply causal properties: an impression of a pink ice cube tends, in view of the causal properties implied by 'ice', to become an impression of a pink cube.

51. Again, where the cause of an impression is one billiard ball knocking another into a pocket, the impression description tends to be watered down into

impression of a white sphere moving towards another white sphere followed by a motion of the latter

and this, in turn, into

an impression of a facing white hemispherical surface moving towards another facing white hemispherical surface followed by a motion of the latter

V

52. If we accept this way of looking at the receptivity involved in visual perception a number of things fall into place. To begin with, we can understand the temptation to assimilate sense impressions to minimal conceptual representations. For neither the sense impression of a red rectangle nor the conceptual representation of a red rectangle is either red or rectangular.

53. In the *second* place the interpretation of the framework of sense impressions as a theoretical framework suggests that the analogy between the attributes of impressions and the perceptible attributes of physical objects is but another case of the role of analogy in theoretical concept formation. Analogical concepts in science are methodologically dependent on a conceptual base to which they are not reduceable.[1]

54. Thus, when we characterize a visual impression as

> an impression of a red rectangle

the use of the word 'red' and 'rectangle' is derivative from the use of the corresponding predicates in the context

> a physical object, the facing side of which is a red rectangle

In this derivative use they form an adjectival expression

> of a red rectangle

which, when joined to the category word 'impression', forms the sortal expression

> (an) of-a-red-rectangle impression

55. Here we must note that there are many who would grant:

(*a*) that there are visual sense impressions;
(*b*) that they are non-conceptual representations;
(*c*) that they can be described only in terms of their standard physical causes;

but who take (*c*) to be equivalent to the idea that the sense of the phrase

> a visual impression of a red rectangle

is simply that of

> a non-conceptual state of the perceiver (mediating between the stimulus and the conceptual outcome) of *the kind which* has as its standard cause a red and rectangular physical object

[1] For an account of analogical concept formation in science see my essay on 'Scientific Realism or Irenic Instrumentalism', in *Boston Studies in the Philosophy of Science*, edited by Robert S. Cohen and Marx W. Wartofsky, New York, 1965, especially §§ 19–37.

This is a radical mistake, for by construing the reference to the characters of the non-conceptual state as a definite description of unknown attributes in terms of their causal connections, *rather than as the analogical introduction of new predicates*, it takes an agnostic stance which plays into the hands of a crude physicalism. Might not *the kind of state which*, etc., be a complicated pattern of the kind of physical processes which go on in hedges and stones?

56. In the *third* place, since in the causal context

> normally caused by a red rectangular (physical) surface

which is the basis (though not the sense) of the description of the corresponding impression; the phrase

> a red rectangular (physical) surface

clearly refers to no particular physical surface, the *apparent* reference of the expression

> an impression of a red rectangle

to a particular red rectangle, which has bemused sense datum theorists, is both explained and explained away. We can understand why visual impressions are *in their way* 'of individuals', and why they have been construed as 'direct' or 'intuitive' representations of individuals as contrasted with representations mediated by general concepts. When, therefore, we understand the role of the phrase 'a red rectangle'; in references to sense impressions proper, we see that the question

> Impression of *which* red rectangle?

makes sense only as a request to know which red and rectangular object is *causing* the impression, rather than how the impression is to be *described*.

57. In the *fourth* place we understand why the fact that philosophers use 'of' constructions involving the same physical object predicates to modify both the category word 'conception' and the category word 'impression', thus

> impression of a red rectangle
> conception of a red rectangle

does not commit them to the idea that these physical object predicates are doing the same kind of job in both contexts.

58. Thus, in the *fifth* place, we understand why the temptation to conflate sense impressions proper with minimal conceptual representations is a temptation to construe an impression of a red rectangle as though it were a special kind of conceptual representation of a particular red rectangle, as though it were a *token* (in Peirce's sense) of the Mentalese phrase

> this red rectangle

or

> this red rectangular thing

that is, as though, in describing sense impressions, the words 'red' and 'rectangle' were being used to mention conceptual items in the vocabulary of inner speech.

59. *Finally*, we understand why, although both the contexts

> impression of . . .

and

> conception of . . .

are, from a logical point of view, intensional (note the 's') for from neither

> Jones has an impression of a red rectangle

nor

> Jones is conceiving of a red rectangle

can we infer that there is a red rectangle in the neighbourhood. Only the latter is 'intentional' (note the 't') from the point of view the philosophy of mind, where the intentional is that which belongs to the conceptual order.

VI

60. Before I return to Kant with this apparatus in mind, one further consequence of the 'causal theme' needs to be noticed, for it reveals additional possibilities of confusion—thoroughly exploited by Hume and not entirely absent in Kant. We are all familiar with Wittgenstein's thesis in the *Tractatus* that at the level

of atomic propositions the conceptual representation of a complex state of affairs is a complex of conceptual representations. Thus, a representing that

x_1 precedes (temporally) x_2

consists of a representing of x_1 related (though not, presumably, by the same relation) to a representing of x_2. I wish to call attention to the fact that a comparable thesis can and has been advanced with reference to sense impressions.

61. Let me begin by postulating a Descartes (let us call him Renatus) who (unlike the historical Descartes) draws a clear-cut distinction between conceptual and non-conceptual states. He rejects, of course, the idea that the sense impression of a red rectangle is literally red or literally rectangular. As we have done, he argues that 'of a red rectangle' combines with 'impression' to form a sortal predicate for a certain kind of mental state. Thus he speaks of

An (of a red rectangle) impression

but proposes a convention, illustrated by the equivalence in ordinary language of 'warm sensation' with 'sensation of warmth', according to which

a red rectangle impression

is to have the sense of

an (of a red rectangle) impression

62. We now ask him to suppose that someone (Jones) is looking, in normal circumstances, at a green square one side of which coincides with a red square, and as a result has

an impression of a green square adjoining a red square

Before exploring the logic of this locution, let us note that language provides us with a way of making complex common nouns out of simple ones, thus from '(a)cat' and '(a)mat' we can form the complex common noun

cat-on-a-mat

which occurs in the sentence

This is a cat-on-a-mat

It is essential to note that the expression

a K_1-R-a-K_2

is an instance of the same general form as that exemplified by

a cat

It is *not* a propositional expression illustrating the form

$x \mathrel{R} y$

A confusion of references to complex objects with relational statements has had serious consequences in both metaphysics and epistemology.

63. Let us return to the above example of

an impression of a green square adjoining a red square

or, otherwise put,

an (of a green square adjoining a red square) impression

or, by the proposed convention,

a green-square-adjoining-a-red-square impression

We now ask Renatus if having this impression entails having an impression of a green square and an impression of a red square. He answers, predictably, yes. We then ask if the original impression *consists of* an of-a-green-square impression and an of-a-red-square impression. Again the answer is yes. Finally, we ask whether, for these two impressions to be parts of the embracing impression, they must be related. The answer is yes; but this time even our co-operative Renatus is recalcitrant enough to insist that the relation of the two impressions is not the adjoining relation—nor any kind of spatial relation. Mental states, he insists, are neither red, green, square, juxtaposed, nor spatial in any way.

64. When, however, it is pointed out that there must be *something* about the relation between the impressions which makes it that they constitute an impression of *adjoining* squares, rather than of *separated* squares, or squares which *meet at corners*, he grants that the relation of the impressions must 'correspond' to *adjoining* in a sense of 'correspond' which turns out, from our point of view, to

be just the *analogy* which has already cropped up in our discussion of the *qualitative* character of impressions. If we represent the genuinely spatial relation of adjoining by 'R_1', we can represent the 'corresponding' relation between the component impressions by 'R_1*'.

65. Thus we must add to our earlier point that the impression of a red rectangle, though neither red nor rectangular, has counterpart attributes, the idea that the impression of a relational complex is a complex (involving a *counterpart* relation) of impressions. Succinctly put, impressions have attributes and stand in relations which are counterparts of the attributes and relations of physical objects and events.

66. These considerations give us the identity:

an impression of a green square R_1 a red square = an impression of a green square R_1* an impression of a red square

Or, using the above convention:

an (a green square R_1 a red square) impression = an (a green square) impression R_1* an (a red square) impression

67. Still more schematically we have

an ($\ldots R_1 - - -$) impression = an ($\ldots$) impression R_1* an ($- - -$) impression

This schema, it will be noted, provides a way of transforming contexts in which relation words appropriate to physical objects occur in phrases which characterize a single impression into contexts in which two (or more) impressions are characterized as related by a counterpart relation.

68. If it is also true, as Wittgenstein held, (*Tractatus*, 3.1432) that conceptual representations of relational states of affairs are to be construed as complexes of conceptual representations of their terms, the question obviously arises 'What is the connection be-

tween the counterpart relations which bind conceptual representations of terms into conceptual representations of complex states
of affairs, thus the conceptual representation that s_1 adjoins x_2,
and the counterpart relation which binds non-conceptual representations into non-conceptual representations of relational
wholes, thus the impression of a green square adjoining a red
square. ?' I shall have something to say on this topic in Chapter IV.

69. The above schema can be seen to amount to the idea that an
impression of a complex is a complex of impressions. If we add
to this the idea that the latter is the 'true' description we have a
characteristically Humean thesis which reappears in Kant.

70. A philosopher who is prepared to insist that at least some
of our concepts are derived by abstraction from the contents of
sense impressions, and who takes the above thesis seriously,
would obviously be hung up on concepts of relation. He might be
impelled to say that concepts of relations have a different 'source'
from concepts of qualities. This, however, would be because he
has failed to note that the same move which takes 'R_1' out of the
context 'impression of' also, as we previously saw, takes 'red' and
'rectangular' out of this context and turns them into counterpart
predicates.

71. Hume, in any case, strode over all these complexities with
seven league boots, for, as is notorious, he confused between:

(1) an impression of a green square;
(2) a conviction that a green square exists;
(3) a green square.

And, correspondingly, between:

(1) an impression of a green square adjoining a red square;
(2) a conviction that a green square adjoining a red square
exists;
(3) a green square adjoining a red square.

72. These confusions also blurred the distinction between
'abstracting' the concept of ϕ from a representation of something
ϕ, and 'abstracting' it from an actually ϕ-item. In this connection
it should be noted that an interesting strand in seventeenth- and
eighteenth-century theories of concept formation is a distorted
form of the sound principle that concepts are *caused* rather than

abstracted. Thus Descartes held that the cause of a concept must be something actually existent which is at least as 'perfect'—in the medieval sense—as what the concept is 'of'. This formulation is clearly designed to permit God to be the cause of mathematical and metaphysical concepts. But many philosophers who rejected innate ideas (e.g. Berkeley and Locke) clearly assumed that our ability to conceive of the various kinds of mental act is caused by the actual occurrence of these acts in our minds, though this causation was usually not distinguished from abstraction. The most interesting example is Hume, who clearly thinks that the concept of an impression is an empirical concept caused by the occurrence of impressions, and the concept of an idea is an empirical concept *caused* by the occurrence of ideas. That he confuses between an impression of a red dot causing an idea of a red dot, and its causing an idea of an impression, bears out the picture of total but useful confusion described above.[1]

VII

73. We are now in a position to comment on some of the more obscure themes in Kant's treatment of sensibility. I shall begin by making the contrary to fact assumption that Kant was clear about the radical difference between sense impressions proper and the intuitions synthesized by the productive imagination. Such a Kant would then have distinguished between:

(*a*) the non-conceptual representations of outer sense proper which, although conveniently described as impressions of spatial complexes, are strictly speaking non-spatial complexes of unextended and uncoloured impressions;
(*b*) the intuitive (but conceptual) representations of extended structures located in space.[2]

---

[1] *A Treatise of Human Nature*, edited by Selby-Bigge, Part I, Book I, Section I, p. 6: 'As our ideas are images of our impressions, so we can form secondary ideas, which are images of the primary; *as appears from this very reasoning concerning them*' (Ital. mine).

[2] It will have been noted that I have had little to say about temporal attributes and relations. I shall be discussing Kant's theory of Time in subsequent chapters. See also the Appendix for a discussion of Time as the form of 'inner sense'. For my present purposes, however, it is sufficient to note that the problems posed are, as Kant saw, parallel to those of Space, and his treatment succeeds and fails in parallel ways.

74. This splitting up of the representations initially lumped together under the heading of 'sensible intuition' into conceptual and non-conceptual representations demands a corresponding splitting in two of the concept of a 'form of sensible intuition'. On the one hand, there would be the intuitive (but conceptual) representations of Space (and Time) which serve as frameworks for the conceptual representation (intuitive or discursive (A68; B93)) of individual objects and events. On the other hand, there would be the attributes of and relations between the impressions of pure receptivity. Though, as has been pointed out, we conceive of certain of these attributes and relations as *counterparts* of spatial attributes and relations proper, they would not literally be the spatial attributes and relations in terms of which we conceptually represent physical objects and events. (That colour and colour relations should have been given a similar treatment is clearly part of the burden of my argument.)

75. Kant's failure to distinguish clearly between the 'forms' of receptivity proper and the 'forms' of that which is represented by the intuitive conceptual representations which are 'guided' by receptivity—a distinction which is demanded both by the thrust of his argument, and by sound philosophy—had as its consequence that no sooner had he left the scene than these particular waters were muddied by Hegel and the Mills, and philosophy had to begin the slow climb 'back to Kant' which is still underway.

VIII

76. It is to be noted that although Kant denies, in the spirit of Hume's principle, that any representation of sheer receptivity is a representation of a complex, and, accordingly, construes all representations of complex items (which he equates with representations of a complex *as* complex, of a manifold *as* manifold) to be acts of spontaneity or the understanding, he nowhere denies, and is not committed to denying, that the manifold of external sense as such is a relational structure. Indeed, the more general point can be made that Kant nowhere denies or need deny that the in-itself has a relational structure. What he does deny, whether for good reasons or for bad, a topic for subsequent discussion,

is that the relations we conceptually represent are the relations which the in-itself exemplifies.

77. With respect to the manifold of outer sense, Kant does not seem to have found the happy medium between the absurdity of saying that Space is a form of outer sense in that the manifold of outer sense is literally spatial, and the overly strong claim that the only way in which spatial relations enter into perceptual states is as contents of *conceptual* representations. This means that the characteristics of the representations of receptivity as such, which is what should *properly* be meant by the forms of sensibility, are never adequately discussed, and the so-called forms of sensibility become ever more clearly, as the argument of the *Critique* proceeds, forms of conceptual representations. By overlooking the importance of analogical concepts—save in theological contexts—and hence by failing to note the analogical character of our concepts of the attributes and relations which sense impressions *must* have to perform their explanatory role, Kant reduces the concepts of receptivity and sensibility to empty abstractions.

78. If, *per impossibile*, Kant had developed the idea of the manifold of sense as characterized by analogical counterparts of the perceptible qualities and relations of physical things and events he could have given an explicit account of the ability of the impressions of receptivity to guide minds, endowed with the conceptual framework he takes us to have, to form the conceptual representations we do of individual physical objects and events in Space and Time. He could thus have argued that when on a certain occasion we come to have an intuitive conceptual representation that this green square adjoins that red square, we do so by virtue of having a complex of non-conceptual representations which, although non-spatial and without colour, have characteristics which are the counterparts of *square*, *red*, *green* and *adjoining*, and which make them such as to account for the fact that we have *this* conceptual representation rather than that of there being a purple pentagon above an orange elipse. That he 'implicitly' gives some such account (or must have done so) has been argued by many, thus, by Professor Paton,[1] though the full scope of the distinctions necessary to pull it off has not always been appreciated.

[1] Kant's *Metaphysic of Experience*, Volume I, Chapter 6, Section 8.

II

APPEARANCES AND THINGS
IN THEMSELVES:

1. MATERIAL THINGS

1. At the heart of the Kantian distinction between things-in-themselves and appearances is the contrast, drawn by Descartes, but by
no means original with him, between formal and (in the medieval
sense) objective reality. This distinction, in some form, is essential
to the idea of a conceptual representation, though a related
distinction, easily confused with it, holds of the non-conceptual
representations of sense. I shall assume that the distinction is a
familiar one, and say just enough about it to show how it, and
related distinctions, illuminate Kant's contrast of things-in-
themselves with appearances, and explain why, in spite of the
retro-causation attempted by many of his admirers, he never even
considered abandoning it. Since both the Cartesian distinctions
and the use to which they were put by Kant can be translated into
contemporary terms, and since the problems with which Kant was
dealing reappear in modern dress, this chapter, like the first, will
be a blend of historical and systematic themes.

2. I shall continue for the time being, at least, to assume the
general validity of the distinction between mental acts or actualities and their overt expression in linguistic and non-linguistic
behaviour. I shall also work, provisionally, with a Cartesian
dualism of body and mind—noting, however, that if it were not
for his ill-advised claim that we 'clearly conceive mind, that is, a
substance which thinks, without body, that is to say, without an
extended substance . . .',[1] almost everything Descartes wanted to

---

[1] *The Philosophical Works of Descartes*, translated by E. S. Haldane and G. R. T.
Ross, Volume II, p. 59.

say could have been put in Aristotelian terms, a mind being a person *qua* subject of mental acts, capacities and propensities, its body a person *qua* subject of bodily states, capacities and propensities. Whether sensory states are sufficiently akin to conceptual thinking proper to be classified as mental, or sufficiently different from both the mental and the bodily to merit a pigeon-hole of their own, is one which any contemporary Aristotelian must face. The dichotomy of predicates of persons into M-predicates and P-predicates[1] is useful for many purposes, but for others is coarse-grained and procrustean. However this may be, Descartes, as is well known, found it appropriate to classify the representations of sense with the representations of conceptual thinking proper as *cogitationes*. The fact that both can be characterized as representations (and have other common features which were explored in the preceding chapter) tempted him to apply to the humbler species the epistemological and ontological categories he applied to conceptual thinking proper, not simply in the spirit of analogy, the positive being counterbalanced by the negative, but literally, the negative analogy being construed as specific difference.

3. The importance of the categories Descartes applies to mental acts lies, as I have indicated, in the fact that they can be seen to be less sophisticated counterparts of distinctions which are drawn with more or less rigour in those contemporary philosophies of mind which have been influenced by formal semantics. The distinctions fall into two closely related, indeed complementary, sets, one focused on concepts pertaining to truth, the other on concepts pertaining to existence—none of which is surprising, since it would generally be admitted that there is the closest of connections between existence and truth, at least in the case of things and their modifications. The first set of categories distinguishes between:

(*a*) a representation *qua* act, i.e. qua represent*ing* or 'operation of the mind';

(*b*) the character by virtue of which it represents what it represents; and,

(*c*) where appropriate, the substance or modification of which the represent*ing*, *qua* representing what it represents, is true.

[1] P. F. Strawson, *Individuals*, London, 1959, p. 104.

1. Material Things

Closely related to the above is a contrast between two ways in which things or substances and their modifications can exist:

(*a*) They can exist 'in' mental acts of representing—i.e. they can be, in Descartes' phrase, 'the objective reality of an idea' by which, he tells us, he understands 'the entity or being of the thing represented by the idea, in so far as the entity is in the idea'.[1]

(*b*) They can, as I shall put it, exist *simpliciter*. In Descartes' terminology, 'the same things are said to be formally in the object of the ideas when they are in them such as they are conceived'.[2]

4. By contrasting existence *simpliciter* with existence 'in' representings (that is, in 'ideas' as Descartes uses the term in the passage quoted above), I do not mean to imply that the concept of 'existence *simpliciter*' has nothing to do with existence 'in' representings. Indeed, I have already suggested that the concept of existence *simpliciter* is internally related to the concept of truth. But the development of this theme requires the more elaborate framework of the next chapter.

5. The first set of distinctions is related to the second as follows:

(1) For a thing or modification to exist 'in' a mental act is for the latter to represent it.

(2) A mental act representing a modification is true of a substance which exists *simpliciter* if and only if the modification exists *simpliciter* as a modification of the substance.

I have deliberately put *these* two points in a make-shift way, since more subtle formulations require distinctions—e.g. between objects and states of affairs—which were not part of Descartes' technical apparatus, though, of course, they made their presence felt.

6. We can tie these distinctions in with the 'new way of ideas' by identifying ideas with entities which are capable of existing 'in' representings, as thus capable. If we do so, however, we must take account of the fact that the term is often used (as in the passage quoted above) to stand for represent*ings*, as contrasted with

[1] Haldane and Ross, Volume II, p. 52.   [2] *Ibid.*, p. 53.

what they represent. If we drop this usage to avoid confusion we can say that 'ideas' in the sense of representables *qua* representables are capable of two interesting relations, the 'in' relation to mental acts, and the 'truth' relation to things and their modifications *qua* existing *simpliciter*.

7. In each of these relations ideas have a one-many aspect which was a constant source of puzzlement:

(*a*) with respect to the 'in' relation, somehow one and the same idea could be 'in' many acts;

(*b*) with respect to the 'truth' relation, one and the same *general* idea could be 'true of' many things.

The former sameness was connected in various ways—most interestingly by Malebranche—with the notion that the primary mode of being of ideas was in God's intellect. What we should now call the public character of concepts was given a theological twist. The second sameness raised the age-old question: How can generals be 'true of' things if, as philosophers have often been tempted to say, there are no generals 'in' things? I shall be concerned in subsequent chapters with both the public character of concepts and the existence of generals.

8. Two final remarks on these Cartesian categories before we apply them to Kant. We distinguished above between a representing *qua* act and a representing *qua* representing something. Since the latter tended to be construed on the model of container to thing contained, the question naturally arises as to what character a 'containing' act might have in addition to its relational property of 'containing' an idea. The dominant Cartesian view seems to have been that *intrinsically* all basic mental acts are alike—all instances, so to speak, of mental-act-ness. (One is reminded of Moore's diaphanous acts.) It should be noted, however, that in a careful passage, in which he is concerned to reply to sophisticated objections, he defines the term 'idea' in such a way that it refers not to a represent*ing* as such, nor to what is 'in' the representing, but rather to the 'form' of the representing, i.e. the character by having which it represents what it represents. Thus he writes, 'By the word "idea" I understand that form of any thought, by the immediate perception of which I am conscious of that same

thought.'[1] Thus used, the term 'idea' is a descendant of the scholastic term 'species' as applied to mental acts. This use is a recessive trait, even in Descartes. After all, the above definition occurs in a reply to objections made from a more traditional point of view. The use of the term 'idea' to stand not for the 'form' of a representing but for what is represented *qua* represented is more akin to the scholastic term 'concept'. In any case, Cartesians could easily put their standard view into scholastic clothing by defining 'idea' in the sense of the form or species of a mental act in terms of what the act 'contains', i.e. in terms of the 'idea', in the more usual sense, which is 'in' them.

9. On the other hand, whether representings are 'informed' by ideas or 'contain' them, representings do have other features—temporal, at least, and, it would seem, such relations as make complex acts out of simpler ones. Here one runs up against the problem, discussed in Chapter I in connection with the representations of sense, of whether a complex representing is complex *qua* act or *qua* representing a complex, where 'representing a complex' is construed as a matter of 'containing' a complex idea. This problem, particularly as it arises with respect to conceptual representations, reappears in ever new guises, and will be discussed in Chapter IV.

10. A second remark is, perhaps, in order. Modern philosophers are often tempted to construe Descartes as, so to speak, a 'thought-is-inner-speech' philosopher *manqué*—to interpret him, that is, in a way which construes the *inesse* of ideas in mental acts as though it were a matter of the acts being tokens (utterances in ones heart) of Mentalese words and sentences. It is clear, however, that the feeling for the logical forms of thought, so clear in the disciples of Ockham, and which revives in Leibnitz and, above all, Kant, is almost totally lacking in Descartes and his British successors. A clear interpretation of intellectual *cogitationes* as 'inner speech' would have made more difficult, if not impossible, many of the exasperating confusions which are characteristic of pre-Kantian philosophy, and by no means totally lacking in Kant.

11. Thus it is exactly the 'containing' model which permitted

[1] *Op. cit.*, p. 52.

the Cartesian blurring of the distinction between sensible and conceptual representations which, as I argued in the preceding chapter, Kant struggles to establish on a sound basis—with only partial success.

II

12. The root notion of 'existing in itself' is that of existing *simpliciter* as contrasted with existing *as represented*, i.e. existing 'in' a representing or as 'idea'.[1] Clearly represent*ings* (conceptual or non-conceptual) as well as non-represent*ings* may be represent*ed*. Thus we can distinguish:

(1*a*) non-representings *qua* existing *simpliciter*;
(1*b*) representings *qua* existing *simpliciter*;
(2*a*) represented non-representings *qua* represented;
(2*b*) represented representings *qua* represented.[2]

13. Let us now introduce the term 'in itself' for anything, representing or not, which exists *simpliciter*, *as* existing *simpliciter*; and let us use the term 'content' for anything, representing or not, which exists 'in' a representing, *qua* so doing. Finally, let us call intuitive representings in themselves[3] (as contrasted with represent*ed* intuitive representings) 'constituting acts'. Notice that it would seem to be possible for an intuitive represent*ing* to be intuitively represent*ed*, i.e. for there to be an 'inner intuition' of an intuition. Indeed, as we shall see, it is necessary for there to be such—but these questions must await a general discussion of inner sense and apperception.

14. We must now take provisional account of the fact that, according to Kant's official position, representings-in-themselves are not in Time. According to this position, Time is, in the *first* instance, the form of intuitively represented representings; and, in the *second* instance, the form of other represent*eds*, both repre-

---

[1] In view of the notorious *ing-ed* ambiguity of words like 'representation' and its German equivalent, '*Vorstellung*', it will be useful, indeed essential, to use the explicit 'ing' or 'ed' form whenever there is a danger of confusion—and to use the technical term 'content' in place of the ambiguous 'idea'.

[2] Notice that there is a further sense in which a representation can exist in 'in' a representing—the 'internal accusative' sense in which a waltz exists in a waltzing. I shall not use this internal accusative sense without making the fact explicit.

[3] Intuitive representings, it will be remembered, are a special class of representings of individuals.

sented representings and represented non-representings (e.g. figures in Space). This thesis was intended by Kant to be the exact counterpart of his treatment of Space as the form of intuitively represented non-representings. And, indeed, the parallel is there, blurred by the ambiguities explored in the preceding chapter, compounded. I argued there that by implicitly requiring that a relation be spatial in a sense which would satisfy a physicist, or else be *in no sense spatial*, Kant dooms to failure his attempt to distinguish the form of outer sense from the Space of mechanics. We shall see that yet other senses in which relations can legitimately be said to be 'spatial' are required by a metaphysics which frees Kant's argument from its historically inevitable limitations.

15. In the case of Time, as Kant himself notes in the second edition, his views encountered greater resistance. He makes the parallel assumption that a temporal relation must be 'chronometric' in a sense congenial to the physicist, or else be *in no sense temporal*. We soon find, however, even more clearly than in the case of Space, that his argument requires two additional uses of temporal expressions. The first of these is required in connection with the form of inner sense, which is confused with the form of inner intuition exactly as the form of outer sense was confused with Space as an intuitively represented framework for the representation of spatial configurations.[1]

16. We soon find, moreover, a *third* kind of temporality peeking out at us from almost every page of the *Critique* from the *Analytic* on. For the *successiveness*, whether it be called temporal or no, of the epistemic acts of the real self in its struggles with the impressions of receptivity, and the *successiveness* of these impressions themselves (and, presumably, of the realities which impinge on our receptivity to cause them), are no mere *façons de parler*, but essential to the very meaning of the argument. Kant's failure to do explicit justice to this successiveness is no accident, and I shall shortly be examining the reasons which account for it. For the moment I simply note that if we were to adopt Kant's official restriction of the vocabulary of Time to the ideal temporal continuum of physical theory we could do no better than follow Bergson's example—though not in all respects—and contrast Time with *durée* and say that the

[1] For an elaboration of this point see the Appendix.

successiveness of representings-in-themselves is *durée* rather than Time.

17. Bergson, indeed, found his cue in Kant, for in B149 Kant writes:

> ... if we suppose an object of non-sensible intuition to be given,[1] we can indeed represent it through all the predicates which are implied in the presupposition that it has none of the characteristics proper to sensible intuition: that it is not extended or in Space, *that its duration is not a time* ... (Italics mine)

Again in B798, after insisting that 'we cannot ... *ursprunglich aussinnen* [which Kemp Smith translates as 'creatively imagine'] any object in terms of any new quality which does not allow of being given an experience', he grants that the concepts of 'a presence that is not spatial, a duration that is not temporal' are not self-contradictory—though, of course, he goes on to say that as far as *our* reason is concerned, they would 'be without an object', since we cannot intuitively represent them.

18. It is possible (as Bergson saw) to insist on the transcendental ideality of *scientific* Time, while affirming the transcendental reality of states of affairs which are temporal in a related, but by no means identical, sense. Indeed, this move is essential to the coherence of a Kantian philosophy, a point I have already argued in the parallel case of Space. The force of Kant's contention that the concepts of such spatiality and such temporality must be without an object because they cannot be illustrated in intuition is a topic for subsequent investigation.

III

19. Now, if the core of the notion of the in-itself is the concept of that which exists *simpliciter* as contrasted with that which exists as idea (content) or representable, it is clear that Kant adds to this core a theme of 'unknowability'. This unknowability, however, must be compatible with the *philosophical* (transcendental) knowledge that there is an in-itself, and that it is structured in a way which can be *abstractly* represented—in some sense of 'abstractly' —and which accounts for the existence and character of experience.

[1] Thus the intellectual intuition which God has of the world.

1. Material Things

20. Correspondingly, the core of the Kantian notion of an appearance is that of an idea or content. Thus, when Kant tells us that spatial objects are appearances his claim is a remote cousin of Berkeley's claim that 'extension and figure . . . are in the mind *only as they are perceived by it,* that is, not by way of *mode* or *attribute,* but only by way of idea . . .'.[1] It should be borne in mind, however, that Kant himself strongly disapproved[2] of this use of the term 'idea' and gives the latter a more sophisticated use. His term 'representation' ('*Vorstellung*') is a rough equivalent, though only when used in the sense of represent*ed* or represent*able* as such.

21. In the preceding chapter I pointed out that Kant's argument requires a distinction between conceptual representings (of which intuition is a special case) and non-conceptual representings. This calls for a corresponding distinction between conceptual and non-conceptual contents.[3] To the extent to which Kant is confused about the distinction between conceptual and non-conceptual representings, to that extent we can expect to find confusion in his treatment of 'appearance'. It will be helpful, however, to introduce the topic of physical appearance in terms of the *conceptual* representation of individuals, where the representations are intuitions in the sense:

(*a*) that they are representations of *this-suches,* i.e. representings in the expression of which predicates do not occur in the properly predicative position;

(*b*) the *suches* are sensible characteristics.

Kant seems to limit these sensible characteristics to spatial characteristics as contrasted, in the *first* instance, with colour (partly because what we intuitively represent, we in some sense 'construct' or 'draw'); and, in the *second* instance, as contrasted with temporal characteristics (another consequence of his confusion between outer sense and outer intuition). Thus he can be construed as holding that nothing is *intuited* as both spatial and

---

[1] *Principles of Human Knowledge,* edited by A. D. Lindsay, London, 1934, p 136 (§ XLIX).

[2] Thus in A319–20; B376–7.

[3] It will be remembered that the 'of'-phrases which 'refer' to the 'content' of a representing are to be construed as adjectives which combine with the category word 'impression' or 'conception' (conceiv*ing*) to classify these representations as of a certain kind.

temporal; which is quite compatible with holding, as he does, that in another mode of conceptual representation items *are* represented as both spatial and temporal.

22. As in the case of the 'in-itself' we must supplement the core notion of a physical appearance as idea (or content), to give it a properly Kantian flavour. Thus we must add that an appearance is an individual which, though it exists primarily as represent*ed* and secondarily as represent*able*, cannot exist *simpliciter* (i.e. in itself). Thus, an individual which is an appearance cannot be identical with anything which exists *simpliciter*. On the other hand, it is essential to note that Kant is *not* claiming that *no* item which exists (or is capable of existing) 'in' a representing can exist *simpliciter* (i.e. in itself). Everything hinges on *how* the item is represented.

23. Thus, an item which is given a purely *transcendental* identification, that is, an identification of the form

the item to which my receptivity responded with an impression which was taken up into this perceiving

can properly be said to exist in itself. But, as Kant sees it, such a purely transcendental description is very thin beer.

24. I have implied that Kant unduly restricts the class of predicates which permit the items of which they are true to exist *simpliciter*, as well as 'in' representings, by overlooking, or at least minimizing, the possibility that spatial, temporal and even colour predicates might be systematically ambiguous. On the other hand, as I have pointed out, he frequently uses language (e.g. in the 'Subjective Deduction') which implies that items-in-themselves can be described in richer terms than the purely transcendental description illustrated above, and exist in themselves as thus described. Acts of 'synthesis' are items-in-themselves, and yet *somehow* they can truly be described as 'successive'. Be that as it may, his official move is to deny that such descriptions can be in spatio-temporal terms.

25. Less puzzling is his treatment of monism and pluralism with respect to the in-itself. What he rejects is not the claim that we have philosophical knowledge that there is a plurality of items-in-themselves but rather monism or pluralism as theses with respect

to the number of *ultimate* logical subjects. It will be remembered that according to the philosophical tradition the 'accidents' or 'modifications' of 'substances' are, to use a contemporary phrase, 'dependent particulars', which themselves can have accidents or modifications. One of Kant's points in the *Paralogisms* is that the 'I' might be a dependent particluar, an aspect of a more fundamental reality, rather than an ultimate logical subject.[1]

26. Thus, although Kant denies that physical appearances, which, in their primary mode of being, are intuitively represented spatial *this-suches*, can exist in themselves, he does seem to think [(B164), (A545; B573)] that the plurality of physical appearances can be said with good reason to correspond to a plurality of *items* (not necessarily *ultimate* logical subjects) in a way which can be expressed by the peculiar relational phrase 'is an appearance of'.

27. Let me complete this initial account by noting that Kant thinks it to be a necessary truth that if there are appearances there are things in themselves. In one sense, although a limited one, he is obviously right, and the point is more interesting than is the superficial one that 'appearance' implies 'something appears', though Kant does sum up his view in this manner. The point is rather that it is an analytic truth that if there are represent*eds* there must be represent*ings*.

28. But might not representings be merely represented representings? The answer is that whether an item be a non-representing or a representing of a non-representing, or a representing of a representing of a non-representing, etc., if it exists merely *as represented*, it must be the content of a representing which, whether or not it is represent*ed*, also exists *simpliciter* or in itself.[2]

29. It must be granted that this argument establishes at most that if there are represent*eds* there must be represent*ings* which exists *simpliciter* or *an sich*. It does not establish that there are non-representings *an sich*, and Leibnitz, for one, and also Berkeley can be construed as holding that everything which exists in itself is, if

[1] See, for example, the note to A364.
[2] In contemporary terms the point is that the concept of the right-hand side of a semantical statement is the correlate of the concept of its left-hand side.

not a representing, at least a representer. Nor does the argument establish that what exists *simpliciter* is in any sense unknowable, nor that represented individuals can only be 'appearances of', rather than identical with, items which exist in themselves. But Kant, of course, thinks he can establish these additional points.

30. One element in his strategy hinges on the fact that the epistemological tools he brings to his task include not only his version of the Cartesian distinction between formal and objective reality but the idea that the human (or any finite) mind is passive with respect to the impressions which initiate its conceptual representation of a world of which it is a part.

31. The following passage from the first edition *Paralogisms* provides a useful summary of the points I have so far made in this chapter:

> Nothing whatever is in Space save in so far as it is actually represented in it. It is a proposition which must indeed sound strange that a thing can exist only in the representation of it, but in this case the objection falls in as much as the things with which we are concerned are not things in themselves, but appearances only, that is, representations (A375).

Although this passage was dropped in the second edition, the significance of this fact must not be overestimated. For Kant came to see that although physical appearances may exist *primarily* as the content of *actual* intuitive representing, they exist *secondarily* as the content of *obtainable* intuitive representings, and, still more remotely, as the abstractly represented system (Nature in its physical aspect) of which *this* and *that* intuitively represented*s* are constituent parts. In this context the more 'primary' is that which is closer to the *actual* as contrasted with the *potential* or *hypothetical*. In another dimension, of course, Nature is primary and our glimpses of it secondary.

IV

32. It has often been noted that when Kant is smoothing the path for his non-critical readers he tends to say *not* that we know *appearances* but that we know things (in themselves) *as they appear*

to us.[1] On the whole, however, his considered formulation is that we know appearances. What is the significance of this change? One explanation, sound as far as it goes, is based on the fact that although Kant is convinced that the implications of practical or ethical discourse entitle us to say that persons are ultimate logical subjects rather than mere features of a mere basic 'substratum', he does not think that reflection on our knowledge of *matter of fact*—even introspective—entitles us to say that what exists in itself is an ultimate plurality of logical subjects.

33. Thus, while Kant undoubtedly thinks that there are features of the in-itself which are, in some sense, the counterparts of the plurality of physical appearances, he finds this notion empty in that, as he sees it, we can have no determinate conception of this plurality. All determinate conception, as far as human minds are concerned, involves spatio-temporal schematization, and, as we have seen, he regards the concepts of Space and Time as un-ambiguous in a way which entails that if Space and Time are transcendentally ideal, *anything* we determinately conceive of in spatial or temporal terms must be transcendentally ideal. This line of thought turns Kant's attention away from the correspondence of the plurality of intuited and intuitable spatial objects with an abstractly conceived plurality of items-in-themselves (which, as we have seen, might be modifications of one single thing-in-itself rather than a plurality of things-in-themselves), to the global relation of spatio-temporal Nature to 'the in-itself' which impinges on our sensibility.

34. Yet there is a more important, though not unrelated, con-sideration which has a direct bearing on the possible relevance today of Kant's contention that the world of physical objects in Space and Time is appearance. Thus, when, at the common-sense level, we distinguish between a thing and how it appears to us, we identify the thing in terms of characteristics it can actually have, and though in any particular case it may only *appear* to have them, it does so by virtue of having competing characteristics which belong to the same families. According to Kant, however, that which exists *simpliciter* can have *none* of the characteristics in terms

---

[1] Both locutions, however, are found throughout the *Critique* (see, e.g., A258; B314), and take on richer meanings as the argument progresses.

of which we represent the objects of perception. As we saw in the preceding chapter, our basic representations with respect to the physical world are of the form

this-cube

and such represent*eds* are incapable of existing *simpliciter*, even as partial aspects of the total 'in-itself'. To say that an object appears to be ϕ implies that the object *as identified* exists *simpliciter*, and, for Kant, nothing identified in spatio-temporal terms can exist as such in itself. As was pointed out above, only that which is identified in purely transcendental terms can exist as such in itself, and transcendental identification, of this kind, though genuine, is, for Kant, completely indeterminate and provides no concrete way of comparing and contrasting one item with any other.

V

35. Another theme in Kant's conception of appearance was not brought fully under control until the second edition *Refutation of Idealism*. A failure to draw clearly and firmly the distinctions we have been elaborating led him to think that the sensible representations of the empirical self have a privileged status which makes them, so to speak, the cash of the world of appearance, even though to be so, they must be represented (and they are, indeed, appearances or represent*eds*) as belonging to a system (Nature) of which they are a vanishingly small part.

36. This idea is akin to that of certain contemporary philosophers, not too far removed from positivistic phenomenalism, who construe the conceptual framework of physical objects as one which, though not *reducible* to the framework of sense impressions, is nevertheless *subordinated* to the latter, and has its cash value in its (probabilistic) power to mediate between sense impression premises and sense impression conclusions. (Compare the instrumentalist conception of microphysical theories as symbolic devices the meaning of which is *constituted by* their power to mediate between premises concerning observables and conclusions concerning observables.)

37. 'After all,' we can imagine Kant to say, 'it is the representa-

tions of outer sense which set the understanding in motion, and although the conceptualized world includes both empirical self and material things, are not the represented sensory states of the empirical self more strictly the phenomenal counterparts of the manifold of outer sense than are the intuitively represented states of material things?' Yet the fact that the impressions of outer receptivity appear in experience as sensory states of the empirical self is quite compatible with the idea that they impel an understanding with our conceptual apparatus to represent *two parallel strands of appearance*: our empirical self *and* material things. For, after all, viewed transcendentally, the representations of outer sense are functions of both the self-in-itself as patient and the non-ego as agent. It must not be overlooked that the states of the empirical self are as much appearances, that is, *contents* of conceptual representings, as are the states of material things in Space.

38. Part of the explanation for Kant's lingering tendency to minimize these considerations is to be found in the idea that states of the empirical self have *content* in a way in which material things do not. The old confusions involved in the distinction between primary and secondary qualities continued to plague Kant. As we have noted, he so construes the figurative synthesis of spatial items by the productive imagination that it excludes colour. It does indeed synthesize degrees of that in appearances which, in the language of the *Anticipations of Perception*, 'corresponds' to 'sensation',[1] that is, the 'real' in appearances (B207) or their 'matter' (A20; B34). But this 'real' or 'matter' is not colour but rather force as a concept of mechanics. At this stage of the scientific revolution it had come to seem a phenomenological truth that the place of colour is (somehow) in the mind. Kant, to use Whitehead's phrase, bifurcated Nature and drew the proper conclusion that since the physical, thus represented, '. . . contains nothing but mere relation' (B66–7), it cannot exist in itself.

39. Kant, of course, would scarcely have held that states of the empirical self are literally coloured, any more than that they are literally extended. Yet he could have held that visual 'sensations'

---

[1] A166. See A20; B34 where he speaks of 'that in the appearance which corresponds to sensation', and calls it the 'matter' of appearance (which corresponds to the phrase 'the real in appearance' of the *Anticipations*).

of the empirical self 'contain' colour in the sense of representing it, and, therefore, that they have content in a sense in which purely physical appearance does not.[1]

40. Kant's discussion of these matters is tangled and confused, and it can be argued that his position is the less drastic one that the productive imagination synthesizes objects which are coloured as well as extended, though there is a difference, bound up with the apparent irrelevance of colour to the mechanical behaviour of material things, between the objectivity of colour and the objectivity of extension.

VI

41. In the first edition, then, Kant was tempted to construe spatial complexes in the fully constituted world of appearance as existing 'in' representings which belong to the history of the temporal self. Since the temporal self is itself appearance, this would amount to the idea that, whatever may go on behind the scenes, we represent spatial complexes in experience *by representing ourselves as representing spatial complexes.* This unfortunate tendency is corrected in the second edition. He there sees clearly that, in spite of their common foundation in the impressions of outer sense, the visual sensations of the empirical self, on the one hand, and the physical events, on the other, are on a par as appearances. They are alike represent*eds*, if I may so put it, of the first degree.[2]

---

[1] How he could have held that the visual sensations of the empirical self 'contain' colour without granting that in the same sense of 'contain' they contain extension is difficult to see. This highlights the difficulty of holding that 'sensations', whether real or phenomenal, granted that they are not extended in the literal way in which physical objects are extended, are 'purely intensive magnitudes'. Yet some of the paradox is removed when it is noted that Kant is prepared to say that the 'real' in appearances (which are obviously extended) 'has . . . magnitude but not extensive magnitude' (A168; B210).

[2] There remains the complication that to the extent to which Kant takes seriously the idea that physical objects are not coloured, colour, as far as the world of appearances is concerned, would be a represent*ed* of the second degree, i.e. we would represent colour only by representing ourselves as representing it. Colour would thus be, in a sense, an appearance to an appearance. This must not be confused with the idea that sensory states of the empirical self are 'appearances of appearances' (*Nachlass*), which finds expression in the 'double affection' theory. The latter is the idea that sensory states of the empirical self as part of Nature are brought about by physical stimulation of the sense organs (mediated by neuro-physiological states), but that this 'bringing about' and the factors it involves are themselves appearances represented by minds under the impact of things in themselves. (See below, § 57.)

46

1. Material Things

42. The second edition *Refutation of Idealism* gives us the key to Kant's interpretation of experience as both knowledge of *appearances* and knowledge of *reality as it appears*. Given our conceptual equipment, we respond to the impressions of sense by conceptually representing a temporal me embedded in a spatio-temporal Nature. The determinate core of this representing consists of intuitive (but conceptual) representings of both *representings* (states of the empirical self) and *non-representings* (states of material things). I shall continue in the present chapter to concentrate on the latter.

43. A 'transcendental realist', as Kant uses this term, holds that, mis-perception aside, intuitively represented objects and events exist *simpliciter* as well as 'in' representings. If such a one were to hear Kant say that reality is such as to lead a being with our conceptual equipment to form the intuitive representings we do, he would say, 'Well, that is because the representings are, by and large, *true*. The things we conceptually represent also exist *simpliciter*, or in themselves, *as we represent them*.' In other words, if I may introduce contemporary terminology to make my point, the transcendental realist would say that the 'obtainability' of both the representings we *actually* have and the representings we *would* have *if* we were to undertake to change our perceptual orientation is grounded in the truth of these representings, the existence *simpliciter* of that which exists 'in' them as idea or content.

44. Notice that the contents of which we are speaking are *conceptual* contents. They are not the contents of non-conceptual representings (sense impressions proper). And they are contents pertaining to states of material things, as contrasted with contents pertaining to the empirical self. They are, in our terminology, represented *non-representings*, not represented *representings* (such as would be the contents of intuitive representings of our inner states).

45. The realist typically denies that concepts pertaining to physical objects are to be analysed in terms of sense contents, i.e. the contents of non-conceptual representings. He can, however, grant that concepts pertaining to physical objects can be analysed in terms of the contents of *outer intuitions*, in Kant's sense of the phrase, without thereby becoming a phenomenalist in the

Berkeleyian or positivistic sense. As for the *obtainability* of these contents, i.e. intuitively represented spatial structures, he would insist, as was pointed out above, that it rests on the existence *an sich* of the spatial structures in question, and the existence *simpliciter* of ourselves as sentient conceptualizing beings in Space and Time.

46. Now Kant himself, as has often been noted, does write on occasion as though physical objects were actual and obtainable sensory states of the empirical self, in other words, as though, in this respect at least, he were a Berkeleyian phenomenalist. This practice was corrected, if not entirely abandoned, in the second edition. Yet Kant remains *in another sense* a 'phenomenalist', though not in quite the sense which Kemp Smith valiantly attempts to define. Kant's phenomenalism can be put, in first approximation, by saying that physical objects and events exist *only* 'in' certain actual and obtainable conceptual representings, the intuitive representings synthesized by the productive imagination in response to the impressions of sense. I say exist *only* 'in' such representings, for no *res extensa* exists *simpliciter* or in itself. A phenomenalism which construes the physical world as a system of available contents in *this* sense differs radically from a phenomenalism which construes the world as a system of available sense impressions, for it construes physical appearances as *irreducibly* physical. It differs from physical realism by denying that these appearances have more than 'objective' or 'representative' being.

47. The transcendental realist, as we have seen, interprets the obtainability of intuitions of spatial structures as grounded in the *an sich* existence of such structures. But while Kant agrees that this obtainability is grounded in the in-itself, he denies that this grounding requires that the in-itself be the spatio-temporal structure we conceptually represent. The strongest interpretation of this claim would be that existence in itself is in no sense akin to the spatio-temporal structures we represent. I see no reason to ascribe this view to Kant, nor does it seem to have any intrinsic merit. A less negative interpretation would be that it is not only *possible* for the in-itself to be, in an interesting sense, *analogous in structure* to the spatio-temporal world but that it is reasonable to think of it as having such a structure.

1. Material Things

48. Something like this view can, indeed, be ascribed to Kant—with some reading between the lines—although his explicit use of the notion of analogical conception is in theological contexts. And even if we attribute to him the view that things-in-themselves are analogous in structure to the world of appearance, the analogy would, for him, be one which could only be 'cashed' by God—much as, according to traditional theology, only He can cash the analogies in terms of which we attempt to conceive Him. God would have a non-analogical grasp of things in themselves by virtue of the fact that His intuitive representations are not passive, but are the very volitions by which they are created.

49. The thesis I wish to defend, but not ascribe to Kant, though it is very much a 'phenomenalism' in the Kantian (rather than Berkeleyian) sense, is that although the world we conceptually represent in experience exists only in actual and obtainable representings of it, we can say, from a transcendental point of view, not only that existence-in-itself accounts for this obtainability by virtue of having a certain analogy with the world we represent but also that in principle *we*, rather than God alone, can provide the cash. For, as I see it, the use of analogy in theoretical science, unlike that in theology, generates new determinate concepts. It does not merely indirectly specify certain unknown attributes by an 'analogy of proportion'. One might put this by saying that the conceptual structures of theoretical science give us new ways of schematizing categories.

50. Kant's own view is the more agnostic one that in our attempt to give an account of how our intuitive representings might be *Erkenntnisse* without being literally true, we are limited to making use of such abstract concepts as *existence-in-itself*, *existence 'in' representings, receptivity, form of intuition, judgment*, etc. One might formulate it as follows:

> Reality is such that finite minds non-arbitrarily, in accordance with their forms of receptivity, and their conceptual frameworks, represent *this-suches* and make judgments about them. Only God, however, knows how reality is. [Compare the idealistic thesis that sound human judgments of the form S is P are to be philosophically re-parsed as Reality is such that (we must represent that) S is P and only the Absolute knows ('feels'?) how things really are.]

49

51. Kant's account implies indeed that certain counterparts of our intuitive representations, namely God's intellectual intuitions, are literally true; but these literal truths can only be indirectly and abstractly represented by finite minds, and there is an impassible gulf between our *Erkenntnisse* and Divine Truth. If, however, as I shall propose in Chapter V, we replace the static concept of Divine Truth with a Peircean conception of truth as the 'ideal outcome of scientific inquiry', the gulf between appearances and things-in-themselves, though a genuine one, can in principle be bridged.

VII

52. Our explication of Kant's phenomenalism is not yet complete. For, if the material world exists only in actual and obtainable representings by individual minds, the problem of its public character becomes acute. It is, in part, the problem of the *intersubjectivity* of the conceptual. Thus, when two minds represent that two plus two equals four, what exactly is the sense in which they are representing *the same*? Metaphorically, one says that two acts in different minds 'have the same content'. But even if Kant could offer a satisfactory account of the intersubjectivity of logical and mathematical concepts and of the representations of Space and Time, this, by itself, would clearly not enable him to distinguish the public character of *possible* states of *possible* material things from the public character of the *actual* course of events in *this* world.

53. His answer clearly lies in a joint appeal to the intersubjectivity of the conceptual framework in terms of which we conceive *possible* states of affairs, and the public accessibility of the in-itself which, by affecting receptivity, generates the manifold of sense and guides the understanding in its use of this conceptual framework to form the intuitive representations of perceptual experience. The argument is a transcendental one to the effect that the very concept of 'objects of experience' as *non-arbitrary representeds which can be shared* unfolds along these lines.[1] It is not always

[1] The connection of 'objectivity' with 'intersubjectivity' stands out most clearly in the *Prolegomena*. See particularly Part II, Sections 18 ff. The importance of these passages is obscured by the confusions involved in his distinction between 'judgments of perception' and 'judgments of experience'.

realized that the philosophical, or higher order, claim that experience requires synthetic necessary principles is, for Kant, an *analytic* truth arrived at by what we would call 'conceptual analysis', but which Kant calls '*Erklaerung*'. Thus, he writes, in the latter part of the *Critique*:

> The German language has for the [Latin] terms exposition, explication, declaration, and definition, only one word, *Erklaerung*, and we need not, therefore, be so stringent in our requirements as altogether to refuse to philosophical explanations the honorable title definition (A730; B758).

Needless to say, however, the definitions in question are not stipulations of use for new sign designs but 'expositions of given concepts'.

54. The above interpretation of the intersubjectivity or public character of appearances is not only compatible with but *requires* the idea that the primary mode of being of appearances is in conceptual representings by *individual minds*. There are, however, those, not uninfluenced by Hegel, who have argued that Kant was moving towards a position which interprets the material world as *somehow* dependent on Mind, without consisting of the contents of actual and obtainable representings by finite minds.

55. It would, I think, be generally agreed that to make the primary mode of being of appearances a matter of being represented by a super-subject—God, the Absolute, or the Red King—is to abandon Kant.[1] Nevertheless, without explicitly making this move, the neo-Hegelian interpretation of Kant's phenomenalism, ignored the Cartesian roots of Kant's conception of appearance, and construed appearances as second-class entities, whose second-class-ness was, indeed, interpreted in terms of a non-arbitrary inadequacy of the thoughts of finite minds, but whose relation to what really is was left notoriously obscure. As appearances, material things and empirical minds were put on a par, and conceived to be causally connected in ways explored by empirical psychology. Instead of being the content of actual and obtainable human representings, grounded in unknowable things-in-them-

---

[1] Which is not to deny that even for Kant, in the last analysis, appearances exist for man because God, in his Providence and Will, conceives of man as representing them.

selves, physical appearance was construed as the ground of the obtainability of human perceptions, and its character as appearance as an unspecified dependence on 'noumenal conditions'.[1]

56. When Kemp Smith argues[2] to some such position from the premise that the actual 'sensations' of finite minds cannot be the 'material' of the world of appearance (since they are only a fragmentary part of it) he is moving from a true premise (that the actual in appearance includes more than the sensory states of empirical selves) and another true, but tacit, premise (that the existence of 'obtainable' sensory states presupposes the existence, in an appropriate sense, of material things) to the false conclusion that the actuality of material things cannot consist in their being actual and obtainable *conceptual* representeds—that is to say, actual and obtainable intuitions (in the Kantian sense) rather than actual and obtainable 'sensations'. For the claim that the world of appearance exists 'in' actual and obtainable intuitions is, as we have seen, by no means equivalent to the idea that it consists of actual and obtainable 'sensations' or 'sense contents', let alone actual 'sensations' only.

57. The doctrine of 'double affection' is an essential feature of Kant's thought. Correctly understood, it simply tells us that the transcendentally conceived non-spatial, non-temporal action of the non-ego on human receptivity, generating the manifold of sense (which action is required to explain how the *esse* of the experienced world can be *concipi* and yet non-arbitrary and inter-subjective) has as its counterpart in the represent*ed* world the action of material things on our sense organs and, through them, on the sensory faculties of the empirical self. Thus, of the two 'affections' one has representative being only, while the other has both representative being 'in' transcendental thought *and* also being *simpliciter* or 'in itself'. This can be put by saying that one 'affection' is the appearance of the other, but unless this is supple-

---

[1] In particular, Kant's valiant attempt to clarify the dependence by means of a 'transcendental' psychology which abstracted from the specific features of human experience as we represent it in the conceptual framework which is natural to us was rejected as involving fictitious mental machinery. Kant's agnosticism is, indeed, to be rejected; but this corrective lies not in dialectical attacks on the concept of an 'unknowable' but in the development of more subtle theories of concept formation.

[2] *A Commentary to Kant's Critique of Pure Reason*, p. 276.

mented by a properly Kantian analysis of appearance it acquires the air of intolerable paradox (a 'two-world' theory) which has led an essential part of Kant's mature teachings to be the subject of fruitless and uninformed controversy, and to be regarded as suspect by many of his more sympathetic students.

VIII

58. But why should we not be transcendental realists? Why should we hold that the *esse* of the material world is *concipi*—more accurately, that it exists only 'in' actual and obtainable representings? (I shall follow Kant in calling the latter the thesis of the transcendental ideality of the spatio-temporal world.) Kant offers a number of arguments for this thesis, all of them interesting but of unequal value and relevance to the contemporary scene. Since I am going to defend a closely related thesis, I shall emphasize those facets of his argument which serve this purpose. Thus I shall not deal directly with the *Antinomies*, which, as Kant saw it, give the *coup de grace* to transcendental realism.

59. Let me begin by discussing the transcendental ideality of Space. Kant, of course, was convinced that Space was not the sort of thing which *could* be transcendentally real, a conviction which found expression in his reference to it as an '*Unding*' (A39; B56) or 'non-thing'. In a certain sense he was absolutely right about this, but mistaken about the conclusions he draws.

60. Let me begin by drawing familiar distinctions. In the first place, between: (*a*) what I shall call, for reasons which will shortly emerge, 'fine-grained' or 'theoretical' Space. It is an infinite individual, consisting of a three-dimensional continuum of points and containing an infinity of lines, surfaces and regions, the chief characteristic of which, for our purposes, is that they are the willing subject-matter for the mathematical technique of Archimedes, Descartes and the inventors of the differential calculus.

61. (*b*) Contrasting with this there is what I shall call 'coarse-grained' or empirical Space. It, too, is an infinite individual, but it is an individual the elements of which are *possibilities*—roughly, possible relations of perceptible material things.

62. As an initial elaboration of this distinction, let me point out that there correspond to it two radically different senses of 'material thing', and two radically different senses in which something can be said to occupy a position in Space. Corresponding to 'fine-grained' Space are what might be called 'fine-grained' objects, systems of point-masses. Fine-grained objects are *related to* regions of fine-grained Space. Here, possibility comes in as the possibility of an object occupying this or that region of Space. Fine-grained Space, unlike empirical Space, does not *consist of* possibilities. Its points and regions are *terms* of possible containments.

63. Coarse-grained (or empirical) Space, on the other hand, *consists of* possible relations of coarse-grained material things to one another. Here, the relation of 'occupying a place' is a special case of that interesting kind of relation which is 'realizing a possibility'.

64. The first point I want to make, then, is that Kant would surely be right to claim that both fine-grained Space and fine-grained objects are transcendentally ideal. Indeed, the only reason I have refrained from calling them *ideal* Space and *ideal* objects is that to do so would make an important point look like a play on words.

65. Kant, however, confused what I will now call ideal Space and ideal objects with the framework of coarse-grained perceptible objects and the Space which is the system of their possible relations. Thus he mistakenly inferred the transcendental ideality of empirical Space—and, correspondingly, the transcendental ideality of perceptible physical things—from the transcendental ideality of their ideal counterparts

66. Notice, however, that there is a legitimate sense in which, given Kant's theory of the modalities, even empirical Space must be transcendentally ideal. For Kant tells us in the metaphysical deduction that:

the modality of judgment is a quite peculiar feature. Its distinguishing character is that it contributes nothing to the content of the judgment . . . but concerns only the value of the copula in relation to thought in general (B100).

1. Material Things

Crudely put, Kant's thesis is that the modalities are meta-linguistic, or, less outrageously, meta-conceptual. It might be put by saying that modal attributes are attributes of propositional representables (judgeables) as such, and not of things or events. I shall have something to say about this later on. For the moment I simply note that *if* Kant is right, then empirical Space, consisting as it does of possibilities *qua* possibilities, is *a fortiori* transcendentally ideal.

67. *But*, it will immediately be noted, it does not follow from the transcendental ideality of empirical Space as a system of possible relations that particular states of affairs involving spatial relations are transcendentally ideal. This is the Achilles' heel of his argument.

68. Why did Kant identify ideal Space with what I am tentatively calling empirical Space? The following considerations seem relevant:

(1) Both are odd kinds of individual or logical subject. Thus they are clearly not substances, if the abilities to act and be acted on are criteria of substance.

(2) Kant does not distinguish the transcendentally ideality due to ideal-ness from the transcendentally ideality due to modality.

(3) There is a platonic theme reminiscent of the *Phaedo* and *Meno*. After all, Kant's whole conception of experience is a sophisticated development of the platonic notion that we experience the world as spatial by responding to sense impression with ideal geometrical concepts which have not been derived from experience. If one (correctly) rejects 'abstraction from sense impressions' as a theory of geometrical concept formation, then why have *two* non-abstracted systems of spatial concepts? This consideration led to the equating of all geometrical concepts with those of mathematical geometry.[1]

69. Kant's sound attack on concept empiricism had the unfortunate consequence that, given certain other commitments, it

[1] Yet, as already indicated, we need at least two systems of geometrical concepts, neither of which can be accounted for in terms of 'abstraction'. (That the acquiring of empirical concepts involves an element of ostensive training can be granted, but this training is only one small facet of the process of acquiring these concepts.)

obscured the difference between two essentially different geometrical frameworks, and two essentially different systems of concepts pertaining to physical things. As a matter of fact, Kant was led to confuse *three* radically different conceptions of 'physical thing', with the result that he failed to notice a further line of argument for the transcendental ideality of perceptible things which really works, and is the one I shall espouse.

70. Yet another confusion, closely related to the above, reinforced Kant's conviction that Space is transcendentally ideal in a sense which requires that all spatial states of affairs be transcendentally ideal. This is the confusion, explored in the last chapter, between Space as a form of intuition and Space as the form of outer sense, that is, the system of attributes of and relations between sense impressions which accounts for the fact that we inituitively represent now *this*, now *that* spatial configuration of objects. These attributes and relations, as was pointed out in the first chapter, are properly construed as 'spatial' only in an analogical sense; yet their structural similarity to spatial attributes and relations proper makes it tempting to equate them with the latter. This, essentially, is what Kant has done. The *subjectivity* of sense impressions which exist *simpliciter* as states of the self in-itself was confused with the transcendental *ideality* (*esse est concipi*) supposedly established by platonic and modal considerations.

71. The upshot of these remarks is that although Kant was right to claim that the individual or logical subject, Space, is transcendentally ideal, he has not shown that particular states of affairs involving *non-ideal* spatial relations must be transcendentally ideal. Correspondingly, though he *has* shown that the ideal material things of Newtonian mechanics are transcendentally ideal, he has *not* shown that perceptible physical objects standing in perceptible spatial relations are transcendentally ideal. If he was right about this, he was right for the wrong reasons.[1]

---

[1] I shall tip my hand by saying that the true ground for the transcendental ideality of the perceptual world lies in the distinction between perceptible physical objects and the objects of theoretical science, a distinction which was blurred by Kant. Thus, his concept of physical appearance runs together not only the idealized counterparts of perceptible things (e.g. systems of point-masses whose velocities and accelerations are amenable to differential equations) but also the object of micro-physics which are as imperceptible as ideal objects, though for radically different reasons.

56

1. Material Things

72. It is also important to note that even if we were to grant him the platonic theme that the Space of perceptual experience is the ideal Space of mechanics, it would still have been open to Kant to say that things-in-themselves, in so far as they affect our sensibility, have, like sense impressions, attributes and relations which are *in their own way* analogous to those of perceptible things, and by virtue of which they elicit sense impressions which are in their *different* way endowed with Space-like characteristics (confused by Kant with the form of outer intuition), and perform the guiding role described above. That Kant implicitly accepted some such view of things-in-themselves is, I think, clear. Yet if the fact had been brought to his attention he would most certainly have claimed that this transcendental use of analogy is *empty*. The abstract concept of such Space-like characteristics could have 'cash value' only for God.

IX

73. Another theme in the Kantian attack on transcendental realism mobilizes an old friend, the distinction between primary and secondary qualities. There seems to be no doubt that Kant, like Descartes, was convinced that material things are properly described in purely spatio-temporal terms; which is not to deny that they have 'secondary qualities' in Locke's sense of the term. He would, of course, insist that our concepts of spatial and temporal characteristics involve the categories or forms of judgment, so that we represent the world in terms of such categorial features as actuality, potentiality, substantial identity, interaction, necessary connection, etc. Or, to put it the other way around, that these characteristics serve as differentia (schemata) for abstract concepts of modes of unity. The point remains, however, that the non-categorial features of represented material things are conceived by Kant to be purely spatial and temporal. Since it is obvious, *pace* Descartes, that nothing which exists 'in itself' can have only spatial or temporal characteristics, the conclusion was reasonably drawn that the world of material things is transcendentally ideal.

74. Now Kant is clearly right to claim that nothing 'consisting of mere relations' can be transcendentally real. Reality must have qualitative content as well as relational form. There is certainly no reason to suppose—unless one is committed to abstractionism, or

to the view that basic descriptive predicates must be ostensively 'defined' or 'learned'—that qualitative content is limited to what humans can perceive. Yet reflection on the nature of empirical Space and spatial attributes (if he had not confused them with ideal Space and spatial attributes, and had not taken the subjectivity of colour for granted) would surely have convinced Kant that the objects of perception are as essentially coloured as they are extended; indeed, that their spatial characteristics essentially involve the contrast of colour with colour. An empirical line, for example, is a white streak on a black background, or the edge of a ruler.

75. Thus Kant should have recognized that colour itself, and not something which 'corresponds' to it, is as essential a feature of the objects of outer intuition as is shape. If, therefore, a sound case can be made for the idea that the colours we conceptually represent in perception are transcendentally ideal, i.e. exist only as conceptually represented,[1] then it would follow that the world of perceived objects is, after all, in the Kantian sense, 'appearance'.

X

76. Perhaps the most interesting argument for the transcendental ideality of the represented world is what might be called the argument from the transcendental ideality of the categories. It goes somewhat as follows:

> Premise I: The categorial forms are forms of what exists in representings, as so existing.
> Premise II: What exists in itself does not, as so existing, exist in conceptual representings.
> Conclusion I: The categorial forms are not forms of what exists in itself, as so existing.
> Premise III: The physical world exists 'in' conceptual representings.
> Conclusion II: The physical world as existing 'in' conceptual representings has categorial form.
> Conclusion III: The physical world has categorial form.
> Conclusion IV: The physical world does not exist in itself.

[1] Notice that this is, of course, compatible with the idea that certain counterpart attributes, conceived by analogy with them, are transcendentally real, though, perhaps, only as in some sense states of the perceiver.

1. Material Things

I have spelled out the argument in such a way as to make it clear that it is formally fallacious. The invalid step is the move from Conclusion II to Conclusion III. Yet although the argument is fallacious, and, more interestingly, *although Kant never uses it*, it is one of the persistent myths of Kant's scholarship. Most of the puzzles about 'Do the categories apply to things in themselves?' rest on a tacit appeal to the following 'principle':

Nothing which as conceptually represented has categorial form can exist *simpliciter* or in itself.

77. This fallacious and quite un-Kantian principle would require, for example, that since things-in-themselves have categorial form as represented, they cannot exist in themselves! It can scarcely be overemphasized that the difficulty Kant finds with things-in-themselves is that, considerations of morals and religion aside, our conception of them is *empty*—not that it is *incoherent*.

78. I have laid stress on the above argument from the ideality of the categories because *although it is not Kantian*, it is not easy to see why. Furthermore, something like it is at the bottom of many contemporary puzzles. Kant's list of categories is notoriously an *omnium gatherum*. There are many who are inclined to say that at least some of the categories or forms are transcendentally ideal. Thus it is said by some that the *modalities* pertain to thought and not to things; that neither *all-ness* nor *some-ness* is 'in the world'; that neither *conjunction* nor *negation* is 'in the world'. There are even those who say that the subject-attribute or subject-relation nexus pertain to thought and not to things. But a fruitful discussion of these topics presupposes an examination of intentionality and truth.

III

THE CONCEPTUAL AND
THE REAL:

1. INTENTIONALITY

1. In the last chapter I was exploring Kant's distinction between appearances and things-in-themselves. The framework of the discussion was the contrast between:

(*a*) representings;

(*b*) contents of representings, i.e. that which exists 'in' representings as so existing;

(*c*) that which exists *simpliciter* as so existing.

It was pointed out that an item may exist, or be capable of existing, 'in' a representing without existing *simpliciter*. It was also pointed out that whereas pre-Kantian philosophy took as its paradigm examples of contents, general contents, e.g., the content *triangular* and the content *wise*, Kant's approach was radically different. Superficially, the most striking change is his insistence that the class of contents should be expanded to include individual contents, e.g., the content of an intuitive representing of *this-cube*, or the content *Socrates*, which, though an individual content, is not the content of an intuitive representing.[1] (There have, of course, been intuitive representings which, though not *strictu sensu* of Socrates, did pertain to him, as when his contemporaries saw him in the Agora.) The class of contents must also include what might be called 'logical contents', though Kant himself would

[1] Notice that the expression 'this cube' picks out a whole family of individual contents which are relative to particular situations of representing in a way made familiar by modern explications of demonstrative phrases. The contents in question might well be called 'fugitive contents', to adopt and adapt a useful suggestion by Austin Duncan-Jones in his paper on 'Fugitive Propositions', *Analysis*, 10, 1949.

have preferred to call them 'forms' rather than 'contents'. We must, however, be careful, for the time being, at least, to distinguish the form *of the content* of a representing from the form of the representing itself *qua* act. It should be borne in mind that Kant's phrase 'form of judgment' lumps together items which must be given quite different treatments. Thus, as we shall see, logical contents (e.g. *not*) must be distinguished from the form (e.g. 'concatenation') which, by combining them with judgmental content, enable them to do their job. I shall therefore, *pace* Kant, speak, for example, of the content *not*, the content *or*, the content *all* and the content *necessary*. Finally, Kant insists on the irreducibility of judgmental to non-judgmental content. This, indeed, was the very heart of his insight. This irreducibility is a function not only of the irreducibility of logical contents but of the irreducibility of the subject-predicate nexus which will be explored in Chapter IV. In accordance with this thesis of the primacy of judgmental content and judgmental form we must give pride of place to such contents as the content *this cube is made of wood* and the content *all bodies are heavy*.[1]

2. In the case of individual contents our original three-fold distinction works reasonably well, thus we have:

acts: a representing of Socrates, a representing of Plato, a representing of Pegasus, . . .

contents: the content Socrates, the content Plato, the content Pegasus, . . .

existents *an sich*: Socrates, Plato, . . .

The fact that Socrates, unlike Pegasus, exists *simpliciter* as well as 'in' our representings finds its expression in the fact that in the third list above we find 'Socrates' but not 'Pegasus'.

3. It is much less obvious, however, what the third category should include in the case of other types of content. For example, when the content is the content *wise*, should we have:

[1] It has not often been noted that Kant's 'derivation' of the substance-attribute category from the form of categorical rather than singular judgments suggests that the category has its roots in Aristotle's conception of 'prime matter' as that " 'which is no longer, in reference to something else, called 'thaten' " (*Metaphysics*, 1049a 23–6). This, in my opinion, is the explanation of his equation of 'substance' with 'matter' in the first Analogy.

existents *an sich*: wise?
existents *an sich*: wisdom?
existents *an sich*: wise people?
existents *an sich*: the wisdom of Socrates, the wisdom of Plato, etc.?

Or should there be no third category, as the Parmenidean tradition would have it in the case of the content *not*? Each alternative has its puzzles, but since the concepts of existence and truth will be the topic of the following chapter, I shall put these puzzles aside.

4. Indeed, I have been getting ahead of my story. My first step must be to translate this vocabulary of 'representings', 'contents' and the like into a terminology which relates the above distinctions I have drawn more perspicuously to contemporary problems. To do this is to raise the question, 'What, after all, does it mean to say that contents exist "in" representings?'

5. If we take seriously the idea that one and the same content can exist in many representings by many minds, which seems to be an implication of the inter-subjectivity or public character of what we conceptually represent, we introduce a platonic theme—the contrast between a *one* which is shared and the *many* which share it. This theme develops of its own accord into the following line of thought:

> We need not only *ones* to be shared by many representings (to do justice to the intersubjectivity of thought), we also need *ones* to be shared by many *things*. We have already noted that even for Kant some general contents must be not only *intersubjective*, but *objective* in the strong sense that they are *true of* (or *capable* of being true of) things in the independent world; true, that is, of things-in-themselves.

6. Why, then, strain at the gnat and swallow the camel. If we admit one *content* 'in' many *representings*, why not admit one *attribute* 'in' many *things*: platonism for things as well as platonism for thoughts? Let us then countenance triangularity and wisdom.

II

7. Platonism is notoriously a heady draught and we must be cautious. We began with the content *wise* and the content *triangular*. We recognized them to be ones in manys. We have just countenanced wisdom and triangularity and recognized them to

62

be ones in manys. Indeed, we were on the point of declaring them to be the *same* ones. And why not? Why not say that the triangularity which is 'in' many triangular things is identical with the content *triangular* which is 'in' many representings.

8. This suggestion has the obvious merit of affirming the closest of connections between the intersubjectivity of representings and their objectivity, their capacity for truth. Sober reflection, however, calls to mind that we have begun the attempt to clarify one metaphorical use of 'in'—the *in-esse* of contents 'in' representings —only to add another, the *in-esse* of attributes 'in' things. For it is clear that the sense of 'in' in which triangularity might be in thoughts can scarcely be the same as that in which it is 'in' things. Thus, if we persist in identifying the content *triangular* with triangularity as an attribute of things we must distinguish two ways in which a single *one* might be 'in' different *manys*.

9. We might seek to mitigate this dualism by finding a generic *in-esse* of which the above are determinate forms, thus assimilating, without identifying, our two 'in's. Thus we might distinguish two attributive ties, one of which ties triangularity to material things (making them triangular), the other tying it to representings (making them representings of triangular things). Such a move, whatever its ultimate merits, has no immediate intuitive foundation, for there seems to be no special copula in actual usage which can join the predicate 'triangular' with expressions referring to thoughts, without committing us to the absurdity of triangular thoughts.

10. As an alternative we might, with early Russell and Moore, abandon the 'in' metaphor altogether and speak of a unique relation, the 'of' relation (as contrasted with attributive tie), between representings and, in our example, triangularity. I shall assume that the dialectic which concludes that the subjective term of such a relation must be a mental act rather than a mind— or for that matter a person—is familiar and compelling. I shall also take for granted that the concept of a diaphanous act, an act which, as far as its epistemic value is concerned, is characterized only by its 'of' relations to such items as triangularity, is unsatisfactory. We are thus led to the notion of a *counterpart attribute* which has already played a key role in our discussion in the first chapter of the non-conceptual representations of sense.

11. To use this model is to say that corresponding to triangularity as an attribute of things there is an attribute of mental acts which is such that mental acts which have it stand in the 'of' relation to triangularity, and, hence, are representings of triangular things. If, in a promisory-note-ish way, we use

'$\phi_{\text{triangular}}$'

to be the predicate of mental acts which corresponds to

'triangular'

as a predicate of material things, and correspondingly in the case of other predicates of material things, we have the schema

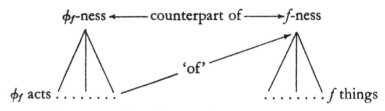

12. We can generalize this procedure. We begin by noting that triangularity belongs to the sort of things which philosophers of logic call 'intensions' (note the 's') and either countenance or try to discountenance. We then identify the various types of content we have so far recognized—individual contents, general contents, state of affairs contents (though not, for reasons which will emerge in a moment, logical contents)—with the corresponding intensions. Thus our list of intensions[1] would include:

Intensions:	*Diagnostic statements:*
individual $\begin{cases} Socrates \\ Pegasus \end{cases}$	$\begin{cases} \text{Socrates exists} \\ \text{Pegasus does not exist} \end{cases}$
universal $\begin{cases} \text{triangularity} \\ \text{diangularity} \end{cases}$	$\begin{cases} \text{Triangularity is exemplified} \\ \text{Diangularity is not exemplified} \end{cases}$
state of affairs $\begin{cases} \text{that Socrates is} \\ \quad \text{wise} \\ \text{that Aristotle is} \\ \quad \text{foolish} \end{cases}$	$\begin{cases} \text{That Socrates is wise obtains} \\ \text{That Aristotle is foolish does} \\ \quad \text{not obtain} \end{cases}$

[1] It should be noted that although my topic in this chapter is intentionality (note the 't'), the term 'intention', though by no means irrelevant, will not occupy the centre of the stage.

1. Intentionality

Corresponding to these intentions we would have another set of intensions, this time all attributes, which are, in accordance with our hypothesis, their counterparts and are attributes of the mental acts which are 'of' the original intensions. Thus, for example,

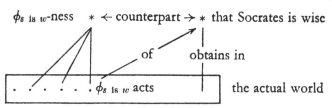

or, schematically

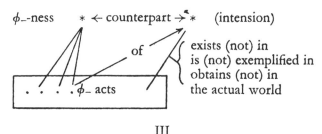

III

13. Having turned most of our contents into intensions, thus mobilizing one range of logical and ontological overtones, let me now turn them into senses, thus mobilizing themes from Frege.[1] For although our initial move away from contents was in a bluntly platonistic direction, introducing triangularity and other intensions as though they were the sort of thing which is altogether independent of thought, i.e. the *esse* of which is in no sense *concipi*, the use of the word 'sense' may rekindle the hope that somehow the objectivity of intensions, illustrated by the facts, for example, that triangularity is exemplified, that the state of affairs that Socrates is wise obtains and that Socrates exists (though Pegasus does not), can be reconciled with a reinterpreted claim that the job of intensions is to be 'in' representings, that their *esse* is, after all, *concipi vel concipi posse*. Thus, although Frege insists that

---

[1] It is now time to notice that in addition to minor differences which will not concern us in this chapter, the notion of *sense* is broader than that of *intension*. Logicians tend to use the latter expression only where it is appropriate to speak of an extension. Thus, triangularity but not negation would be spoken of as an intension. I shall, however, speak indifferently of senses or intensions save where I am explicitly discussing the senses of expressions which cannot be said to denote an extension.

the entities he calls senses have a being which is independent of being conceived by particular minds on particular occasions—thus correctly insisting on their public character—he does not seem to take the tough early Russell line that they are independent of thought altogether. That he nowhere spells out their dependence on thought is an indication of the difficulty of the problem; and he certainly realized that to say that they depend on *Bewusstsein überhaupt* or Objective Spirit is scarcely illuminating.

14. But more than this, the adoption of Frege's terminology implies that, properly understood, our original idea-contents turn out to be the sort of thing which serve as the senses of linguistic expressions (as contrasted with their reference or denotation, where these are appropriate). This implication carries with it two interesting programmatic corollaries:

(1) An attempt should be made to construe the relation between mental acts and their intensions or senses as a form of the relation between linguistic episodes and *their* intensions or senses.[1] In other words, the first programmatic corollary is to the effect that conceptual episodes are to be construed as *in their way* standing for senses or intensions. This gives us the schema:

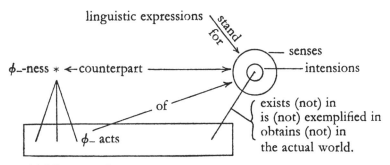

(2) The second programmatic corollary is that the counterpart attributes of conceptual episodes, by virtue of which they,

---

[1] If we take this course, it will be unwise to use the term 'express' for the relation of a form of words to their sense, for this term is more obviously fitted for the relation of a conceptual episode to the verbal behaviour which, in candid speech, is its overt culmination. I shall, therefore, use 'express' only in the latter sense, and say, therefore, that linguistic episodes 'stand for' their sense, and that where appropriate they 'refer to' their referent or 'denote' their extension.

in their own way, stand for their senses, are to be construed on the analogy of whatever it is about linguistic episodes by virtue of which they stand for their senses.

These programmatic corollaries are, of course, guide-lines rather than theses. Yet they unfold in such a way as to indicate certain demands which must be satisfied if the programme is to be achieved.

15. But before undertaking this programme, it will be helpful to stand back and view it in the setting which gives it point. The idea that conceptual episodes are analogous to speech is an ancient one. It can be traced to Plato and, perhaps, to the Sophists who began the study of language and its powers. The interpretation of thought as 'inner speech' has taken different forms, and has been used to clarify a variety of problems—thus problems pertaining to the logical forms of thought and the connection of thought with things. All these problems retain their vitality, but to each age its paradigmatic problem, and to our generation it has been that of the public and the private, the conceptual relationships and, in particular, priorities involved in the existence of epistemic privilege in the public domain.

16. Thus, in the days before 'other minds' and 'one's own case' became phrases to be reckoned with it would have been possible for an 'inner-speech' philosopher to interpret the analogy between thought and speech as a *discovered* analogy, as one might discover analogies between colours, sounds and tastes. A Cartesian might have articulated these analogies in great detail, but turned things upside-down by claiming that our *primary* concepts of those features which are common to thought and speech pertain to thought. He might, indeed, concede that in practice we describe thoughts by using, in a derivative way, the language in which we characterize verbal episodes, but he would insist that this is a purely practical matter, based on the fact that language, being public, provides a common reference point for discourse about private thoughts. His thesis would be the counterpart of the contemporary view which finds our use of the vocabulary of physical objects to characterize the impressions of sense to be a convenience which implies no conceptual priority of discourse about physical objects to discourse about sense impressions.

17. A post 'other minds' philosopher might make rather similar remarks, but deny the conceptual priority of categories pertaining to inner episodes. Beginning with the sound phenomenological points that the world contains both thought and language as it contains both pains and wounds and that certain forms of linguistic behaviour are logically adequate criteria for the occurrence of certain conceptual episodes, as certain forms of behaviour are logically adequate criteria for the occurrence of pain—he might go on to insist that there is here *no question of conceptual priority*. It is, for him, a conceptual truth that thoughts are the sort of thing which find their expression in linguistic behaviour, and that, *ceteris paribus*, linguistic behaviour is the expression of thoughts. The tie between the 'overt' and 'convert' is 'logical' rather than 'empirical'—yet 'logical' in a way which involves no commitment to logical behaviourism. He insists that his difference from the logical behaviourist does not simply consist in his generous use of such notions as *open texture* and *cluster concept*, as contrasted with *jointly sufficient* and *separately necessary conditions*. As he sees it, the connections between the private and the public are *logical* without being even *in principle*, or from the point of view of God, substitution instances of 'subject matter independent' logical truths.

18. But if this approach is sound phenomenology, it is, like most sound phenomenology, a doctrine of synthetic necessary truth—if we mean by the latter phrase, as I believe we must, necessary truth which is subject matter *dependent*. And this, surely, is what proponents of synthetic necessary truth have intended, more or less clearly, all along. This core notion of synthetic necessary truth must not be confused with attempts to explain its possibility in terms of 'intuition', '*Wesensschau*' or the like. On the other hand, those who defend the idea of synthetic necessary truth are surely responsible for giving us *some* account of the status of such truths. In a sense the present chapter is an effort in this direction.

19. It was a major step forward to see that the connection between mental episodes and behaviour cannot be understood on the model of either instantial induction or even sophisticated forms of reduction. It was also a major step forward to show

68

convincingly that this is so, by making it clear that retail doubts about particular cases presuppose general connections which, since they are neither inductive nor reductive, must be synthetic necessary connections.[1]

20. Now since, to come to the heart of the matter, it is clear that the idea that there are conceptual episodes does serve as a means of explaining what people say and do, and since it is clear that the models of instantial induction or of the 'corroboration' provided by surviving instantial tests do not work, the suggestion naturally arises that the relation of the framework of conceptual episodes to what people say and do can be compared, though not in all respects, to that of a framework of micro-physical entities to such perceptible things as trees, tables and chunks of refined pitch-blende.

21. For the latter connection is:

(*a*) subject matter dependent; yet,

(*b*) in an interesting sense, a matter of conceptual truth.

The suggestion has the additional merit that, as in the case of the framework of sense impressions, the fact that analogy with publicly observable phenomena is a striking feature of conceptual episodes would be accounted for by the essential role of analogy in theoretical concept formation.

22. The suggestion, then, is that, just as in the theory of sense impressions, the predicates of physical objects are given a new use in which they form sortal predicates pertaining to impressions, thus,

an (of a red rectangle) impression

a use which, embedded in informal principles, contributes to the explanation of the correlations of our preceptual responses with the environments to which we respond—so certain predicates which apply to linguistic episodes are given a new use in which they form sortal predicates pertaining to conceptual acts, and are

---

[1] If we take into account (as I believe we must) the fact that synthetic necessary connections can be statistical as well as universal we see that the sceptic, when he is not arguing invalidly from the absence of contradiction to physical possibility, is arguing invalidly from the consistency of 'exceptions' with statistical necessity to the consistency of the latter with a hypothetical 'universal exception'.

embedded in informal principles which contribute to the explanation of rational (and irrational) behaviour.

23. In each case the analogical predicates, combined with informal principles concerning the connection (causal in a very broad sense) of, in the one case, impressions and, in the other, conceptual episodes with overt behaviour, make possible the fuller understanding of a certain range of phenomena.

24. In the case of conceptual episodes or mental acts (in the proper sense of this phrase) the analogical predicates are, if my programme is sound, the cash for the promissory note issued above, when it was suggested that it is

ϕtriangular acts

which stand for triangularity as *somehow* both the sense of an expression ('triangular') and an attribute of things; that it is

ϕSocrates acts

which stand for *Socrates* as both a sense (or, more realistically, one or other of a family of senses) and an individual intension which was realized in Athens some two and one-half millennia ago; that it is

ϕSocrates is wise acts

which stands for the sense[1] *that Socrates is wise*, which is also a state-of-affairs intension which obtained in the same place and period; and last, but by no means least, in the series of examples, that it is

ϕnot acts

which stand for the sense *negation*.[2] 'Not' stands for an *operator* rather than an *attribute*, but the understanding of its status will

---

[1] I leave aside the filagree which, as indicated in connection with the previous example, a finer grained analysis would display.

[2] I have already pointed out that although 'not' has a sense, it does not have an 'intension', when the latter term is used in the specialized way in which it contrasts with 'extension'. Some, but not all, senses are intensions. I must now add that, strictly speaking,

ϕnot acts

should be said to stand for not-ness, since what stands for negation is rather the concatenating of a 'not' with a statement. However, in the context of this chapter the distinction is not essential to the argument, though its importance will grow.

turn out to be the key to understanding the status of all other senses and intensions, a fact which Plato grasped in the *Sophist*, and a programme which has been on the philosophical agenda since Parmenides.

IV

25. Now, since it is obvious that the idea that there are conceptual episodes or mental acts (and corresponding capacities, dispositions and propensities) did not arise as a formally proposed and deliberated hypothesis, and equally obvious that it is not the sort of thing we would normally put in a box labelled 'highly confirmed theories', the suggestion we have been nibbling at has a very odd ring to it. One is put in mind of the status of 'contract' theories in political philosophy. And, indeed, the programme on which we are embarked amounts to an attempt to 'reconstruct' the conceptual framework of mental acts in such a way as to show how it might have achieved its present status by a series of steps none of which violates accepted standards of rationality, and none of which, in particular, involves those moves (e.g. the argument 'from one's own case') which have so convincingly been shown to be incoherent. Success along these lines would escape between the legs of the trilemma:

    logical behaviourism
    the synthetic *a priori*
    the *global* argument from analogy

26. We can readily spell out two demands which must be met if such a programme is to be realized:

(1) It requires that a form of linguistic behaviour be describable which, though rich enough to serve as a basis for the explicit introduction of the framework of conceptual episodes, does not, as thus described, presuppose any reference, however implicit, to such episodes. In other words, it must be possible to have a conception pertaining to linguistic behaviour which, though adapted to the above purpose, is genuinely independent of concepts pertaining to mental acts, as we actually can conceive of physical objects in a way which is genuinely free of reference to micro-physical particles. Otherwise the supposed 'introduction' of the framework would be a sham.

(2) It requires an account of how a framework adopted as an explanatory hypothesis could come to serve as the vehicle of direct or non-inferential self-knowledge (apperception). In spite of appearances, this second requirement is, from a philosophical point of view, the less interesting of the two, for even a logical behaviourist must give some account, in principle, of privileged access, in other words, of how language pertaining to behavioural dispositions and propensities can acquire the use by which one's possession of such dispositions and propensities is avowed. Since, as will emerge, I believe that logical behaviourism does reconstruct a dimension of our concept of mind, I shall stipulate that the acquisition of the avowal role by the framework of mental episodes proper is of a piece with the acquisition of this role by a framework of behavioural dispositions and propensities.

27. What these demands amount to, spelled out in concrete terms, is the possibility of describing a community whose initial concepts of rationality coincide with concepts pertaining to overt linguistic behaviour and the corresponding capacities, dispositions and propensities. *We*, of course, making use of the Strawsonian framework we learned at our mother's knee, know that the members of this community have a rich inner history of which they are totally unaware, though they are aware of certain related episodes which we (though not, of course, they) can confuse with this history. The latter confusion is the essence of logical behaviourism as an account of not just one dimension of the concept of mind but of the concept of mind *sans phrase*.

28. For the term 'episode' is elastic enough to cover a great deal of territory. If anything which occurs or takes place is to count as an episode, then whenever an object changes from having one disposition to having another the change is an episode. Thus the logical behaviourist can correctly point out that he, too, believes in 'conceptual episodes'—though for him this means, for example, that a person may change from having the propensity at 5 p.m. to say 'It will rain tonight' if asked to forecast the weather, to having the propensity at 5.02 p.m. to answer 'It will snow'. It is clear that logical behaviourism cannot even get off the ground

unless it grants (as, of course, it does) that waking life is a steady stream of such changes in one's verbal propensities. Dreams provide additional problems, as witness Norman Malcolm's pressing of the brow, and even the dreamless sleep of mathematicians is not unproblematic, for mathematical thinking in sleep is no more dreaming than mathematical thinking when awake is perceiving.

29. Clearly the episodes in which we are interested are not shifting behavioural propensities; they are connected with such shifts, but the connection is synthetic, as is the connection of molecular motion with the shifting propulsive propensities of a volume of gas.

30. Again, even when an episode is an episode in a tougher sense which precludes that it is a mere shift in propensity, a shift, in Peirce's phrase, from one *would-be* to another, it may be described in a way which carries a burden of hypotheticals. Ryle makes this point in connection with publicly observable episodes, but it obviously holds in the case of covert episodes proper—if such there be. Thus it should not be assumed that one who defends the notion of mental episodes in a non-Rylean sense is thereby committed to the view that their character as conceptual is, so to speak, a purely categorical character. On the contrary, I shall argue almost everything that can be said about the conceptual character of conceptual episodes is as mongrel, as fraught with hypotheticals or *would-be*'s, as Ryle could wish. But not *everything*, for to bear the burden of these hypotheticals they must have a determinate episode-ishness which I shall explore in Chapter VI.

V

31. The crux of a philosophical argument often appears to be a Dedekind cut between a series of 'as I will show's and a series of 'as I have shown's. In a sense the preliminaries *are* the argument, and there is no crux apart from their perspicuous deployment. A few more introductory remarks, therefore, and my job will be done.

32. The concept of linguistic performances is very much in the air, and rightly so. Yet the importance of the concept should not blind us to the fact that not every linguistic episode is an act in a sense of performance or piece of conduct. The role of language in

the articulation of social relationships should not blind us to the foundation of essentially unperformable episodes which supports this role—which is not, of course, to say that the performatory and non-performatory aspects can be separated as with a knife.

33. The importance of this point is, or should be, obvious. It would be a radical mistake to construe mental acts as actions. There are, indeed, such things as mental actions; thus, there is deliberating, turning one's attention to a problem, searching one's memory, to mention some clear-cut cases. An action is the sort of thing one can decide to do—though, of course, in particular cases one may do it without deciding, as one may salute an acquaintance without the question whether or not to do so crossing one's mind. But mental acts, in the basic sense, though they may be elements of mental actions, are not themselves actions. Thus, perceptual takings, e.g. taking there to be a book on the table (and I have in mind *not* the dispositional but the occurrent sense of 'taking' to which there corresponds the achievement word 'notice'), are not actions. It is nonsense to speak of taking something to be the case 'on purpose'. *Taking* is an act in the Aristotelian sense of 'actuality' rather than in the specialized practical sense which refers to conduct. A taking may be, on occasion, an element of a scrutinizing—which latter is indeed an action in the practical sense. To take another example, one may decide to do a certain action, but it is logical nonsense to speak of deciding to will to do it; yet volitions, of course, are mental acts. Again, when one draws a conclusion from given premises there occur mental acts which may be elements of thinking about a problem, yet, if the process has been correctly described, the act which is the thinking of the conclusion is not, in that context, at least, the sort of thing one can be said to decide to do.

34. If one construes all linguistic utterances on the model of actions, then, since actions are essentially the sort of thing which can be done 'on purpose', one will think that every linguistic utterance is the sort of thing which can be done 'on purpose'. A possible source of confusion is the fact that every linguistic episode falls under a description such that an episode of *that* description *can*, indeed, be a performance. One may also be misled by the fact that, after reaching years of discretion, a person's utterances just

might *all* be actions, performed in the presence of his auditors to achieve perhaps devious, perhaps noble, ends.

35. I say, 'after reaching years of discretion', because it is a familiar fact, though not always taken as seriously as it should be, that we must learn to lie. The point is a more general one, and I shall immediately put it to use by characterizing my hypothetical community as one for which the basic concept pertaining to linguistic behaviour is that of what we might call spontaneous or candid 'thinking-out-loud'; where the phrase is hyphenated, and its equivalent in *their* language would not suggest to them, as it does to us, that in thinking-out-loud covert conceptual episodes proper are, so to speak, coming to the surface and finding their appropriate expression in speech.

36. Thus, corresponding to our concept of, for example, such a mental act as perceptual taking would be their concept of what we would call 'taking-out-loud', that is, of spontaneous verbal responses to perceptual situations. The latter are no more to be construed as actions than are the mental episodes which *we* conceive to find expression in such spontaneous and candid speech. Our primitive community, which belongs to what I shall call the Ryleian age, also has such concepts as 'willing-out-loud', 'concluding-out-loud' and, of course, concepts pertaining to linguistic actions proper, thus 'deliberating-out-loud', 'searching-one's-memory-out-loud'—not to mention such other-oriented actions as 'telling', 'stating', 'promising', etc., which, of course, can *only* be done out loud.

VI

37. The topic of linguistic performances not unnaturally introduces the topic of linguistic rules. This concept has come in for some hard knocks, some of them deserved. Linguistic rules, as contrasted with the uniformities they promote, are, in a familiar sense, meta-linguistic. Thus, those of our Fregean senses which are rule-senses are 'stood for' by meta-linguistic practical sentences and by the meta-linguistic practical thoughts which, in our terminology, find expression in them. That there are linguistic rules, and that they are 'stood for' by both thoughts and speech episodes will be argued, if only by implication, in the final chapter.

My present concern, however, is the vital distinction between rules for *doing* and rules for *criticizing*. The distinction is essentially akin to that which has been drawn between 'ought to do' and 'ought to be'. Thus the two kinds of rule are internally related in a way which parallels the fact that ought-to-be's imply (with additional premises) ought-to-do's, and ought-to-do's imply ought-to-be's.

38. To use a hackneyed example, one ought to feel gratitude for benefits received, though feeling grateful is not something which one *does*, save in that broad sense in which anything expressed by a verb in the active voice is a doing. (One thinks of the 'act of existing' on which Thomistic Existentialists lay such stress.) One ought, however, to criticize (an action proper) oneself for not feeling gratitude and to take steps (again an action proper) to improve one's character.

39. The point I wish to make is the obvious one that if a species of linguistic episode is not a doing in the practical sense, a performance, then the relevant rules *must* be rules of criticism rather than rules of performance. Ryleians do not follow rules of performance in their takings-out-loud, nor *could* they—a logical 'could'. If a Ryleian child's linguistic responses are incorrect, its parents set about improving its linguistic character, a process which can be continued by the child on his own hook after reaching linguistic maturity.

40. A final preliminary remark, which pulls together most of the foregoing considerations. Our programme, it will be remembered, is that of construing the counterpart attributes of conceptual episodes, by virtue of which, in their own way, they stand for senses or intensions, on the analogy of whatever it is about linguistic episodes by virtue of which the latter stand for senses or intensions. Since it is obvious that linguistic episodes do not stand for their senses merely by virtue of what Carnap calls their sign designs, but rather by virtue of the patterns they make (when produced in a language-using frame of mind) with other designs, with objects (in a suitably broad sense) and with actions, the counterpart attributes of conceptual episodes are to be construed along parallel lines.

1. *Intentionality*

41. Particular linguistic configurations are correct or incorrect (in that they are subject to criticism) in a way which is illuminated by, although not defined in terms of, these general patterns or correlations. Since we are concerned with that distinguishable (if not separable) *stratum* of linguistic episodes which are essentially non-performatory, the correctness we have in mind involves rules of criticism; and since we are not concerned with questions of taste, morality, perspicuity or wisdom, we can provisionally characterize the correctness relevant to 'standing for a sense' as *semantical* correctness, and the corresponding uniformities as semantical uniformities—though without the specifically Ziffian overtones of this phrase.

VII

42. Technical semantics of the Tarski–Carnap variety, because of its original orientation towards the foundations of mathematics, has tended to concentrate on extensions rather than intensions, on classes rather than properties, on truth values rather than propositions and on truth-functional connectives rather than modal predicates. There are signs that these self-imposed limitations are being outgrown, though, to shift metaphors, some who are at home in the desert may feel that the land of milk and honey is a jungle.

43. My ultimate aim is to argue that extensions are limiting cases of intensions and cannot be understood apart from them. Thus, classes, in the logistic sense, cannot be understood apart from properties, nor truth apart from propositions. As I see it, Quine's attempt to by-pass intensions simply misses the point. He has looked for intensions in Plato's beard, but, like the bluebird of happiness, they have always been in his own backyard.

44. Let us put ourselves in Ryleian shoes and consider 'negation'. We are strongly inclined to think-out-loud that this abstract singular term does not stand for anything in the non-linguistic world, that in the world 'being alone is, not-being is not'. On the other hand, we are reluctant to tie one hand behind our back by refusing to use this term—refusing, for example, to say

'Not' stands for[1] negation

_____
[1] See footnote to § 24.

or that, in the dialect of the East

'*Niet*' stands for negation

45. Of course, if we decide to restrict the left-hand side of the context '. . . stands for – – –' to expressions which denote or have extensions we shall still be able to make interesting semantical statements in which we mention the word 'not', thus,

'Not-*p*' is true ⟷ '*p*' is not true

but this does not alter the fact that 'not' has a sense in a sense of 'sense' to which intensions belong.

46. What kind of statement is

'Not' stands for negation?

To answer this question we must take account of the fact that in the semantical uniformities of our language such words as 'not', 'all', 'some', etc., have a unique role. While it is true that we find uniformities in which utterances in which they occur are *directly* linked with extra-linguistic situations—thus people notice-out-loud: 'Tom is not here' 'This is not a dog'—yet they are not correlated in isolation as 'red' is, for example, with red things or 'gavagai' with rabbit-slices. More important is the fact that the purely intra-linguistic uniformities in which they are mutually involved seem to be the heart of their functioning. If logical words played a purely intra-linguistic role the 'noticing-out-loud' uniformities in which they occur would be replaced, without loss of expressive power, by indirect or inferential uniformities, thus, in the presence of a cat: 'Lo! This is a cat; so it is not a dog.' Thus, for our purposes, we can assume that the uniformities exhibited by logical words can be described in purely syntactical terms.

47. In these purely syntactical descriptions, of course, we will not use the locution

'Not' stands for negation

and, if we were hasty, we might assume that this is because the latter form of words, if taken seriously, would commit us to the proportion

$$\frac{\text{`not'}}{\text{negation}} = \frac{\text{`Fido'}}{\text{Fido}} = \frac{\text{`Rational Animal'}}{\text{Featherless Bipeds}}$$

i.e. we might equate 'stands for' with 'names' or 'denotes'. Yet it is surely clear that there is a perfectly good sense in which 'not' stands for negation, although it neither names, nor denotes, nor has, in the technical sense, an extension.

48. I said at the beginning of this chapter that if we can get clear about 'not' and negation we will have the key to the status of senses generally, both of those senses which are intensions and of those senses which are extensions. It is therefore of the utmost importance that in the case of negation the truth is simple and, in a sense, just beneath the conceptual surface.

49. What kind of singular term is 'negation'? What kinds of singular term are there? Demonstratives, proper names, definite descriptions, indefinite descriptions, . . . and distributive singular terms. Consider the common noun 'bishop'. We can say

(In chess) bishops move along diagonals

or we can say

The bishop moves along diagonals

50. What kind of general term is formed by the use of quotes? A common noun. Must we construe it as merely standing for the kind of design which it illustrates? No, for while in some contexts it can be construed in this way, it often stands for this design as subject to unspecified semantical correctnesses and, hence, as taking part in the corresponding uniformities in some language or dialect. In this respect the common noun

'not'

resembles the common noun

soldier

for though a soldier must have *some* rank and function in *some* army or other, the expression does not specify which.

51. Furthermore, to be a 'not' in our language an item need not have the visual shape illustrated between the quotes. It can have an auditory shape, or, even, a different visual shape. This permissiveness, however, is compensated for by the requirement that to be a 'not' in this permissive sense a linguistic design must function

with other designs in a way which parallels the functioning of
'not's in our language.

52. Let us use dot quotes to embody quotation thus construed.
In this sense the 'niet's of the East could well be ·not·s. After all,
a bishop need not be made of wood nor look like London. A
bishop must, however, be distinguishable from knights, pawns,
etc., and capable of deployment in patterns which parallel, however abstractly, those which are found in the Bureau of Standards
in Moscow.

53. Thus,

    'Niet's (in the East) are ·not·s

would, by virtue of the dot quote convention, tell us, who use
'not's, how 'niet's function in the East. Indeed, it would give the
same information to anyone who knows how 'not's function in
our language. If spelled out, of course, this information would be,
as we have seen, formulated in terms of semantical uniformities
(and correctnesses) of a purely syntactical kind, for 'not's have a
purely syntactical job.

54. What does all this have to do with negation? Suppose that
our word for negation was 'neg' rather than 'not', and let us form
the distributive singular term

    the ·neg·

We have already pointed out that statements with distributive
singular terms in the subject position are equivalent to general
statements. If there were a similar convention according to which
statements with a distributive singular term in the *predicate* position were equivalent to statements involving the corresponding
common noun, perhaps somewhat as

    Tom loves the brimming glass

stands to

    Tom loves brimming glasses

we could construe

    'Niet's (in the East) stand for negation

as

    'Niet's (in the East) stand for the ·neg·

In other words, we could construe the suffix of the abstract singular-term negation having the force of dot quotes.

55. If we follow the above suggestion,

'Niet's (in the East) stand for the ·neg·

would be equivalent to

'Niet's (in the East) stand for ·neg·s

And if we construe the latter as a way of saying

'niet's (in the East) are ·neg·s

we get an interpretation of abstract singular term which is a powerful tool for dealing with problems in the philosophy of language and the philosophy of mind. For to make this move is to construe 'stands for' as a specialized form of the copula 'to be', the surface features of which (*a*) indicate that the subject matter is linguistic rather than, for example, military or religious; (*b*) make possible such contrasts as those between 'stands for', 'connotes', 'denotes', 'refers to' and 'names', on which I shall comment in the next chapter.

56. The above technique of reconstruction can readily be extended to all the Fregean senses into which our original 'contents' were transformed. Thus, the individual intension

Socrates

becomes

the ·Socrates·

the attributive intension

wisdom

becomes

the ·wise·

and the state of affairs intension

that Socrates is wise

becomes

the ·Socrates is wise·

57. According to this reconstruction, statements of the *surface* form

(the) '– – –' (in L) stands for (abstract singular term)

are classificatory in nature, and have, from a more searching point of view, the form

'. . .'s (in L) are '– – –'s

VIII

58. I have defended this reconstruction in some detail on other occasions,[1] and shall have more to say about it in the following chapter. My present aim is to draw its consequences for the problems with which this chapter began.

59. In the first place, if this reconstruction is correct, it follows at once that semantical statements of the Tarski–Carnap variety do not assert relations between linguistic and extra-linguistic items, though, in the case of expressions which stand for senses which are intensions, it will also be true (and necessarily so) that these expressions are involved in semantical uniformities (actual or potential) with the appropriate extra-linguistic items. Thus in order for it to be true that

'Dreieckig's (in German) stand for triangularity

i.e. that

'Dreieckig's (in German) are ·triangulars·

German 'Dreieckig's must participate in uniformities with triangular things, uniformities which parallel those involving our word 'triangular'. But this does not mean that these statements themselves have the form

(Linguistic item) R (non-linguistic item)

60. In the case of

'Niet's stand for negation,

---

[1] See, for example, 'Notes on Intentionality', *Journal of Philosophy*, Volume LXI, No. 21, 1964 [reprinted, with minor alterations, in *Philosophical Perspective* (Springfield, Illinois, 1966)].

on the other hand, the semantical information conveyed by virtue of the function (as we are construing it) of the abstract singular-term 'negation' is intra-linguistic or syntactical, and only surface grammar makes it look as though, by countenancing such a statement, we were growing a beard.[1]

61. It may be objected to the above that whereas I may have made my case with respect to the schema

(expression) (in L) stands for (sense)

i.e. have shown that neither

'Niet' (in Russian) stands for negation

nor

'Dreieckig' (in German) stands for triangularity

has the form

(Linguistic item) R (non-linguistic item)

I have not yet shown that the same is true of statements belonging to semantics of the Carnap–Tarski type. For, it will be pointed out, the latter concerns *not* what it is to 'stand for' a Fregean sense but rather what it is to 'denote' or be 'true of' an extension. After all, I will be reminded, Carnap–Tarski semantics doesn't even consider such statements as

'Und' (in German) stands for conjunction

though it does, of course, throw light on the sense of truth-functional connectives by specifying the truth conditions for statements involving them. Surely, it will be said,

'Rational animal' (in E) denotes featherless bipeds

and, even more obviously

'Plato' (in E) denotes the teacher of Aristotle

do have the form

(Linguistic) R (non-linguistic)

62. The general lines of the answer can be sketched as follows.

[1] This metaphor appropriately enough is not as pejorative as it once was.

We introduce a variable 'S' (read 'sense') which takes as its substituends common nouns formed by dot quoting. We use this variable to make such quantified statements as

For some S, 'niet's (in Russian) are S's

i.e.

For some S, 'niet' (in Russian) stands for S

Other examples would be

For some S, 'Plato' (in English) stands for S
For some S, 'rational animal' (in English) stands for S

63. We also introduce the form

S_i is materially equivalent to S_j[1]

examples of which would be

·Rational animal· is materially equivalent to ·featherless biped·

which is true if and only if

(x) x is a rational animal $\equiv$ x is a featherless biped

and

·Plato· is materially equivalent to ·the teacher of Aristotle·

which is true if and only if

$(f) f$ (Plato) $\equiv f$ (the teacher of Aristotle)[2]

64. In this framework we can explicate

'Man' (in E) denotes featherless bipeds

---

[1] Note that not all substituends for 'S_i' and 'S_j' make sense in this context. For example, we would want to rule out all statements beginning

·not· is materially equivalent to . . .

and, presumably, such statements as

·Socrates· is materially equivalent to ·featherless biped·

We could do this by subdividing senses into propositional senses, connective senses, predicate senses, individual senses, etc., and laying down appropriate formation rules in terms of these distinctions.

[2] Note that this object language statement can be rewritten, using the Leibnitz–Russell definition of identity as

Plato = the teacher of Aristotle

as

For some S, 'rational animal' (in E) stands for S, and S is materially equivalent to ·featherless biped·

and

'Plato' (in E) denotes the teacher of Aristotle

as

For some S, 'Plato' (in E) stands for S, and S is materially equivalent to ·the teacher of Aristotle·

65. This analysis amounts to the idea that the difference between

'. . .' (in L) stands for – – –

and

'. . .' (in L) denotes – – –

is not a matter of what goes on the right-hand side, for in each case it is an expression for a sense, but rather in the diluted character of 'denotes' as contrasted with 'stands for'. Thus, surface grammar not withstanding,

'Rational animal' (in E) denotes featherless bipeds

has the form

'Rational animal' (in E) R_1 ·featherless biped·

and

'Rational animal' (in E) stands for *featherless biped*

has the form

'Rational animal' (in E) R_2 ·featherless biped.

Of these two statements only the former is true, given the usual zoological assumption. It unpacks into

For some S, 'Rational animal's (in E) are S's, and S is materially equivalent to ·featherless biped·

which is true because

'Rational animal's (in E) are ·Rational animal·s, and ·rational animal· is materially equivalent to ·featherless biped·

where the second clause is logically equivalent to

(x) x is a rational animal $\equiv$ x is a featherless biped

On the other hand,

'Rational animal' (in E) stands for *featherless biped*

falsely tells us that

'Rational animal's (in E) are ·featherless biped·s

66. I claimed early in this chapter that extensions would be found to be a variety of sense, indeed, a variety of intension. This was, I hope, not too misleading a way of saying that it is intensions which are denoted as well as stood for. It was misleading in that it seemed to imply that not every intension can be denoted. But while not every *sense* can be denoted, every intension can stand to an expression in a weaker 'relation' (defined with reference to material equivalence) than being stood for, and it has become customary to use 'denote' in such a way that to the examples already given we can add the pair

'Snow is white' (in E) stands for (the sense) that snow is white

'Snow is white' (in E) denotes (the sense) that the moon is round

Any true statement can replace 'the moon is round' in the second context, for it unpacks into

For some S, 'Snow is white' (in E) stands for S, and S is materially equivalent to ·the moon is round·

67. The above is a preliminary defence of the claim that the concept of an intension (as a variety of sense) is conceptually prior to that of an extension (or 'reference' or 'denotation' or 'designatum', etc.). In the next chapter this point will be pressed home in connection with the concept of truth.

68. To sum up, it is, as I see it, a mistake to suppose, as Carnap does, that semantical statements in *his* sense, i.e. statements which involve such expressions as 'denotes' or 'designates', are semantical statements in the sense that they formulate (ideal) semantical uniformities. They do not have the form

(Linguistic) **R** (non-linguistic)

86

as, in the case of denoting expressions, do semantical statements in the latter sense. On the other hand, that Carnapian statements *convey*, with conceptual necessity, information which is *formulated* by the latter has been an equally important part of my story. This conceptual necessity can, in our reconstruction, be traced to the fact that the criteria for the application of dot-quoted expressions ('This is a ·not·' 'This is a ·triangular·') consist in being subject to the same semantical correctnesses as the expressions within the dot quotes.

IX

69. Let us return to our character as members of the Ryleian community pondering the fact that our propensities to think-out-loud now this, now that are constantly changing as they would have changed had we been noticing-out-loud what was going on, reasoning-out-loud in both the theoretical and the practical mode, and willing-out-loud to act in various ways. And, to cut a long story short, let us consider the hypothesis that we are the subjects of imperceptible episodes which are:

(*a*) analogous to thinkings-out-loud;
(*b*) culminate, in candid speech, in thinkings-out-loud of the kind to which they are specifically analogous;
(*c*) are correlated with the propensities which are realized in such thinkings-out-loud.

70. Let us classify such episodes as, for example,

representings of Socrates
representings of wisdom
representings of that Socrates was wise

or, more perspicuously, by making an analogical use of 'stand for' and of dot-quoted distributive singular terms,

thoughts standing for the ·Socrates·
thoughts standing for the ·wise·
thoughts standing for the ·Socrates is wise·

that is,

·Socrates· thoughts
·wise· thoughts
·Socrates is wise· thoughts

and let us, leaving perspicuity aside for subsequent generations of philosophers to worry about, train ourselves and our children to say

I have a thought of Socrates
I have a thought of wisdom
I have a thought of that Socrates is wise

where we now say

I have a disposition to think-out-loud of Socrates, etc.

71. It is now 1966. Millennia have passed since the Ryleian community in which we placed ourselves, espoused the new way of mental acts and began the training which shaped the Strawsonian framework in which we live, move and have our being.

X

72. A concluding postscript. I introduced promissory note predicates of the form

ϕ-'

to stand for the counterpart attributes of mental acts by virtue of which they stand for the senses they do. We have just seen that, perspicuously represented, these predicates are common nouns formed by an analogical use of our original dot quotes. Thus,

ϕtriangular acts

become

·triangular· acts

Our argument suggests that

·Triangular· acts stand for triangularity

should become

·Triangular· acts stand for the ·triangular·

which, amounting to

·Triangular· acts are ·triangular·s

would be as analytic as one could wish. But we must be cautious, for the Ryleian triangularity with which we began was

the ·triangular·

where the dot-quoted expression applies not to inner episodes but to thinking-out-loud. On the other hand, in

·Triangular· acts are ·triangular·s

the dot-quoted expression on the right-hand side is an analogical extension of its Ryleian counterpart and applies only to mental acts. To avoid two triangularities we must coalesce our original and our analogical use of dot quotes to form sortal expressions which apply to both thinkings-out-loud and inner speech. Only then can we say that

·triangular· thoughts-out-loud

as well as

·triangular· inner episodes

stand for

the ·triangular·

where the latter expression is unambiguous; and only then can we say, given our reconstruction, they stand for the same

triangularity

73. It should also be noted that the counterpart attribute of mental acts,

ϕtriangular-ness

by virtue of which they stand for triangularity becomes, on our reconstruction,

·triangular·-ness

the explication of which, along parallel lines, requires a double use of dot quotes, thus

the ··triangular··

74. A final word to conclude this chapter and introduce the next. What about the right-hand side of the diagram in § 12 above? What are we to make of the relation between intensions, construed as having the form

the ·– – –·

where the dot quotes have the comprehensive use adumbrated in the preceding paragraph but one, and the world? How, that is, are we to interpret 'exists', 'is exemplified' and 'obtains'? This, as has already been indicated, involves the problem of truth to which I now turn.

IV

THE CONCEPTUAL AND
THE REAL:

2. TRUTH

1. At the beginning of the last chapter I pointed out that the 'content' of representings—individual contents, general contents, state-of-affairs contents, etc., must be construed as *ones* in *manys* in order to do justice to the intersubjectivity of thought, the fact that different persons, and the same person at different times, can represent the *same*, even though the representings (as acts) are numerically different. Thus one and the same content must be capable of existing 'in'—in some sense of 'in'—many representings.

2. I then pointed out that this platonic theme concerning contents and representings would seem to call for a parallel countenancing of attributes as *ones* in *manys* with respect to the things which exemplify them, one and the same attribute—e.g. triangularity—being capable of existing 'in' many things.

3. At this point the suggestion naturally arose, at least in connection with general contents, that it might be possible to identify the *ones* which are shared by many representings with the *ones* which are shared by many things, the content *triangular* with triangularity. To do so, it was pointed out, would have the virtue of ensuring the closest of connections between the *intersubjectivity* of contents with respect to representings and their *objectivity* with respect to things.

4. It took but a moment's reflection, however, to see that even if that which is shared by representings were identical with that

which is shared by things the *mode* of sharing could not be the same. The sense in which triangularity is 'in' representings could scarcely be the same as that in which triangularity is 'in' things. That a thing shares in triangularity implies that it is triangular, but that a representing shares, in its way, in triangularity can scarcely imply that the representing is triangular.

5. The hypothesis of the identity of general contents with attributes requires, in other words, a dualism of two modes of *in-esse*, the *in-esse* of attributes in representings and the *in-esse* of attributes in things, thus

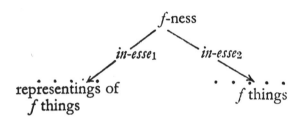

6. Before exploring this hypothesis, we generalized it by extending it to contents other than general contents. Thus, noting that attributes, such as triangularity, are special cases of intensions (with an 's'), we enriched the above schema with individual intensions, state-of-affairs intensions, etc., and distinguished, correspondingly, between three (and potentially more) sub-modes of *in-esse$_2$*.

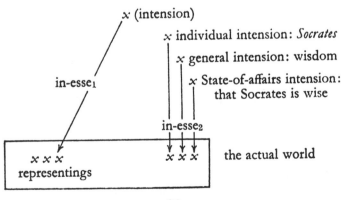

2. Truth

Individual intensions are real or not real depending on whether or not they exist in the actual world.
General intensions are exemplified.
State-of-affairs intensions obtain or fail to obtain.

7. Having made this classic, but for our purposes provisional and problematic, move with respect to intensions and their in-esse in the world, we turned our attention to the primary topic of that chapter, which was the *in-esse*$_1$ of contents, now construed as intensions, in representings. We introduced a theme from Frege by suggesting that contents be construed as *senses*, hoping in this way to revitalize the conceptualistic claim, characteristic of the new way of ideas, that the job of contents is to exist 'in' representings, though in a way which is compatible with genuine inter-subjectivity, compatible, that is with the view that literally one and the same content can exist 'in' many representings by many minds. We followed up this theme in a single-minded way, leaving to the present chapter the implications for the *in-esse*$_2$ of intensions in the world of such results as might be achieved.

8. The general strategy was to construe the *in-esse* of contents in representings on the model of *standing for* as a relation between linguistic expressions and their senses. Intensions were construed to be a sub-class of senses, consisting of those which can meaningfully be contrasted with *extensions*, as triangularity can be contrasted with the class of triangular things. (How the extensions corresponding to individual intensions and state-of-affairs intensions were to be construed was left open, though it was suggested that, in general, extensions are special cases of intensions and, *a fortiori*, of senses.) It was emphasized, however, that in addition to intensions, in this technical sense, the class of senses includes the items which were originally introduced as 'logical contents' and, perhaps, others which have not yet been mentioned, thus 'contents' pertaining to practical thought.[1]

9. The hypothesis that the relation of representings to their

[1] Our original list of contents, generated by the Kantian table of forms of judgment, included, besides connectives, quantifiers and the subject-predicate *nexus*, such modal contents as the content *necessary*. The content *true*, which does not occur in Kant's list of categories save, perhaps, under the guise of 'actuality', is the subject of this chapter.

contents is to be construed on the model of the relation of linguistic expressions to their senses, thus

(representing) of (content)

on the model of

(expression) stands for (sense)

was followed by an analysis according to which to say what an expression stands for is to classify it.

10. It was noted that among the varieties of singular term available as possible models for understanding the force of the abstract singular terms which follow 'stands for' in statements of this form are what I proposed to call distributive singular terms, thus

the bishop
the pawn

Statements which have such terms in the subject position, e.g.

The pawn captures *en passant*

are reducible[1] to general statements having as their subjects the plural form of the corresponding common noun, thus

Pawns capture *en passant*

This gives us the schema

The K is $f \longleftrightarrow$ Ks are f

11. When a distributive singular term occurs in the predicate, and our example was

Tom loves the brimming glass

the reduction occurs in accordance with the schema

x R the K $\longleftrightarrow x$ R K's

which, like the preceding equivalence schema, requires a commentary to bring out the distinctive flavour added by the distributive singular term.

[1] I have explored the qualifications which this blunt formulation requires in 'Abstract Entities', *Review of Metaphysics*, Volume XVI, 1963 [reprinted in *Philosophical Perspectives* (Springfield, Illinois, 1967)].

12. Our fundamental hypothesis was that abstract singular terms can be construed as unperspicuous distributive singular terms formed from common nouns of a very special sort. The latter resemble the common nouns formed by ordinary quoting, thus

'the'

as in

There are four 'the's on this page

save that, unlike the latter, they involve a special quoting device by virtue of which they apply to expressions in any language which play the linguistic role played by the design which occurs between them in a familiar language, to be called the 'base language'. Dot quotes were introduced to form these common nouns.
Thus,

·not·

would be a common noun applying to expressions in any language which function[1] as does our word 'not',

·triangular·

a common noun which applies to expressions in any language which function as does our word 'triangular' and

·two plus two equals four·
·Socrates is wise·

common nouns which apply to expressions in any language which function as do the corresponding English sentences. It will be remembered that with respect to such functioning we limited our attention to candid thinking-out-loud—in other words, we concentrated our attention on the epistemic function of language as contrasted with its performatory role in interpersonal relationships.

[1] It is important to note, for future reference, that provision can be made for degrees of likeness of function—indeed *must* be made, not only if the account is to be realistic but if the evolution of conceptual frameworks is to be taken into account, and, hence, the 'identity' of our framework with the more adequate frameworks of the future, which must be an element in any penetrating account of truth.

13. The operation of dot quoting is unperspicuously performed in English by such suffixes as '-ity', '-hood' and '-ness', and the word 'that'. The latter also turn these unperspicuous common nouns into distributive singular terms. Thus the *abstract* singular-term character of such expressions as 'triangularity' and 'that Socrates is wise' is explicated by reconstructing them (in Reichenbach's sense) as *distributive* singular terms formed from dot-quoted common nouns.

Thus,

> Triangularity = the ·triangular·
> That 2 plus 2 equals 4 = the ·2 plus 2 equals 4·
> (The individual intension) *Socrates* = the ·Socrates·
> Negation = the ·nego·ing (i.e. the ·not·ing)

The last of these examples amounts to the intuitively sound idea that to negate a statement or statement form is to 'operate' on it, modifying it in a way which parallels, in the relevant language, what *we* do when we concatenate a statement with a 'not'.

14. Our next step was to construe statements of which the surface form is

> (Expression) (in L) stands for (sense)

to illustrate,

> '*sage*' (in F) stands for wisdom

as having the depth form illustrated by

> The '*sage*' (in F) stands for the ·wise·

which, in accordance with our principles for 'reducing' statements involving distributive singular terms, becomes

> '*Sage*'s (in F) stand for ·wise·

15. Our final step was to interpret 'stand for' as a specialized form of the copula 'are'—specialized in that it is tailored for linguistic contexts and can serve as a contrast to such other 'semantical connectives' as 'denotes', 'designates' and the like. Thus, to use another example,

> '*Deux et deux font quatre*' (in F) stands for (the proposition) that 2 plus 2 = 4

becomes, according to this 'rational reconstruction',

'*Deux et deux font quatre*'s (in F) are ·2 plus 2 = 4·s

Once again, to say what an expression stands for is to classify it. The classification, however, is a subtle one, as is the depth grammar of the classification expression.

16. We devoted most of our attention in the preceding chapter to construing the language of conceptual episodes proper (mental acts) as though it had been introduced, in a community whose conceptions of rational behaviour were purely Rylean, as a theory to explain the fact, among others, that a person's verbal propensities and dispositions change during periods of silence as they would have changed if they had been engaged during these periods in specific sequences of candid linguistic behaviour, thus noticings-out-loud and reasonings-out-loud. Although the purpose of the argument was to attack logical behaviourism as an adequate account of the mental *überhaubt*, the strategy of the argument involved conceding that a distinguishable stratum of discourse about the mental can be reconstructed along Rylean lines; just as a distinguishable stratum of scientific discourse can be reconstructed in a way which makes no reference to the entities of micro-physical theory. I argued, indeed, that this Rylean stratum provides a basis for the development of a theory of non-Rylean inner episodes, just as the stratum of description and explanation in terms of 'observables' provides a basis for the introduction of the imperceptible entities of micro-physical theory.

17. My general thesis, then, is that concepts and categories pertaining to mental acts can be construed as analogical extensions of Rylean concepts and categories pertaining to candid overt speech. Assuming that this thesis has been given some measure of plausibility, I shall follow the strategy it implies in my exploration of *in-esse₂* and its modes. In other words, my discussion of the relations between 'thoughts' (intensions) and the world will be in purely Rylean terms. If my programme is correct, however, the results can be extended, by analogy, to the mental acts ('inner speech') of which candid speech episodes are, in a broadly causal sense, the expression. In other words, the representings with which we shall be concerned are linguistic representings, their

'contents' are the senses of linguistic representings and the relations of intensions to things and events are the relations of the intensions of linguistic representings to the world of which candid speech episodes are a part.

II

18: According to our reconstruction, the *in-esse*$_1$ of senses and, in particular, of intensions in representings is a matter of classification, thus

(representing) stands for wisdom

becomes

(representing) is a ·wise·

and

(representing) stands for that 2 plus 2 equals 4

becomes

(representing) is a ·2 plus 2 equals 4·

We now turn to the question: What, given the validity of this reconstruction, are we to make of the in-esse$_2$ of intensions and things?

19. I have already implied that the strategic case to consider is that of truth or, as we are tempted to put it, the relation between a state-of-affairs intension and the world by virtue of which the intension can be said to 'obtain'. And, indeed, I shall argue that the explication of this relation, if such it can be called, brings with it, almost as corollary, an account of what it is for an attribute to be exemplified and an individual intension to be real.

20. But first a terminological point. The intensions which obtain or fail to obtain in the world (in our terminology, state-of-affairs intensions) are a sub-set of propositional intensions. Also included among the latter are logical and mathematical propositions. These can, indeed, be said to 'obtain' or 'be the case', but not, we are inclined to say, 'in the world' or, at least, not in a way in which the intension that Socrates is wise obtains in the world.

2. *Truth*

21. Let us therefore begin by considering the more general case of propositional intensions. Our reconstruction of intensions as classifications commits us to construe such statements as

> *Socrates* is real
> Wisdom is exemplified
> That Socrates is wise obtains

in terms of contrived statements which begin

> The ·Socrates· . . .
> The ·wise· . . .
> The ·Socrates is wise· . . .

But how are they to continue? The third case, fortunately, is sufficiently perspicuous to give us a clue. For given the momentum of the argument,

> That Socrates is wise obtains

must surely be 'reconstructed' as

> The ·Socrates is wise· is true

22. Indeed, the predicate 'obtains' (or 'is the case') corresponds to what Carnap[1] calls the 'absolute' sense of 'true', which he contrasts with the 'semantical' sense. Truth in the absolute sense he takes to be an attribute of non-linguistic entities, propositions in the tough platonic sense of early Russell and Moore. And, as Moore points out in *Some Main Problems of Philosophy*,[2] we do indeed use the expression 'true' in the sense of 'obtains' or 'is the case', thus

> That Socrates is wise is true

23. In drawing his contrast between the 'absolute' and the 'semantical' sense of 'true', Carnap had in mind the distinction between the use of 'true' just illustrated and that which is found in

> '*Socrate est sage*' (in F) is true

where reference is made to a specific language. From the standpoint of our analysis he mistakenly infers from the absurdity of

> That Socrates is wise is true in English

[1] *Introduction to Semantics*, Cambridge (Mass.), 1942, § 17. But see *Meaning and Necessity*, Chicago, 1947, p. 24 n.   [2] London, 1953, p. 297.

that the expression 'that Socrates is wise' here stands for a *non*-linguistic entity. According to our account, *that Socrates is wise* is *inter*-linguistic rather than *non*-linguistic, its inter-linguistic character being constituted by the use of 'that' to form a singular term which we have reconstructed as 'the ·Socrates is wise·'. Our concern, therefore, is with the contrived statement,

The ·Socrates is wise· is true

III

24. In technical semantics an essential role is played in the explication of truth by equivalences of the form illustrated by

'Snow is white' is true ⟷ snow is white

In order to be adequate, it is said, a definition of truth with respect to a given language must be such that equivalences of this form are its 'consequences'.

25. From our point of view the subject of the statement on the left-hand side of the above equivalence is a singular term, indeed, a distributive singular term. Thus the equivalence should read

The 'snow is white' is true ⟷ snow is white

Furthermore, since to make its point, i.e. if 'true' is to have a sense which is common to English and French, the equivalence must translate, say, into French as

Le 'la neige est blanche' est vrai ⟷ la neige est blanche

which it would not do unless the quotation marks were, in effect, our technical quotes, and French contained a parallel device, our attention turns to the equivalence

The ·snow is white· is true ⟷ snow is white

26. Now it is clear, I take it, despite rumblings on the horizon, that such equivalences, in their ordinary garb, thus

That snow is white is true ⟷ snow is white

do not formulate identities of sense. On the other hand, they *are* conceptually necessary. The account of this conceptual necessity

I wish to recommend is that these equivalences 'follow' from the 'definition' of truth in that for a proposition to be true is for it to be assertible, where this means not *capable* of being asserted (which it must be to be a proposition at all) but *correctly* assertible; assertible, that is, in accordance with the relevant semantical rules, and on the basis of such additional, though unspecified, information as these rules may require. The phrase 'semantical rule' is used in the sense defined in the preceding chapter, but which will be further explicated as the argument proceeds. 'True', then, means *semantically* assertible ('S-assertible') and the varieties of truth correspond to the relevant varieties of semantical rule.

27. From this point of view,

> The ˙snow is white˙ is true

has the sense of

> The ˙snow is white˙ is S-assertible

and the implication

> That snow is white is true → snow is white

is not an element in an *extensional* definition of 'true', a recursive listing of truth conditions, as, in effect, it is on Carnap's account, but is rather a consequence of the above *intensional* definition of 'true', in the sense that the assertion of the right-hand side of the implication statement is a *performance of the kind authorized by the truth statement on the left.*

28. In this respect the sequence of inscriptions

> ⋮
> The ˙snow is white˙ is true
> Snow is white
> ⋮

differs from an *inferential* sequence in that whereas in the latter, thus

> ⋮
> If it is day, it is light
> It is day
> It is light
> ⋮

the inscribing of 'It is light' is warranted by a leading principle (*modus ponens*) which does not occur *in the sequence*, in the case of the so-called 'truth inference', the so-called 'premise' is a statement which *of itself* authorizes the inscribing of the consequence.

29. It is, as has often been noted, as though the force of 'true' in

'Snow is white' is true

were to *say* that the quotation marks which precede it, together with itself, may be erased. This way of putting it, though suggestive, is awkwardly self-referential, and must be construed as an epigrammatic way of summarizing some such account as the above, according to which the concealed presence of common nouns in that-clauses explains the general or 'season-ticket' character of the licence which is given by 'true'.

IV

30. Now it is clear that the above account of truth applies to all kinds of propositions, ranging from singular state-of-affairs intensions to the propositions of mathematics and even the propositions of practical discourse. Thus the sequence of licence and performance

The ·causing pain is *prima facie* wrong· is true (S-assertible)
————————————————————————————————————
Causing pain is *prima facie* wrong

is no less correct than

The ·2 plus 2 equals 4· is true (S-assertible)
————————————————————————————
2 plus 2 equals 4

and this, in turn, no less correct than

The ·snow is white· is true (S-assertible)
————————————————————————
Snow is white

31. But before we take a closer look at the way in which varieties of semantical correctnesses and uniformities correlate with the varieties of truth, let us see how the above discussion of 'obtains' or 'is the case' might illuminate the context

Wisdom is exemplified

32. Since to be exemplified is to be exemplified by one or more individuals, let us consider the statement

Wisdom is exemplified by Socrates

Now there is the closest of relationship between this statement and

That Socrates is wise obtains (or is the case, or is, in the 'absolute' sense, true)

a closeness which is made apparent by the intermediate form

That he is wise is true of Socrates

We are therefore tempted to construe the latter as

The ·he is wise· is true of Socrates

but a note of caution is struck when we consider that the expression 'he' is functioning in a peculiar way. Clearly *something* like the step from

That he is wise is true of Socrates

to

That Socrates is wise is true

is involved, but how is it to be understood? The expression 'Socrates' has in some sense been 'substituted' for the expression 'he', and clearly the former statement in some way tells us that the result of this substitution is a true proposition. This suggests that, in approximation, the 'he' is serving as a variable, and that the statement

That he is wise is true of Socrates

is to be construed as saying

The result of replacing the ·x· in an ·x is wise· by a ·Socrates· is true, i.e. S-assertible.

And while this will not do as it stands, for reasons which emerge when one asks what it would be to replace the ·x· in the fleeting utterance of an ·x is wise· with a ·Socrates·, it is close enough to the truth to serve my purpose on the present occasion.

33. For that purpose is to argue that although the statement

Wisdom is exemplified by Socrates

appears, by its surface form, to assert that a certain relation or, if you prefer, *nexus* or tie, holds of the objects wisdom and Socrates, the actual situation is quite different. For whereas in

Plato is admired by Socrates

the expression 'Socrates' is occurring as a first-level referring expression, and stands for its ordinary sense – – – is, in other words, a ·Socrates· – – –, in the context

Wisdom is exemplified by Socrates

it stands for a second-order sense and is, in our terminology, a ··Socrates··. Using a bludgeon instead of a scalpel, we may say that in the context

Plato is admired by Socrates

the word 'Socrates' is *used* whereas in

Wisdom is exemplified by Socrates

it is *mentioned*.

34. In more technical terms the exemplification statement fails to assert a relation (*nexus* or tie) between Socrates and an object, because its reference to Socrates is in a special way indirect, being mediated by the truth performance

$$\frac{\text{The ·Socrates is wise· is true (S-assertible)}}{\text{So, Socrates is wise}}$$

V

35. The statement 'Wisdom is exemplified by Socrates' fails to assert a relation, tie or *nexus* between Socrates and an object for the additional but related reason that wisdom is not an object. Thus if we agree with Frege in thinking of an object as the sort of thing which can be named, wisdom is not an object, because 'wisdom' is not, in this use, a name. To avoid the appearance of turning distinguished philosophers into un-persons, I shall change my example. If triangularity is not an object, what is it?

36. If it is an object it is an odd one, as witness all the perplexity it has caused. Yet if my analysis is correct, this oddness falls into

place. For it is a *distributive* object—in which respect it belongs in the same box as *the pawn*.

37. Thus, if we use the word object in a broad sense, according to which all singular subjects of predication[1] are objects, we can say

The ·the pawn· is a singular term, specifically a distributive singular term (DST)

similarly, we can say

Triangularity is an object, specifically a distributive object

which is the material mode of speech for

The ·triangularity· is a singular term, specifically a distributive singular term

38. Reflection on this latter statement calls attention to an ambiguity in the use of the expression 'triangularity', which has often been sensed, but never, to my knowledge, clarified. In the contexts we have so far considered it has had the sense of

the ·triangular·

[1] Corresponding, of course, to the distinction between objects proper and distributive objects there are, of course, two senses of 'predication', the one derivative from the other, as distributive singular terms are derivative from common nouns. If we represent

Socrates is a man

by

Socrates ∈ man

we might represent

The K_1 is a K_2

by

The K_1 E K_2

also

x belongs to the K

as

x ɯ the K

also

K_1's belong to the K

as

K_1 ⊏ the K

and

The K_1 belongs to the K_2

as

The K_1 m the K_2

105

But if our analysis is correct, in the context

> Triangularity is an object

it has the sense of

> the ·the ·triangular··

for

> The ·triangularity· is a DST

unpacks into

> The ·the ·triangular·· is a DST of the second level

39. This distinction, as I see it, is the cash value of the medieval distinction between predicative and formal universals. Thus, it is said that

> *Animal* is a predicative universal

whereas

> *Animality* is a formal universal

This corresponds to our distinction between

> The ·animal· is a predicate

and

> The ·the ·animal·· is a DST

40. The thesis I have been advancing can be put by saying that all abstract entities are distributive objects. On the other hand, not all distributive objects are abstract entities, as this phrase is ordinarily used. Thus, *the pawn* is a distributive object, but does not belong in the same category as attributes, propositions, senses, intensions, classes, individual concepts and the like, which are the concern of logical theory. The latter, unlike *the pawn* and *the lion*, are *linguistic* distributive objects. Notice, however, that not all linguistic distributive objects are abstract entities in the usual sense, but only those which belong in the framework of discourse about *implication, meaning, truth* and such related epistemic notions as *verifiability, decidability* and *confirmation*, to mention but a few.

41. The above thesis, if correct, has the corollary that just as all statements beginning with

The pawn . . .

could, in principle, be eliminated in favour of statements beginning

Pawns . . .

and these, in turn, in favour of statements about permissible configurations and sequences of configurations of objects satisfying certain general conditions of distinguishability and combinability —statements which define a mode of rule-governed activity called a game, *so* all statements beginning with expressions such as

triangularity
that Socrates is wise
etc.

could, in principle, be eliminated in favour of statements beginning

·triangular·s
·Socrates is wise·s
etc.

and these, in turn, in favour of a system of statements about permissible configurations of inscriptions and utterances with other inscriptions and utterances, with objects and events and with non-linguistic behaviour—statements which define a mode of rule-governed behaviour which it is illuminating to call, by analogy, a language game.[1]

VI

42. All of the above logic-chopping, however persuasive it might be for the moment, would soon be swept away by the feeling that

---

[1] The above eliminability would hold even in the case of statements involving variables whose substituends are abstract singular terms, and expressions, such as 'attribute₁', 'state of affairs₁₅', etc., which stand for specific abstract entities without being formed by a quoting device. The exception, and it is an important one, is that where such variables and constants occur in a context which involves the predicate 'true', the latter, when made explicit, is not eliminable *by the truth move*. It remains, however, eliminable through being replaced by 'S-assertible', which can, in turn, be further explicated.

'triangularity' is the 'name' of an 'object' in the 'world', if it were not reinforced by the theory of predication which Wittgenstein developed in the *Tractatus*, the revolutionary implications of which, as far as I can see, he never completely grasped. Not only is triangularity an odd object in the above sense, it is odd in a yet more radical way, failure to appreciate which generates ever anew the conception of universals as a special sub-set of ordinary, or non-distributive, extra-linguistic objects.

43. After all, it might be said, the fact that there are contexts in which the word 'Socrates' is used, not to mention a person, but to refer to the sense for which it ordinarily stands, and to stand for a second-level sense, odd objects, perhaps even distributive objects—all this is compatible with the hard-core fact that in its basic use it does refer to something in the extra-linguistic world, a man who lived a long time ago and started the hare you are chasing.

44. Similarly, it might be said, the fact that there are contexts in which 'triangular' is used to stand for very odd objects in Frege's hierarchy of senses—perhaps, if you are right, distributive objects—all this is compatible, surely, with the idea that in its basic use it does refer to an object proper in the world, though, of course, a universal rather than a particular.

45. Now what Wittgenstein established[1] was that whether one does it perspicuously or not, one can only say of two objects that they stand in a certain relation by placing the corresponding referring expressions in a counterpart relation. Thus, whether we say

a is larger than b

or

a_b

in either case what we have done is form an expression which,

[1] I developed the following interpretation of Wittgenstein's theory of predication in a series of seminars on the *Tractatus* in the 1950s. It was published in 'Naming and Saying', *Philosophy of Science*, 29, 1962 [reprinted as Chapter 7 in *Science, Perception and Reality*]. It was developed independently by Erik Stenius in his *Wittgenstein's Tractatus*, Cornell, 1960, but he failed to clarify its significance for ontology.

from the standpoint of its semantical functioning, is a dyadic configuration of the names '*a*' and '*b*'; it is, in other words, an

$$R* [\cdot a \cdot, \cdot b \cdot]$$

where this is a common noun which applies to items consisting of an ·*a*· and a ·*b*· related in a way which does the job, in the language to which it belongs, which is done in our subject-predicate language by concatenating these names with a predicate.

46. Thus, in an idealized form of English we would bring it about that the ·*a*· and the ·*b*· were related as having the design 'larger than' between them. But, as indicated, there could be a non-subject-predicate language in which the ·*a*· and the ·*b*· were made to form a statement having the same, or at least a closely related, sense, by placing them in a configuration which involves no use of an additional sign design.

47. The conclusion Wittgenstein correctly drew is that predicate expressions are ancillary expressions, and are dispensible in a way in which referring expressions are not.

48. Let me emphasize that this is not to say that singular statements could, in principle, 'consist of referring expressions' in the sense of being a mere list—the crudest possible form of nominalism. It is rather the more subtle point that one says *how* objects are by inscribing or uttering the corresponding referring expressions in a certain manner. Thus, one might say what we say by concatenating a ·wise· with a ·Socrates· by writing the referring expression ·Socrates· in bold face or italics.

49. Of course, the point Wittgenstein was making is a general one, and leaves open the question as to whether the basic referring expressions of a language refer to two types of objects proper— particulars and universals—or particulars only. Thus, a platonic realist could grant Wittgenstein's general point, and yet insist that, in the statement (in the PMese dialect)

Triangular *a*

both expressions refer to objects proper, and that the statement tells us that these objects stand in the exemplification *nexus*, by being a concatenation of these two referring expressions without the use of an auxiliary expression, thus saying perspicuously what would be said unperspicuously by

Triangularity is exemplified by *a*

50. If, however, my argument is correct, this sophisticated position is a misapplication of Wittgenstein's insight, applying it at the level of distributive linguistic objects rather than at the level of objects proper.[1]

51. Of course, if one is convinced on other grounds that the extra-linguistic order includes particulars and universals standing in the exemplification *nexus*, or tied by a characterizing tie, one will construe universals as well as particulars as objects proper. But if my argument is correct, and exemplification belongs in the same box as truth, and is a matter of the semantical correctness of a certain performance—roughly the de-quoting of a quoted expression, then, instead of being, as is often claimed, irrelevant to the problem of abstract entities, Wittgenstein's insight provides the keystone which can keep philosophical semantics from collapsing ever anew into a rubble of fruitless discussion.

52. From the vantage point we have reached we see that the primary member of the family of abstract entities, the member the understanding of which brings with it the understanding of all the others, is the proposition, and the key predicate is 'true'. For when it is seen that the reality of individuals, the exemplification of universals, attributes having extensions, the obtaining of states of affairs, propositions denoting the actual world (or The True), etc., etc., are all to be explicated in terms of truth, the temptation to regard these items as extra-linguistic states of affairs must surely be diminished.

---

[1] Notice that Wittgenstein's point does apply equally well to non-linguistic distributive objects, such as the knight and the bishop in chess. Thus, instead of saying

The knight is more powerful than the bishop

we could say

The knight

      The bishop

VII

53. Before I conclude this chapter with some remarks on semantical uniformities and the rules of criticism which keep them under control, a comment, in the light of the above, on the philosophical concept of a linguistic convention is in order. There is, indeed, a legitimate sense in which it is a matter of convention that the design 'circular' stands for circularity. It makes perfectly good sense to suppose that some other design, say 'brillig', might have stood for this attribute; indeed, we can imagine a lisping reformer to propose that we use 'brillig' to stand for circularity, and to succeed, by virtue of, say, his political authority, in persuading us to adopt his proposal.

54. But, and this is the crucial point, it is no more illuminating to describe the adoption of the proposal as the bringing it about that 'brillig's (in our language) have the *stand for* relation to circularity than it would be illuminating to describe the adoption of a proposal that kopeks be used to play the pawn, as the bringing it about that kopeks have the *play* relation to the pawn.

55. The cash value of adopting the proposal is, in each case, that items of a certain description come to be involved in configurations and uniformities with human behaviour, which are subject to rules of criticism. Indeed, if our reformers were to boast

    'Brillig's (tomorrow) will stand for circularity

and

    Kopeks (tomorrow) will play the pawn

these boasts, on our analysis, would be equivalent to the boasts

    'Brillig's (tomorrow) will be ·circular·s
    Kopeks (tomorrow) will be pawns

where the criteria by virtue of satisfying which, 'brillig's in the one case will be ·circular·s and kopeks on the other will be pawns, are specified in terms of the relevant configurations, uniformities and rules of criticism.

56. If we know, for example, that

    '*Sage*'s (in F) are ·wise·s

we know, by virtue of our knowledge of what 'wise's do in our language, that the French word '*sage*' must occur in uniformities[1] involving both tokens of '*sage*' and extra-linguistic objects. But the uniformities do not consist of tokens of 'sage' *standing for* wisdom but are rather to be characterized as complex uniformities involving many configurations of many French words and forms of behaviour, on the one hand, and, not wisdom, but wise people, on the other.[2]

57. I have argued that no semantical statement in the Carnap–Tarski sense, properly understood, formulates either an idealized semantical uniformity or a semantical rule in *our* sense of the term. Notice, on the other hand, that what Carnap calls a 'syntactical system'[3] is an abstract formulation of possible ideal intra-linguistic uniformities, and *can* be construed as a sub-set of the rules of criticism for a possible language. Indeed, it is because the ideal uniformities and correctnesses formulated in the logical syntax of a language are purely intra-linguistic that the temptation arose to construe the sense in which Semantics, as a theory of extensions, intensions, designation and truth, is richer than Syntactics as a matter of the supposed fact that semantical statements (in the Carnap–Tarski sense) formulate ideal uniformities and correctnesses involving *extra*-linguistic as well as linguistic objects. This, if I am right, is a mistake. Statements involving these important logical concepts do not formulate such uniformities or rules of criticism, though where these statements are about expressions to which the distinction between 'extension' and 'intension' applies they do *imply* statements which formulate such uniformities and rules, by virtue of the function of abstract singular terms and the predicate 'true'.

58. To supplement the syntactical characterization of a language with classificatory of the form

[1] It will be remembered that we are concerned with that conceptually distinguish able stratum of configurations and uniformities which is involved in what we have called the epistemic function of language, as contrasted with its role as social glue.

[2] It might have been better to call the uniformities I have in mind 'semeiotic' rather than 'semantical' because to speak of them as 'semantical' may lead the unwary to suppose that 'semantical' statements in the Carnap–Tarski sense formulate such uniformities (though 'idealized' in a way which makes them parallel to statements about ideal gases). But the word is a good one, and appropriate, and should outlast the effects of bad philosophy.

[3] *Introduction to Semantics*, p. 12.

(Expression) (in L) stands for (sense) e.g. 'Dreieckig' (in G) stands for triangularity

would not, by itself, however 'semantical' its ring, provide the basis for an explication of the concepts of denotation, extension, satisfaction, exemplification and other concepts of this family. One *must* introduce, in addition, a predicate having the distinctive function of 'true'.

59. On the other hand, the classificatory function of abstract singular terms is equally essential, for it is only because our semantical statements about a given language, say French, include statements of the form

( ) stands for ( )

which, on our interpretation, classify its expressions with respect to a base language which we know how to use, thus

'*La neige est blanche*'s (in F) are ·snow is white·s
'Deux et deux font quatre's (in F) are ·2 plus 2 equals 4·s

that the truth moves

$$\frac{\text{The ·snow is white· is true}}{\text{Snow is white}}$$

$$\frac{\text{The ·2 plus 2 equals 4· is true}}{\text{2 plus 2 equals 4}}$$

are connected with the French expressions

'La neige est blanche'

and

'Deux et deux font quatre'

so that we can say

'La neige est blanche' (in F) is true $\longleftrightarrow$ snow is white
'Deux et deux font quatre' (in F) is true $\longleftrightarrow$ 2 plus 2 equals 4

60. This primacy of classification and the truth performance can be obscured by misleading axiomatizations of semantical theory, but it exists none the less, and makes its presence felt. Failure to

appreciate it accounts, in my opinion, for the fact that technical semantics, when it has not been philosophically barren, has spawned new forms of outworn metaphysics.

VIII

61. If we idealize and simplify—as indeed we must—and concern ourselves with the kind of language which Wittgenstein describes in the *Tractatus*, the language of *Principia Mathematica* with a vocabulary of undefined descriptive terms and the basic vocabulary of practical discourse (about which Wittgenstein has little which is helpful to say), the semantical uniformities and rules of criticism of which I have been speaking can be classified as follows:

I. *Intra-linguistic uniformities:*

(*a*) Formative (formation rules).
(*b*) Consequential (transformation rules).
   (α) Logical rules in the narrow sense (L-rules).
   (β) Law-like statements construed as principles of inference (P-rules).
   (γ) Consequence rules relating names, demonstratives and the language of Space and Time.

II. [*World → Language*] *Uniformities:*

(*a*) Language-entry (responsive):
   (α) Demonstrative: responding to situations of different kinds with sentence tokens of the kind ·this is – – –·.
   (β) Sortal: responding to different kinds of situation with tokens of correspondingly different demonstrative sentences—that is, since PM is a subject-predicate language, sentences with correspondingly different predicates.
(*b*) Mediated by combination of II (*a*) with I (*b*) (β) and I (*b*) (γ).

III. [*Language → World*] *Uniformities.*[1]

---

[1] An earlier version of these distinctions is to be found in 'Some Reflections on Language Games', *Philosophy of Science*, 21, 1954 [reprinted as Chapter XI in *Science, Perception and Reality*].

IX

62. A realistic account of these semantical rules precludes that every proposition of the relevant variety is either true or false. Indeed, in the case of logical and mathematical propositions, *where S-assertability means provability*, the law of bivalence can be defended only by defining a sense in which propositions in one axiomatic framework can be 'identified' with propositions in a more inclusive axiomatic framework. This topic is but one part of the broader topic of the 'identifiability' of items in one framework with items in another, which is crucial to the understanding of the Peircean dimension of the concept of truth, its relation to on-going inquiry. This will be the topic of the next chapter.

V

THE CONCEPTUAL AND
THE REAL:

3. PICTURING

1. I have emphasized that the concept of truth as S-assertibility is universal in its scope, applying to propositions of the most divergent types. On the other hand, as a generic concept it takes specific forms which are functions of the semantical rules which govern these different types of propositions. My concern in this chapter will be with what might initially be called 'factual truth'. This phrase is intended to cover both the truth of propositions at the perceptual and introspective level, and the truth of those propositions which, though 'empirical' in the broad sense that their authority ultimately rests on perceptual experience, involve the complex techniques of concept formation and confirmation characteristic of theoretical science.[1]

2. Since the term 'fact' is properly used as a synonym for 'truth' even in its most generic sense, so that we can speak of mathematical and even ethical facts, 'factual', in the more specific sense indicated above, should be thought of as short for 'matter-of-factual', and as equivalent to Leibnitz' technical term *verité de fait*.

3. Notice that if the phrase 'factual truth' is introduced to contrast with '*a priori* truth' or '*verité de raison*' it would be quite

[1] Thus, this chapter is an attempt to give a unified treatment, which coheres with the argument of the remainder of the book, of issues separately discussed in 'Truth and "Correspondence",' *Journal of Philosophy*, 59, 1962 [reprinted as Chapter 6 in *Science, Perception and Reality*], and 'Scientific Realism or Irenic Instrumentalism' for reference see note on p. 21 above].

appropriate to classify substantive ethical truths, granting there to be such, under this heading. Indeed, according to the theory to be advanced in the final chapter, ethical truths are the projections of 'matter-of-factual' truths, in the narrower sense adumbrated above, into the framework of intentions and purposes.

4. Even this narrower sense, however, in which we contrast the ethical 'ought' with the matter-of-factual 'is', does not bring us to the end of the series of chinese boxes which make up factual truth. For the domain of 'is' also has its 'oughts'. Thus, though I shall not defend the analysis here, law-like propositions tell us how we ought to think about the world.[1] They formulate rules of criticism, and if, as such, they tell us what ought or ought not to be the case, the fact that it is what ought or ought not to be the case with respect to *our beliefs about* the world suffices to distinguish them from those rules of criticism which tell us what ought or ought not to be the case in the world. The fact that our beliefs about the world are themselves in the world does not undermine this distinction, though it emphasizes the care with which it must be drawn.

5. The conceptual form of a law-like statement is roughly indicated by the following example:

For all temporal senses *t*, one ought not to accept both the proposition that there is lightning at *t* and the proposition that there is not thunder at *t* plus Δt

This is, in first approximation at least, equivalent to

(*t*) that there is lightning at *t* implies that there is thunder at *t* plus Δt

where '*t*' ranges over the appropriate temporal senses or intensions. Thus law-like statements are at the meta-linguistic (and meta-conceptual) level, and must be carefully distinguished from quantified statements at the first level of discourse. As indicated, they involve quantification over intensions or senses. Thus the above implication statement must not be confused with the object language statement

(*t*) there is lightning at *t* $\rightarrow$ there is thunder at *t* plus Δt

[1] I have discussed this topic at length in 'Counterfactuals, Dispositions and the Causal Modalities', *Minnesota Studies in the Philosophy of Science*, Volume II, Minneapolis, 1957, and 'Induction As Vindication', *Philosophy of Science*, 31, 1964.

where '→' stands for material implication, and '*t*' ranges over moments of time.

6. If something like this analysis stands up, it follows that law-like statements are, in our sense of the phrase, 'semantical rules', and are, *ceteris paribus*, reflected in uniformities pertaining to the verbal behaviour (and conceptual acts) of those who espouse them. These uniformities would be characterized by the absence, *ceteris paribus*, from overt and covert propositional episodes of pairs which violate linguistic ought-not-to-be's of the kind illustrated above.

7. In philosophy one thing always leads to another, and it is tempting, at this point, to embark on an extended discussion of induction. What is the rationale of accepting law-like statements thus construed? How is this rationale grounded in the end-in-view of scientific inquiry? The attempt to answer these and related questions is a notoriously intricate and controversial enterprise. I have attempted to carry it through in some detail on another occasion.[1] I shall limit myself now to pointing out that the above account of law-like statements would seem to imply that their truth (S-assertibility) involves a semantical rule or rules relating the accepting of them to the accepting of the corresponding evidential statements. If so, the rationale of accepting *this* higher order rule (or rules) must involve the job which law-like statements, construed as we have construed them, perform. Since this job is to govern, as rules of criticism, semantical uniformities involving factual statements in a deeper sense of 'factual', to understand the point of inductive reasoning one must understand the distinctive functions of matter-of-factual statements belonging to the level below that of law-like statements.

II

8. Although Wittgenstein's *Tractatus*, by lacking a theory of the normative aspects of matter-of-factual discourse, fails to do justice to the complex interrelationships between the different levels of such discourse, it does contain essential clues to an understanding of the distinctive functions of first-level matter-of-

[1] 'Induction As Vindication', *Philosophy of Science*, 31, 1964.

factual discourse. These clues are contained in his discussion of language as a means of constructing 'logical pictures' of the world.

9. I speak of the distinctive *functions* of first-level matter-of-factual discourse; for even within this level essential distinctions must be drawn if we are to grasp the difference between the *primary* concept of factual truth (truth as correct picture), which makes intelligible all the other modes of factual truth, and the *generic* concept of truth as S-assertibility, which involves the quite different mode of correspondence bound up with illustrating propositional expressions and the truth performance, as in

$$\frac{\text{That 2 plus 2} = 4 \text{ is S-assertible}}{\text{2 plus 2} = 4}$$

in terms of which the 'correspondence' statement (i.e. equivalence statement)

That 2 plus 2 $= 4$ is true $\longleftrightarrow$ 2 plus 2 $= 4$

is to be understood.

10. The key distinction pertaining to matter-of-factual statements of the first level is a familiar one, easy to indicate, but difficult to refine. It is that between atomic and molecular statements. In first approximation it is atomic statements which make up 'linguistic pictures' of the world. These pictures are correct or incorrect in terms of the semantical rules of the framework within which they are statements. They are true (S-assertible) if correct, false if incorrect.

11. Molecular statements, on the other hand, have their own specific way of being S-assertible. They pick out sets of pictures within which they play no favourites, and are true if the set of pictures they pick out includes the correct picture, false if they pick out a set of pictures which does not include this picture. Tautologies pick out *all* pictures and hence *pick out* none. Contradictions pick out no pictures for, to use a metaphor and an Irish Bull, the pictures they pick out are red and green all over.

12. Basic factual predicates come in families of competing predicates, one or other of which must be satisfied by every object

which *can* satisfy a predicate of that family. If a is not f_1 it must be f_2 or f_3. Hence

$$f_1 a \cdot \sim f_1 a$$

implies

$$f_1 a \cdot (f_2 a \vee f_3 a)$$

that is

$$f_1 a \cdot f_2 a \vee f_1 a \cdot f_3 a$$

Thus one misses the point if one argues that a contradiction picks out all pictures on the grounds that 'a contradiction implies every proposition'.

13. The S-assertibility of molecular statements which are neither tautologies nor self-contradictory is a function of the syntactical moves which connect them with disjunctions of conjunctions of non-negative and non-competing atomic statements, and of the S-assertibility of these conjunctive complex *qua* complex pictures.

14. Thus, if the two families are ['f_1', 'f_2', 'f_3'] and ['g_1', 'g_2', 'g_3']

$$\sim (f_1 a \cdot \sim g_1 b)$$

becomes the disjunction of conjunctions

$$(f_1 a \cdot g_1 b) \vee (f_2 a \cdot g_1 b) \vee (f_2 a \cdot g_2 b) \vee (f_2 a \cdot g_3 b) \vee (f_3 a \cdot g_1 b) \vee (f_3 a \cdot g_2 b) \vee (f_3 a \cdot g_3 b)$$

and is S-assertible if any of the disjuncts constitutes an S-assertible picture.

15. Notice that the mode of composition by virtue of which a number of atomic statements join to make a complex picture must not be confused with the mode of composition by virtue of which a number of atomic statements join to make a molecular statement. In other words, we must distinguish 'pictorial' from 'logical' complexity. Thus, the complex picture of which the elements are an ·fa·, an ·aRb· and a ·gb· must not be confused with the conjunctive statement

$$fa \cdot aRb \cdot gb$$

3. Picturing

16. It was pointed out in the preceding chapter that to be an ·*fa*· is, strictly speaking, to be an ·*f*· [·*a*·], where the latter is a common noun, analogous to 'white dog', which applies to items which are both ·*a*·s and possessed of a character by virtue of which they do the job done in the base language by '*a*'s which are concatenated to the left with an '*f*'. I am assuming that the base language is a subject-predicate one because of the convenience of expressing how things are by giving referring expressions the how of being concatenated in a one-dimensional order with predicative expressions, though the latter are in principle eliminable in favour of more complex devices. Redundancy also is convenient, but, in principle, dispensible. With redundancy the complex picture corresponding to the molecular statement

fa · *aRb* · *gb*

might be, for example,

fa.aRb.gb

where the dots are periods rather than ·and·s.

17. Without redundancy the picture might be, for example,

R*fagb*

and in a non-subject-predicate language it might be, for example,

aᴮ

where the fact that the ·*a*· is in bold face makes it an ·*fa*·, the fact that the ·*b*· is in upper case makes it a ·*gb*· and the fact that the ·*a*· is to the upper left of the ·*b*· makes them an ·*aRb*·.

III

18. The point I have just been making can be put by saying that logical connectives and quantifiers do not occur *as such* in pictorial complexes. Thus, when the conjunctive statement '*fa* · *aRb* · *gb*' is considered *qua* picture the connectives, though physically present, no longer function as such, but become so to speak mere punctuation. This suggests that there might be other ways in which logical operators 'occur' in pictures without occurring in them *as operators*.

19. We are all familiar with problems concerning the sense in which 'it is raining' occurs in such intensional contexts as 'Jones believes that it is raining'. Less attention has been paid to problems concerning the sense in which the quantificational apparatus of definite description occurs in contexts which are *prima facie* purely extentional. The topic is an important one, for unless we are clear about it the Tractarian account of matter-of-factual truth is likely to appear so remote from ordinary usage as to be absurd.

20. It seems reasonable, as a first step, to interpret

The g is f

and

The g is not f

not as contradictories but as contraries, by construing them as the informal counterparts, respectively, of

$$(Ex)\, gx \cdot (y)\, gy \rightarrow y = x \cdot fx$$

and

$$(Ex)\, gx \cdot (y)\, gy \rightarrow y = x \cdot \sim\!fx$$

This would mean that to negate 'The g is not f' we would have to say something like 'It is not the case that the g is f'.

21. On this analysis both 'The g is f' and 'The g is not f' would be false if the uniqueness condition is not satisfied. If we distinguish, with Russell, between

(a) $\sim\!f[(\imath x)\, gx]$

and

(b) $\sim\!\{f[(\imath x)\, gx]\}$

the latter would correspond to 'It is not the case that the g is f',[1] the former to 'the g is not f'.

22. It will be remembered that we have been abstracting from the 'dialectical' assertibilities which are grounded in the require-

[1] Strictly speaking, of course, 'It is not the case that the g is f' is in the metalanguage. If we were to remain in the object language we would have to say something like 'Not the g is f'. Notice that while (b) involves standard propositional negation, (a) involves a contextually defined use of negation.

ments of unambiguous communication. If we are prepared to take into account a dimension of 'dialectical' assertibility (D-assertibility), it is tempting to suggest that

It is false that the g is f

is not D-assertible in a dialogue, if the speaker's ground is that the uniqueness condition is not satisfied, *and* this fact has not yet been brought out in the dialogue. It becomes D-assertible when this occurs. Since S-assertibility abstracts from this type of consideration, it would follow that although both

It is false that the g is f

and

It is false that the g is not f

are true (S-assertible), neither is, in specifiable circumstances, D-assertible. If we take 'false' to imply 'not D-assertible' neither

It is true that the g is f

nor

It is false that the g is

would be D-assertible. This fact must not be confused with the idea that when the uniqueness condition is not satisfied, 'The g is f' is neither true nor false.[1]

23. Now in the case of informal arithmetical statements, thus

(1) The square of 2 is even
(2) The square of 2 is not even
(3) The square root of 2 is not rational
(4) It is not the case that the square root of 2 is rational

we can reasonably say that the sense of these statements is captured by the PMese counterparts

(1) (Ex) sq $(x, 2) \cdot (y)$ sq $(y, 2) \to y = x \cdot ev(x)$
(2) (Ex) sq $(x, 2) \cdot (y)$ sq $(y, 2) \to y = x \cdot \sim ev(x)$
(3) (Ex) sqr $(x, 2) \cdot (y)$ sqr $(y, 2) \to y = x \cdot \sim rat$ (x)
(4) $\sim \{(Ex)$ sqr $(x, 2) \cdot (y)$ sqr $(y, 2) \to y = x \cdot rat$ $(x)\}$

[1] For an earlier attempt along these lines see my 'Presupposing', *Philosophical Review*, 63, 1953.

According to this analysis, (1) would be true, (2) false, (3) false and (4) true but, perhaps, not D-assertible in a given dialogue.

24. When, on the other hand, we turn our attention to first-level matter-of-factual statements which resemble the statements we have been calling pictures in every respect *save that the subject term is a definite description*, we need to recognize that although

The *g* is *f*

can be perspicuously represented as

$$f[(\imath x)\, gx]$$

neither 'the *g*' nor '$(\imath x)\, gx$' is occurring *as a logically complex expression, but rather as a simple expression which, if the uniqueness condition it indicates is satisfied, can be used to form linguistic pictures of a certain object.* Failure to appreciate this point leads to the mistaken view that 'existential quantification is the referential tie between language and the world'. The relation between existential quantification and reference is, indeed, close, but it is not that of identity.

25. The point stands out more clearly when we note that instead of using 'the *g*' or $(\imath x)\, gx$' we could introduce an expression, say '*a*', which has no internal logical complexity, and specify that '*a*' has denotation if and only if E! $(\imath x)\, gx$, in which case it denotes $(\imath x)\, gx$.

26. The fundamental job of singular first-level matter-of-factual statements is to picture, and hence the fundamental job of referring expressions is to be correlated *as simple linguistic objects* by matter-of-factual relations with single non-linguistic objects. The difference between '*a*', on the one hand, and 'the *g*' and '$(\imath x)\, gx$', on the other, is that the latter carry on their sleeve the logical and empirical information relevant to their correct use.

27. Thus, even in the absence of considerations pertaining to the 'open texture' of criteria for the use of specific referring expressions there is reason to deny that the *sense* of referring expressions is given by definite descriptions, for their sense is, at bottom, their job, and their job is to be linguistic representatives of objects. It is this, rather than open texture, which is the fundamental

reason for speaking of definite descriptions as providing 'criteria' for the use of names, rather than giving their sense.

28. We have thus defined a sense in which

The g is f

presupposes, rather than *asserts*, that there is one and only one g. Presupposition in this sense must be distinguished from the dialectical sense explained above, in which *presupposing* uniqueness is compatible with *asserting* it.

29. Although much more could be said on the general topic: '. . . the logical constants do not represent', enough has been said to indicate how Wittgenstein's thesis that atomic statements alone are pictures can be reconciled with his otherwise puzzling statement:

> 5.526 One can describe the world completely by completely general propositions, i.e. without from the outset coordinating any name with a definite object.
>
> In order then to arrive at the customary way of expression we need simply say after an expression 'There is one and only one x, which . . .': and this x is a.

IV

30. To be an ·a· is to be an expression which does the job done in the base language by 'a's. It is true, but unilluminating, to say that this job is that of referring to a; for, as was argued in the preceding chapter,

'a's (in L) refer to a = $_{Df}$ (ES) S $\subset$ INSENSE · 'a' $\subset$ S · S materially equivalent to ·a·

Thus, in explaining the job of referring expressions in the base language, it is unilluminating to say that their job is to refer to certain objects. We must look instead to the semantical rules and uniformities in which they are involved. Thus:

(1) Non-demonstrative referring expressions must themselves belong to the 'natural' order and be connected with objects

in a way which involves language entry transitions, intra-linguistic moves (consequence uniformities) and language departure transitions (willings-out-loud).[1]

(2) There must be a relatively stable, if skeletal, framework of propositions (involving these referring expressions) which describe the spatio-temporal location of these objects with respect to each other'.

(3) A proper part of this skeletal framework must 'specify location of the language user in his environment'.

(4) Rehearsings of this skeletal framework must gear in with the use of demonstratives to 'specify the location with respect to *here-now* of the objects with which the referring expressions are correlated'.

31. The above remarks are obviously but a first instalment of the explanation, an attempt to give an informal or intuitive account of how referring expressions function in first-level matter-of-factual discourse. Thus it will have been noticed that (2), by speaking of propositions as 'describing the spatio-temporal location of objects with respect to each other', is of a piece with explaining the job of '*a*' to be that of referring to *a*. 'Describe', like 'refer', does not stand for a specific linguistic job, but rather a job classification. Thus the job in question must ultimately be put in terms of uniformities pertaining to the use of spatio-temporal predicates. Similar considerations apply to (3) and (4).

32. The above points, however, do serve to emphasize that the job of referring expressions cannot be explained without taking into account the job of characterizing expressions, and, in parti-cular, those characterizing expressions which stand for spatial and temporal relations; nor can the job of these, in their turn, be explained without taking into account the responsive role of linguistic expressions (language entry transitions) which is the key to the analysis of 'here' and 'now', and the consequence rules which give the 'axiomatics' of spatio-temporal discourse, not to mention the language departure transitions which reconstruct the voluntary participation of the language user in the course of events which pragmatism has stressed from its inception.

---

[1] These willings pertain to changing one's situation with respect to object making possible new and, perhaps, surprising language entry transitions.

3. Picturing

33. Thus, in order for '*a*', '*b*', etc., to be correlated with objects, the spatio-temporal story-tellings in which they occur, however schematic, must be depictings. This means that certain matter-of-factual relations, satisfied by '*a*'s, '*b*'s, etc., as elements in the language, must be counterparts of relations satisfied by the objects which they represent in the pictures.

34. Furthermore, as we have seen, non-demonstrative referring expressions must be associated with criteria which authorize, for example, moves of the form

This $= a$

In other words, the fact that '*a*'s represent O_1 cannot be a matter of purely spatio-temporal relations and their linguistic counterparts. Individual constants must have a *sense* as well as a *denotation*. That this involves the neck-sticking-out move from

This is $f_1 \ldots f_n$

to

This is *the* $f_1 \ldots f_n$

is no more surprising than that inductive neck-sticking-out is an unavoidable feature of factual discourse.

V

35. We saw in the preceding chapter that for a predicate to stand for an attribute or a relation is for it to be of a certain kind. Thus, to stand for triangularity is to be a ·triangular·. What is it to be a ·triangular· ? It is to be an item which does the job done in the base language by 'triangular's. Specifically, it is to give a singular term concatenated with it a counterpart character, T'. It is T' individual constants which correctly picture triangular objects, provided that the individual constants are correlated, as above, with the objects.

36. But although T' individual constants are correlated with T objects, the concept of this correlation is not the *analysis* of what it is for T' individual constants to *stand for* triangularity, nor does it explain what it is for T' individual constants to *denote* triangular objects. The correlation between objects and their linguistic

pictures must not be confused with the pseudo-relations *standing for* and *denoting*. Thus, that 'triangular's stand for triangularity essentially involves the intra-linguistic consequence uniformities governed by the consequence rules (axiomatics) of geometrical predicates. The crudest form of the contrary position consists in taking the language entry role of a perceptual predicate, the fact that statements involving the predicate are correct responses to objects which exemplify the perceptual character for which it stands, to *constitute* the fact that it stands for this character. For T' individual constants to stand for triangularity essentially involves the consequence patterns in which T' individual constants participate.

VI

37. It is now time to take into account the fact that since the job of abstract singular terms is to classify linguistic and conceptual episodes by comparing the jobs they do with the jobs done by expressions in the base language, the use of abstract terms admits of a dimension of flexibility which, though it has not been unnoticed, particularly by the Hegelian tradition, has never been given an adequate explanation, though the materials for this explanation have long been at hand.

38. One needs only connect the two ideas that triangularity is the ·triangular·, and that the function of 'the ·triangular·' is analogous to that of 'the pawn', to mobilize the familiar fact that it can make very good sense to say that a piece in a certain game is a pawn without implying that it works in *exactly* the same way as pawns do in standard chess. Is a pawn which cannot capture *en passant* a pawn? Is the game in which it belongs chess? There is room here for a decision. More important is the fact that there is room for argument. Considerations of various kinds can be advanced, the most interesting of which pertain to the *point* of classifying games in one way rather than another. One may decide, all things considered, to say 'no', but in the same breath say also that a common-noun 'prawn' could be introduced such that 'standard prawn' and, supposing the non-standard game to be called Jess, 'Jess prawn' would be subordinate classifications.

39. We speak of Euclidian triangularity and contrast it with,

say, Riemannian triangularity. Clearly, this distinction falls in a different dimension from that between scalene triangularity and isosceles triangularity. To say that the design 'triangular' in two different geometries stands for two different triangularities is, in our terms, to do two things. In the first place, it is to classify the design as it functions in these two contexts under a common heading, thus

'triangular's (in G_1) are ·triangular·s
'triangular's (in G_2) are ·triangular·s

On the other hand, it is also, in the second place, to qualify the common nouns under which both uses are subsumed (·triangular·), thusly,

'triangular's (in G_1) are G_1 ·triangular·s
'triangular's (in G_2) are G_2 ·triangular·s

where the expressions on the right-hand side are analogous to 'Guernsey cow' and 'Jersey cow'. The former tells us that 'triangular's in G_1 are ·triangular·s of the G_1 variety, the latter that 'triangular's in G_2 are ·triangular·s of the G_2 variety.

40. This situation must be carefully distinguished from that of ambiguity, as when one distinguishes between geometrical cultural squareness. A person who spoke both 'teen English and fogy English might say

'square' (in 'teenese') stands for squareness, i.e. are ·square·s

and

'square' (in fogese) stands for squareness, i.e. are ·square·s

but the two '·square·s' would be unperspicuously different common nouns, which is not true of '·triangular·' in the above example.

41. The point stands out clearly in number theory, where we say, for example, that there are a number of Two's. There is the natural number Two, the integer Two, the rational number Two, the real number Two, not to mention the imaginary number Two.

42. Furthermore, abstract entities, *pace* Plato, change. Obviously it is in no ordinary sense that they change, yet it is a legitimate one at that.[1] I shall have more to say on this topic before the chapter is over. For the moment it will suffice to note that the base language with respect to which abstract singular terms are introduced is part and parcel of the natural order, the world of 'process' or 'becoming'. Its mode of being is as historical as that of the social institutions it makes possible. The expressions which are embedded in abstract singular terms of the illustrating variety, reconstructed by our dot-quoting device, belong to a cross-section of the history of the language, though the cross-section need not be, in the ordinary sense, 'contemporary usage'.

43. Thus, abstract singular terms, built from designs which once played, but no longer play, the role of the expressions the singular term is designed to single out, can still do the job they originally did, if one knows how the designs were originally used. For those who do not, these abstract singular terms must be connected ('by definition') with others which contain *understood* designs. For, *ultimately*, abstract singular terms must relate to the 'truth move' in which the non-illustrating component falls away, as in

> That snow is white is true
> ————————————————
> Snow is white

44. Thus, if abstract singular terms are to do their job without crutches, the expressions which are built into them must be expressions which those who use the abstract singular terms understand—which, again, does not mean that they are in 'ordinary usage' or that 'everybody' understands them.

45. The fact that a predicate in a certain language may play a role which is generically alike, but specifically different from, that played by '*f*' in the base language, and yet be correctly said to 'stand for *f*-ness', can be given an historical twist illustrated by the history of science. Thus we distinguish between Newtonian simultaneity and Einsteinian simultaneity; and between the

[1] One is tempted, indeed, to say that it is not abstract entities which change but rather our concepts of them. But according to the account we have given, the contrast between 'concepts' and 'abstract entities' is not as straightforward as on more platonic positions.

members of a large family of oxidations ranging from Lavoisierian oxidation to oxidation *à la* chemistry of 1966. (Once again, it is important not to confuse the modifiers with the differentia of ordinary specification.) Thus, as the historian of science looks back he can, on the one hand, make statements of the form

'– – –' (in L_{1800}) stood for f-ness, i.e. were $\cdot f \cdot$s
'– – –' (in L_{1860}) stood for f-ness, i.e. were $\cdot f \cdot$s
'– – –' (in L_{1966}) stands for f-ness, i.e. were $\cdot f \cdot$s

and, on the other hand, introduce qualifiers corresponding to the 'Euclidean' and 'Riemannian' of our previous example.

46. An equivalent formulation can be given by introducing the concept of degrees of 'standing for', and pinning down the criteria to the exact way in which 'f' is used in the base language. Ultimately, we shall see both kinds of move must be made in order to give a complete clarification of the concepts of truth and reality.

47. To say that the semantic rules governing 'f's in our language could change over a period of time, and yet that the 'f's could all be $\cdot f \cdot$s, is what is meant by saying that f-ness has changed over this period. Just as we have the concept of a developing language or conceptual scheme, from which the concept of a language as studied in current formal semantics is an abstraction, so we have the concept of a developing linguistic or conceptual role from which the usual concept of a 'sense' or 'intension' is also an abstraction. To be an $\cdot f \cdot$ (stand for f-ness) does not require in this context that the expression to be classified plays the identical *determinate* role currently played by 'f', but that its function in the earlier stage of the language is sufficiently similar to the current function of 'f' to warrant classifying them together. Roughly, 'f's at t_1 stand to L at t_1 as 'f's at t_2 stand to L at t_2.

VII

48. The explication of truth as S-assertibility raises the question: assertible by whom? With respect to the concept 'true statement (in L)', the obvious, but superficial, answer is: by users of L. But since, as we have seen, this explicitly language relative concept is to be explicated by means of the schema

'– – –' (in L) is true ←→ '– – –'s (in L) are ˙. . .˙, and ˙. . .˙s
are true

i.e. in terms of what is misleadingly called the 'absolute' sense of
true, the more penetrating answer is: S-assertible by *us*. For truth
in the 'absolute' sense is, *in its own way*, language relative, relative
to *our* language. Thus the

˙. . .˙s are true

on the right-hand side of the above schema has the sense of

˙. . .˙s are S-assertible by us

where *we* are users of the language in terms of which specific propositional expressions are introduced.

49. Thus, to characterize a statement in a foreign language, for
example, French as true is, in effect, to treat this language as a
'dialect' of a language game which *we* play, i.e. to treat speakers
of French as speakers of *our* language, as players of a common
game. Since the term 'language' as it is ordinarily used refers to
the specific linguistic materials (sign designs and surface grammar)
which differentiate, e.g. French from German, we need another
term for the common game which is played by users of such
differing resources. I shall use the expression 'conceptual structure'[1] to serve this pupose. Thus the above schema, made explicit,
becomes

'– – –' (in L) is true ←→ '– – –'s (in L) are ˙. . .˙s
and ˙. . .˙s are S-assertible proposi-
tions belonging to our conceptual
structure.

50. We must now refine our analysis by taking to account the
fact that since even the 'absolute' sense of truth has the form

S-assertible proposition belonging to our conceptual structure

---

[1] It should be borne in mind that 'conceptual structure' in this sense refers to language games. It does not refer to conceptual activity in the sense of 'inner episodes'.
I am assuming, as before, that once the epistemic and ontological categories with
which we are concerned have been clarified in their application to Rylean items the
extension of this clarification to 'inner-episodes' poses no difficulty of principle.

which can be simplified into

S-assertible in our conceptual structure

the fundamental form of 'true' is

true in conceptual structure CS_i.

The 'unqualified' sense of 'true' pertains to the special case where CS_i is *our* conceptual structure (abbreviated, in what follows, as CSO), thus

true = S-assertible in CSO

51. We are now in a position to supplement our previous explanation of the relation between the (so-called) 'language relative' and the (so-called) 'absolute' sense of 'true'—in which we were limiting our attention to the special case of *one* conceptual structure embedded in two different systems of linguistic resources, English and French was involved—with a more penetrating analysis of truth which takes into account difference of conceptual structure as well as difference of sign designs and surface grammar. To do so we must draw on the above discussion of the evolution of conceptual structures.

52. The point stands out most clearly in the case of the evolution of a scientific theory. Here it makes obvious sense to say that a certain concept belonging to the theory at one stage is a development of a concept belonging to the theory at an earlier stage. Let us suppose that the theory is one which we accept, and hence that what, for the moment, we shall think of as the 'latest' stage of the theory, is part of our conceptual structure as it now stands (CSO). Let us refer to the conceptual structure which includes a certain earlier stage of the theory as CS_1. Finally, let us introduce the concept of a family of propositions (PRFAM) which are the counterparts of each other at different stages in the development of the theory. We can now introduce the following rough definition of the truth of a proposition in CS_1 in terms of the 'absolute' sense of 'true'—which, as we have seen, amounts to 'true proposition belonging to CSO', thus

$PROP_j$ (in CS_1) is true $\longleftrightarrow$ for some PRFAM and for some PROP, PROP belongs to CSO, $PROP_j$ (in CS_1) $\subset$ PRFAM, PROP $\subset$ PRFAM, and PROP is true

Here the truth of $PROP_j$ in the less developed conceptual structure is defined in terms of the truth of its counterpart in our current conceptual structure.

53. This approach can be generalized still further by introducing a concept of 'true *quoad* CS_i'. Notice that 'true *quoad* CS_i' must not be confused with 'true in CS_i'. We are introducing a sense in which a proposition in one conceptual structure can be true not only with respect to our current conceptual structure, which is what the so-called 'absolute' sense amounts to, but with respect to any suitably related conceptual structure. Thus we can define a sense in which a proposition in our current conceptual structure (CSO) is true *quoad* the earlier conceptual structure CS_1, thus

$PROP_k$ (in CSO) is true *quoad* CS_1 $\longleftrightarrow$ for some PRFAM and for some PROP, PROP belongs to CS_1, $PROP_k$ (in CSO) $\subset$ PRFAM, PROP (in CS_1) $\subset$ PRFAM and PROP is true *quoad* CS_1

We thus distinguish between the conceptual structure to which a proposition *belongs* and the conceptual structure *with respect to which its truth is defined*. Notice, however, that however many sophisticated senses of 'true' may be introduced, and however important they may be, the connection of truth with *our current conceptual structure* remains essential, for the cash value of S-assertibility is assertion by us *hic et nunc*.

VIII

54. There is a sense in which it is correct to say that truth does not admit of degrees. A statement in our conceptual structure is either S-assertible or it is not. (If it is in principle undecidable, neither it nor its negation is S-assertible.) On the other hand, one conceptual framework can be more 'adequate' than another, and this fact can be used to define a sense in which one proposition can be said to be 'more true' than another. Once again I find myself in the position of attempting to revitalize central themes in nineteenth-century Idealism.

3. Picturing

55. My primary aim in this chapter is to explain this 'comparative' sense of truth with respect to matter-of-factual propositions, but it is worth noting that the concept is also relevant to mathematical truths. In the case of arithmetic, for example, the concept of truth (S-assertibility) coincides with that of provability. It follows, of course, from Goedel's results that, with respect to the conceptual structure (in the sense of axiomatics) to which it belongs, not every arithmetical proposition is either true or false. It also follows that not every arithmetical proposition which is in some sense true is true in the absolute sense, i.e. with respect to our current conceptual structure, if this is taken to be an axiomatics. On the other hand, a proposition which is not provable in a weaker axiomatics, A_i, and hence which is not true *quoad* A_i, can be said to be true in a derivative sense, if its counterpart in a richer axiomatics, A_j, which is also, in a sense difficult to define, an axiomatics of arithmetic, is provable in A_j. Thus a proposition in A_i can be said to be true *quoad* A_j. In the case of arithmetic there is no end to the series of 'more adequate' axiomatic systems. On the other hand, in the case of factual propositions we are haunted by the ideal of *the* truth about the world.

56. Truth, we have seen, is not a relation. Picturing, on the other hand, is a relation, indeed, a relation between two relational structures. And pictures, like maps, can be more or less adequate. The adequacy concerns the 'method of projection'. A picture (candidate) subject to the rules of a given method of projection (conceptual framework), which is a correct picture (successful candidate), is S-assertible with respect to that method of projection. Thus the S-assertibility of a matter-of-factual proposition formulated by the schema

The ·*fa*· is S-assertible *quoad* CS_i

is a matter of ·*fa*·s being elements of correct pictures of the world in accordance with the semantic rules of CS_i. The concept of basic matter-of-factual truth, however, is not *identical* with the concept of a correct picture, because it involves the generic notion of the correctness of *assertion*. As we have seen, the concept of a linguistic or conceptual picture requires that the picture be brought about by the objects pictured; and while bringing about of linguistic pictures could be 'mechanical' (thus in the case of sophisticated robots), in thinking of pictures as correct or incorrect we are thinking of the uniformities involved as directly or indirectly subject to rules of criticism.

57. Linguistic picture-making is not the performance of asserting matter-of-factual propositions. The *criterion* of the correctness of the performance of asserting a basic matter-of-factual proposition is the correctness of the proposition *qua* picture, i.e. the fact that it coincides with the picture the world-cum-language would generate in accordance with the uniformities controlled by the semantical rules of the language. Thus the *correctness* of the picture is not defined in terms of the *correctness* of a performance but vice versa.

58. The concept of a linguistic picture is meta-linguistic in a sense which must be carefully distinguished from meta-linguistic statements in the Carnap–Tarski sense, however closely they are related. Thus

'*fa*'s (in L) correctly picture O as ϕ

must be carefully distinguished from

'*fa*'s (in L) stand for that ϕO, and that ϕO is true

The former tells us that (in L) utterances consisting of an '*f*' concatenated with an '*a*' are correlated with O, which is ϕ, in accordance with the semantic uniformities which correlate utterances of lower-case letters of the alphabet with objects such as O, and which correlate utterances of lower-case letters of the alphabet which are concatenated with an '*f*' with objects which are ϕ. These correlations involve the complex machinery of language entry transitions (noticings), intra-linguistic moves (inference, identification by means of criteria) and language departure transitions (volitions pertaining to epistemic activity),[1] and must not be confused with the pseudo-relation of *standing for* or *denoting*. Picturing is a complex matter-of-factual relation and, as such, belongs in quite a different box from the concepts of denotation and truth.

[1] Compare the tautolizingly obscure but suggestive account of the relation of doing to knowing in William James' *Pragmatism*, New York, 1907, *passim*.

3. Picturing

59. A statement to the effect that a linguistic item pictures a non-linguistic item by virtue of the semantical uniformities characteristic of a certain conceptual structure is, in an important sense, an object language statement, for even though it mentions linguistic objects, it treats them as items in the order of causes and effects, i.e. *in rerum natura*, and speaks directly of their functioning in this order in a way which is to be sharply contrasted with the meta-linguistic statements of logical semantics, in which the key role is played by abstract singular terms. Thus it is essential to note that whereas in

'*a*' (in L) denotes O

the 'O' of the right-hand side is a meta-linguistic expression, in

'*a*'s (in L) represent O

it is not.

60. The same is true of the right-hand side of

'R (a, b)' (in L) correctly pictures O_1 and O_2

Furthermore, if we proceed to justify such a statement we must say

... because R* ('*a*', '*b*') and R (O_1, O_2)

rather than

... because Concat ('R', '*a, b*') and Exempl(R-ness(O_1, O_2))

The 'R' of 'R(O_1, O_2)' stands for a complex matter-of-factual relation and not the pseudo-relation of exemplification.

61. The objects which are pictured by a linguistic picture can thus be genuinely extra-linguistic (though, of course, linguistic episodes as items *in rerum natura* can also be pictured). *The concepts* of these objects are, of course, relative to a conceptual scheme, but the form of these concepts is not

O (in our conceptual scheme)

On the other hand, the 'O' of

'*a*' (in L) denotes O

has the form '·O·', which, by virtue of the considerations advanced in the above discussion of truth, does have the form

INSENSE (in our conceptual scheme)

We must not repeat Berkeley's mistake when he wrote, '. . . but it does not show that you can conceive it possible the object of your thought may exist without the mind: to make out this, *it is necessary that you conceive their existing unconceived or unthought-of, which is a manifest repugnancy.*'[1]

62. According to our previous analysis

  '*a*' (in L) refers to O

has the form

  For some INSENSE, '*a*' (in L) $\subset$ INSENSE, and INSENSE materially equivalent to ·O·

We must now take into account the fact that the individual sense in question belongs according to that analysis to our conceptual structure, as does ·O·. This enables us to take into account the fact that we can define a sense in which expressions in a different but related conceptual structure can be said to refer to or denote that which is denoted by expressions in our conceptual structure. Using, once more, the informal or intuitive notion of a family of counterpart individual senses, we have

$INSENSE_j$ (in CS_i) denotes O $\longleftrightarrow$ for some INSENSE and for some INFAM, INSENSE belongs to CSO, $INSENSE_j$ belongs to CS_i, INSENSE $\subset$ INFAM, $INSENSE_j$ belongs to INFAM, and INSENSE materially equivalent to ·O·

63. As in the case of truth, the importance of this analysis lies in the fact that it permits the extension of epistemic notions to conceptual items in a framework which is other than, but related to, the conceptual structure which is embedded in our language as it now stands. In other words, the connection of these epistemic notions with our current conceptual structure (which is necessarily the point of view from which we view the universe) is loosened in a way which makes meaningful the statement that our current conceptual structure is both more adequate than its predecessors and less adequate than certain of its potential successors.

[1] *Principles of Human Knowledge*, XXIII.

64. Thus the fact that, using the conceptual framework of common sense, we quite properly say,

Jones saw that O was red

does not commit us to the idea that there is such a thing as O *as conceived in the framework of common sense*, nor that O is red *as redness is conceived in this framework*. Jones sees that O is *f* involves that Jones has a conceptual episode of the ·O is *f*· kind. This includes a component which refers to O, and, assuming that the conceptual structure in question is of the subject-predicate kind, a component by virtue of which it characterizes O as *f*. That there is no such thing as O as conceived in the framework of common sense, is compatible with the idea that there is such a thing as O as conceived in another framework, thus that of physical theory.

IX

65. It is a truism that we don't speak a more adequate language than we do. On the other hand, it makes sense to speak of people who speak a more adequate language than we do. The putative concept of a linguistic structure which permits a more adequate picturing of objects than we are able to do raises the question: In which framework are these objects conceived? If in CSO, then how can they be more adequately pictured than they are in CSO, i.e. by its method of projection? How, it might be asked, can ? common-sense object be more adequately pictured than in common-sense terms?

66. Are the individual variables we use tied exclusively to the individual senses of our current conceptual structure? Are the predicate variables we use tied exclusively to our conceptual resources? It is obvious that the only *cash* we have for these variables is to be found in our current conceptual structure, but it is a mistake to think that the substituends for a variable are limited to the constants which are here-now possessions of an instantaneous cross-section of language users. The identity of a language through time must be taken seriously, and a distinction drawn between the *logical* or 'formal' criteria of individuality which apply to any descriptive conceptual framework, and the more specific (material) criteria in terms of which individuals are

identified in specific conceptual frameworks; and, similarly, between the logical criteria which differentiate, say, *n*-adic from *m*-adic predicates generally, from the conceptual criteria (material rules) which give distinctive conceptual content to predicates which have the same purely logical status.

67. Thus the purely formal aspects of logical syntax, when they have been correctly disentangled, give us a way of speaking which abstracts from those features which differentiate specific conceptual structures, and enables us to form the concept of a domain of objects which are pictured in one way (less adequate) by one linguistic system, and in another way (more adequately) by another. And we can conceive of the former (or less adequate) linguistic system as our current linguistic system.

68. It should be noted that statements to the effect that one linguistic system generates more adequate pictures of these objects than another, though in one sense a 'meta-linguistic' statement, is an object language statement in the sense explained in paragraph 59 above.

69. Let us now go one step further and conceive of a language which enables its users to form *ideally* adequate pictures of objects, and let us call this language Peirceish. Indeed, let us conceive of the conceptual structure which would be common to English Peirceish, French Peirceish and even Mentalese or inner episode Peirceish.

70. We might, to begin with, look at Peirceish 'externally', and construe the semantical uniformities it involves in terms of the electronic propensities of Peirceish robots, by means of which their tapes are filled with 'information' reflecting their environment and reflected in their behaviour. There is, however, another way in which we can conceive of Peirceish. To bring this out, notice that we can conceive of less perfect robots, robots which are programmed along Austinian lines: ordinary language robots.

71. It was pointed out above that when we characterize a statement made in French, thus,

La neige est blanche

as true, we conceive of it as belonging to a linguistic kind, thus,

·Snow is white·-kind

which is represented in the language game we play. We conceive, so to speak, of ourselves and Frenchmen as playing different forms of the same game and, indeed, 'the same game' in a stronger sense than that which is illustrated by two pairs of people playing chess. The conception is rather to be compared with that of team-mates on the same football field. Thus we translate not only French arithmetic but French statements involving such expressions as '*ici*', '*la*', '*maintenant*', '*hier*' and '*moi*', and respond to these statements as we do when we turn Jones' 'I am here' into 'He (Jones) is there'.

72. To apply epistemic terms to Peirceish expressions we must think of it, too, as 'the same game', this time, however, in a more developed, more adequate form. We conceive of Peirceish speakers as a successor generation in a continuing scientific community or, at least, as an 'adopted' generation (as we might 'adopt' Martians).

73. If we represent the Peirceish conceptual structure by 'CSP' we can sketch the following additional concepts of truth

$PROP_i$ (in CSP) is true *quoad* CSP $\leftrightarrow$ $PROP_i$ (in CSP) is S-assertible by users of CSP.

$PROP_j$ (in CS_i) is true *quoad* CSP $\leftrightarrow$ for some PROP, and for some PRFAM, PROP belongs to CSP, PROP belongs to PRFAM, $PROP_j$ (in CS_i) $\subset$ PRFAM, and PROP is true *quoad* CSP.

74. Two principles relating 'true *quoad* CSP' to other senses of 'true' with respect to basic matter-of-factual propositions would seem to be valid:

(*a*) If a proposition in CSO is true its counterpart in CSP is true *quoad* CSO, and true *quoad* CSP. (Roughly, if a system of natural linguistic objects tokening a proposition in CSO pictures certain objects, then tokens of the counterpart proposition in CSP also picture these objects.)

(b) If a proposition in CSP is true *quoad* CSP its counterparts in such frameworks (CS_i) as contain a counterpart are true *quoad* CSP, but not necessarily true *quoad* CS_i, though not false *quoad* CS_i. (The law of bivalence analytically holds for matter-of-factual propositions in CSP, but it need not hold for matter-of-factual propositions in less developed conceptual frameworks.)

75. Notice that although the concepts of 'ideal truth' and 'what really exists' are defined in terms of a Peirceian conceptual structure they do not require that there ever be a Peirceish community. Peirce himself fell into difficulty because, by not taking into account the dimension of 'picturing', he had no Archimedeian point outside the series of actual and possible beliefs in terms of which to define the ideal or limit to which members of this series might approximate.

76. Nor need ideal matter-of-factual truth be conceived of as one complete picture existing in simultaneous splendour. The Peirceish method of projection must enable picturings (by observation and inference) of *any* part, but this does not require a single picturing of *all* parts.

77. What of statements such as 'a drop of water fell into the Pacific at place *s* and time *t*', where '*t*' refers to a time before the human race began? Does S-assertibility with respect to *us* require that we be able, in principle, to infer this statement from observations we might make in the future? No, it requires only that if we had been at the appropriate place and time with our conceptual framework we could have observed it to be the case. Thus, to generalize, although Peirceians are our conceptual descendants, truth defined with respect to them does not require that Peirceians be able to infer the previous history of the world from their observations, though, of course, to the extent that they actually do picture the past which they have not observed, their pictures will be constructed by inference.

78. The concepts of ideal matter-of-factual truth and of what there really is are as fraught with subjunctives pertaining to con-

ceptualization as the idealists have ever claimed. But *no* picture of the world contains *as such* mentalistic expressions functioning *as such*. The indispensibility and logical irreducibility of mentalistic discourse is compatible with the idea that in *this* sense *there are no mental acts*. Though full of important insights, Idealism is, therefore, radically false.

X

79. I shall conclude this chapter with some remarks on the truth of scientific theories. This will enable me to make a token payment on the promissory note issued in Chapter II, where I agreed with Kant that the world of common sense is a 'phenomenal' world, but suggested that it is 'scientific objects', rather than metaphysical unknowables, which are the true things-in-themselves.

80. I emphasized at the beginning of this chapter that the crux of the problem of matter-of-factual truth concerns the truth of singular statements. This point holds not only of statements belonging to the perceptual framework (common sense) but also, though in a more complicated way, of statements belonging to ampliative theories, thus micro-physics.

81. I have also emphasized that a correct account of matter-of-factual truth, even at the perceptual level, must contain 'instrumentalist' components. Both law-like statements (in the metalanguage) and molecular (and quantified) statements in the object language were construed as, in a sense, 'instruments' for constructing pictures of objects in the world. Thus the idea that an adequate account of the meaning and truth of theoretical statements will also contain an instrumentalist component should cause no surprise. The fundamental issue in the debate between 'instrumentalist' and 'realist' is, from this point of view, *not* whether theories can be fruitfully compared to instruments—for this is true even of the conceptual framework of common sense —but whether basic singular statements (in a sense to be defined) in the language of such a theory can meaningfully be said to 'correspond' to the world in the 'picture' sense of 'correspond' (as contrasted with the Carnap–Tarski sense of 'correspond', the

extension of which to theoretical statements of all types seems to be quite unproblematic).

82. The instrumentalist, from our point of view, is one who holds that theoretical statements of *all* kinds, including singular statements, are *essentially* instruments for generating statements *in the observation framework*. Thus, if he went along with our distinctions he would hold that (ampliative) theoretical statements are simply more sophisticated instruments which along with molecular, quantified and law-like statements in the observation framework are means of constructing *observation framework* pictures of objects and events. Picturing, to put it bluntly, would be the inalienable prerogative of the perceptual level of our current conceptual structure.

83. Instrumentalists (and philosophers of science generally) lay little stress on the role of singular statements in micro-physical theories. They concentrate, rather, on the relation of theoretical principles to empirical laws; and the singular statements they emphasize are observation framework statements. Again, for the most part, they do not explicitly recognize the picturing dimension of factual truth, or fail to distinguish it clearly from the '*p*' *is true* ⟷ *p* dimension. Thus, even when they recognize the existence of properly singular statements in theoretical discourse, and recognize that the latter are properly characterized as true or false, this does not raise for them the question whether these statements can be regarded as conceptual pictures in their own right.

84. This failure, as we have seen, is aided and abetted by a naïve realism which, as we have seen, construes the meaningfulness of perceptual predicates as a relation between persons, sign designs *and attributes construed as independent entities*. Naïve realism conceives of this relation as brought about by a learning process in which acquaintance with facts involving these attributes enables sign designs to be associated with them.

85. In effect naïve realism construes

S sees that *a* is *f*

as

S sees that *a* exemplifies *f*-ness

where exemplification is taken to be a relation (or 'tie') between extralinguistic objects. But this, according to our analysis, is on a par with construing 'S sees that *a* is *f*' as

S sees that it is true that *a* is *f*

86. Since the coming to have meaning of theoretical predicates obviously involves no such process of association, and since these predicates are not introduced by explicit definition, however broadly construed, their very meaning becomes, for these philosophers, *essentially* instrumental with respect to the perceptual level of our current conceptual framework. The sophisticated instrumentalist does not, indeed, deny that theoretical predicates have 'cognitive' meaning; any more than he denies that theoretical statements are true or false. But by interpreting theoretical meaning and truth as essentially instrumental with respect to the observation framework, construed in naïvely realistic terms, he gives this meaning and truth an *essentially* derivative or second-class status.

87. I say *essentially* derivative or second-class status, for although there is a legitimate methodological sense in which micro-physical theory is dependent on, and instrumental with respect to, the perceptual level of our current conceptual framework, it is vital not to transform this *methodological* dependence into an *ontological* thesis to the effect that 'real' (as contrasted with 'instrumental') existence, meaning and truth are limited to objects as conceived at the perceptual level of our current conceptual structure.

88. *Prima facie*, it makes just as much sense to speak of basic singular statements in the framework of micro-physics as pictures, according to a complicated manner of projection, of micro-physical objects, as it does to speak of basic singular statements in the observation framework as pictures of the objects and events of the world of perceptible things and events. The instrumentalist, however, even if he recognizes that there is a sense in which there can be theoretical pictures of theoretical objects, must interpret the picturing as *itself* essentially second class. For the statements which formulate this picturing relation are contaminated by the Pickwickian character, analysed above, of the reference to the micro-physical entities which serve as the non-linguistic terms of the picturing relation.

89. 'Language entry' uniformities are, as we have noted, essential to the meaning and truth of singular statements in the common-sense or observational framework. Thus, if singular statements in the framework of micro-physical theory could *independently* be shown to be *in principle* the sort of statement which is inferred, by the machinery of the theory, from singular statements in the observation framework, this would reinforce the instrumentalist contention. Actually, however, the arguments which are given are invariably reformulations of the naïvely realistic theory of concepts and concept formation criticized above.

90. Thus the Scientific Realist need only argue that a correct account of concepts and concept formation is compatible with the idea that the 'language entry' role could be played by statements in the language of physical theory, i.e. that in principle this language could *replace* the common-sense framework in *all* its roles, with the result that the idea that scientific theory enables a more adequate picturing of the world could be taken at its face value.

91. Needless to say, the epistemological thesis that such a direct use of theoretical language in perceptual response to the world could stand on its own feet and not presuppose the 'stand-by' presence of the common-sense framework to underwrite its reasonableness must not be confused with the methodological thesis, appropriate to a developing science, that it would be irrational, at least for the foreseeable future, to abandon the dualism of observational and theoretical frameworks which the instrumentalist transforms into an ontology.[1]

XI

92. The idea that singular statements in the language of microphysics might constitute pictures of micro-physical objects and events is open to a number of more or less obvious objections. Thus, (1) it might be argued that the requirement that pictures not be molecular or quantified statements, i.e. that their complexity be

[1] I have argued this point in a series of papers, most recently in 'Scientific Realism or Irenic Instrumentalism: a critique of Nagel and Feyerabend on Theoretical Explanation', in *Boston Studies in the Philosophy of Science*, Volume Two, edited by Robert S. Cohen and Marx W. Wartofsky, New York, N.Y., 1965.

matter-of-factual rather than logical, rules out the idea that the language of micro-physics could permit the formulation of pictures. For, it might be said, no singular statement about individual micro-physical particles can occur in a language entry transition, or observation. Statements formulating observations, if in micro-physical terms, would have to be logically complex, and enormously so. This objection assumes, however, that statements which are basic as the constituents of pictures must also be epistemically basic in the sense that they formulate observable states of affairs. It is, indeed, true of the common-sense framework that statements which are basic in one sense are also basic in the other. Yet the two senses of 'basic' are different, and a transcendental philosophy which rises to a level of abstraction which distinguishes the generic character of epistemic concepts (e.g. language entry transition, conceptual picture, object) from the specific forms they take in common-sense discourse will not assume that the basic constituents of conceptual pictures must be statements of the kind which occur as conceptual responses to sensory stimulation.

93. A more serious objection, (2) is that properly singular statements in micro-physical theory would be about 'ideal objects' in the sense in which the point-masses and instantaneous events of macro-mechanics are ideal objects. Unlike the case of point-masses, however, there would seem to be no non-ideal counterparts of which they are the idealization. Thus one who takes an 'instrumentalist' view of the 'ideal objects' which the mathematics of the Space–Time continuum manipulates so handily would seem to be forced back to Instrumentalism just when we seem to have cleared the way for Scientific Realism. This objection raises serious issues about the conceptual structure of micro-physical theory, issues which are so intricate that I can do little but look them in the eye and walk on.

94. I distinguished in Chapter II between idealizing and ampliative theories. Micro-physics is an ampliative theory. Is it also *essentially* an idealizing theory? I.e. does it *essentially* involve the structure of real number theory and the continuum? Or can we conceive that in principle a 'finitist' micro-theory could be formulated which would stand to the framework which uses all the

resources of mathematical analysis, as a mechanics of finite differences stands to the idealized macro-mechanics of Newton and Einstein? I wish I could say something helpful on this point. I can only confess that it seems to me that the possibility of such a micro-physics is an unavoidable implication of Scientific Realism. If this looks a 'transcendental' deduction of 'finitism', I can only plead that I am not alone in thinking that the issue is not an empirical one.[1]

XII

95. The claim that the common-sense framework is transcendentally ideal, i.e. that there really are no such things as the objects of which it speaks, can now be reassessed and reformulated. We must distinguish carefully between saying that these objects do not really exist and saying that they do not really exist *as conceived in this framework*. For they do really exist as conceived in what, omitting the qualifications which were introduced in the preceding section, we have called the Peirceian framework, the framework which is the regulative ideal which defines our concepts of ideal truth and reality.

96. Just as we distinguish between truth with respect to CS_t, truth *simpliciter* in the sense of truth with respect to *our* conceptual structure (CSO), and (ideal) truth in the sense of truth with respect to a Peirceian framework, so we must draw corresponding distinctions with respect to such related epistemic concepts as denotation and existence. The latter is the one which concerns us here. If we use 'ATT' to refer to attributive senses, as 'INSENSE' refers to individual senses, something like the following seem to capture the relevant concepts of existence (which must not be confused with the concept of 'something' which is captured, the 'existential' quantifier):

[1] It might seem that if the above is a transcendental deduction of 'finitism' it is also a transcendental deduction of 'quantism'. I do not think that this is so. To deny the physical reality of Cantorian entities one does not need to construe a Cantorian conceptual framework as a useful tool for dealing with a quantized world (cf. Whitehead). One can suppose that the world is continuous in a more Aristotelian sense, and, hence, that though any mesh in terms of which we conceptually cut up the world into objects to be pictured will have a finite grain, it can, however, be replaced, in principle, by a still finer mesh. In this case the concept of an *ideally* adequate method of projection would be an 'idealization' in the sense in which mathematical geometry is an idealization.

INSENSE$_i$ (in CSO) exists *quoad* CSO ⟷ for some ATT, ATT belongs to CSO, and ATT [INSENSE$_i$] is true *quoad* CSO

INSENSE$_i$ (in CSP) exists *quoad* CSP ⟷ for some ATT, and for some INSENSE$_j$, and for some INFAM, ATT belongs to CSP, INSENSE$_j$ belongs in CSP, INSENSE$_i$ belongs to INFAM, INSENSE$_j$ belongs to INFAM, and ATT [INSENSE$_j$] is true *quoad* CSP

97. Corresponding to the principles concerning 'true *quoad* CSO' and 'true *quoad* CSP', which were formulated in paragraph 74 above, we would have:

(*a*) If INSENSE (in CSO) exists *quoad* CSO, then its counterpart in CSP exists not only *quoad* CSO, but *quoad* CSP.

(*b*) If INSENSE (in CSP) exists *quoad* CSP, then its counterpart (if any) in CS$_i$ exists *quoad* CSP, but not necessarily *quoad* CS$_i$.

98. To say that an object doesn't exist *as conceived in CSO* (as opposed to saying that it doesn't exist *period*) is to claim that there are significant differences between the way in which the object is conceived in CSO and the way in which it is conceived in CSP— i.e. the conceptual form of its counterpart in CSP.

99. On the other hand, to say that an object doesn't *really* exist is to make the stronger claim that its counterpart in CSP is not an object but, say, a virtual class of objects, in which case the counterparts would stand to one another as

·*a*·

to

·$\hat{x}fx$·

100. But why not construe the counterpart in CSP of an observable thing as a *whole* of micro-particles, for example, rather than a virtual *class* of molecules? Notice that *within* CSO we can choose between saying that a wall is a class of bricks, and that it is a whole of which bricks are parts. If we say that the counterparts of physical objects in CSP are wholes rather than virtual classes, then these counterparts would also be objects and we could use the 'doesn't exist as conceived in CSO' locution as contrasted with the 'doesn't really exist' locution.

101. Is there any reason for supposing that the concept corresponding in CSP to the concept of a material object in CSO must be a class concept rather than a whole concept? I think there is, for, after all, the logic of whole and part doesn't replace the logic of predication, but builds on it. Discourse about wholes and their parts presupposes subject-predicate talk about the objects which are to be described as 'parts'.

102. To what extent does the positive account I have been giving amount to a Kantian-type phenomenalism? Should I say that the *esse* of the common-sense world is *concipi*? It is not too misleading to do so provided that this is taken to be a vigorous way of stressing the radical differences in conceptual structure between the framework of common sense and the developing framework of theoretical science. Yet, according to the picture I have been sketching, the concepts in terms of which the objects of the common-sense or 'manifest' image[1] are identified have 'successor' concepts in the scientific image, and, correspondingly, the individual concepts of the manifest image have counterparts in the scientific image which, however different in logical structure, can legitimately be regarded as their 'successors'. In *this* sense, which is not available to Kant, save with a theological twist, the objects of the manifest image do *really* exist.

[1] For an earlier exploration of the relations between these two 'images' of the world which touches on important topics not dealt with in this book see my essay on 'Philosophy and the Scientific Image of Man', in *Frontiers of Science and Philosophy*, Robert Colodny (ed.) (Pittsburgh, 1962), reprinted as Chapter I in my *Science, Perception and Reality* (London and New York, 1963).

VI

APPEARANCES AND THINGS
IN THEMSELVES:

2. PERSONS

1. In the third and fourth chapters we were concerned to understand what it means to say of candid overt speech episodes that they *stand for* various kinds of *senses*, thus attributive senses, state-of-affairs senses, individual senses, logical-connective senses, etc., and to understand what it means to say of those senses which can be called intensions—i.e. those which correspond to extensions—that, depending on what they are, they *obtain*, or are *exemplified* or *exist*.

2. The broader context in which this endeavour was embedded was an attempt to construe the language of conceptual episodes proper as though it had been introduced, in a community whose conceptions of rational behaviour were purely Ryleian, as a theory to explain the fact, among others, that a person's verbal propensities and dispositions change during periods of silence as they would have changed if he had been engaged in specific sequences of various types of candid linguistic behaviour called 'thinkings-out-loud' by our Ryleians, though the hyphenated phrase, useful for our purposes, did not imply to them, as it does to us, that this candid linguistic behaviour is the manifestation at the overt level of imperceptible conceptual episodes.

3. We distinguished the sense of 'manifestation' in which a perceptible episode is a manifestation of a disposition or propensity, as the dissolving of salt is a manifestation of solubility,

from the sense in which a perceptible episode is a 'manifestation' of imperceptible episodes. The latter corresponds, in a way which is not without a strong negative analogy, to the sense in which the motion of a perceptible physical object is the manifestation of the motion of a cloud of electrons and nuclear particles. We also distinguished between a broader and a narrower sense of 'episode', in the former of which an object's change from having one propensity to having another, or even its unchanging possession of a given propensity for a certain period of time, would count as an episode; whereas, in the narrower sense, to count as an episode, the change or abiding state must admit, in principle, of a 'core' description in non-hypothetical terms—must admit, that is, as we put it, of a purely categorical description. The distinction is, of course, an Aristotelian one, though his formulations must be refined and polished to fit contemporary needs.

4. The fact that an episode, in the narrower sense, admits, in principle, of a purely categorical description is, of course, compatible with the idea that most if not all of our work-a-day descriptions of the episode are, in Ryle's useful phrase, of a mongrel hypothetical–categorical character. Indeed, it might well be the case that almost everything we could say about certain episodes proper which was of any but the most recondite interest was thoroughly mongrel and fraught with hypotheticals. Something like this is true of perceptible physical objects, though here it does seem possible to isolate, at least for purposes of philosophical analysis or 'reconstruction', a stratum of relatively determinate categorical descriptions in terms of such perceptible qualities as colour and shape. In the case of conceptual episodes proper the categorical element is abstract or generic in the extreme. It was argued that our classification of these episodes (by the use of abstract singular terms) was essentially functional involving an analogical extension to them of the semantical uniformities which specify the jobs done by the thinkings-out-loud which are their models. Indeed, it is characteristic of functional classification that, although it requires that the items classified have characteristics which enable them to perform the relevant functions, it does not require that these characteristics be determinately specified. Yet a generic categorical description is a categorical description for a' that.

2. Persons

5. Thus, it was pointed out, a philosopher who defends the notion that there are conceptual episodes in a non-Ryleian sense is not thereby committed to the idea that their character as conceptual is, so to speak, a purely categorical one. Indeed, almost anything which can be said about the conceptual character of conceptual episodes, without reaching into the domain of a speculative neuro-physiology, is as mongrel as Ryle could wish. But not *everything*, for to bear the burden of these hypotheticals these episodes must have a determinate categorical character, though, of course, our *conception* of this categorical character need not be (and is not) determinate.

6. Thus, when told that Texans play chess with odd pieces on odd boards, we infer that these pieces and boards have determinate features, but, knowing Texans as we do, it would be well that our conception of the pieces and the boards not pin them down to specific materials.

II

7. Our strategy has been to use the structure of the reasoning by which, in sophisticated science, a framework of imperceptible things and processes (which may in interesting cases be quite un-thingish and very odd processes) is introduced to explain certain perceptible phenomena as a model for explicating the situation which confronts us in the philosophy of mind when, after pains-taking phenomenology, conceptual analysis and transcendental argument, we find ourselves convinced that there are covert episodes proper (mental acts and sense impressions) which are such that overt behaviour of certain sorts provides 'logically adequate criteria' for the ascription of these episodes to others. These criteria, of course, are unnecessary for reliable self-ascription, though they are involved in explaining why it *is* reliable. Given that the episodes in question are indeed episodes proper (as contrasted with the Ryleian propensity-clusters with which they are associated), it follows that the relation of overt behaviour to them is not only logically synthetic (which would be true even in the case of the relation of overt behaviour to propensity-

clusters—as is seen by reflecting on the simple case of '*x* has lengthened' and '*x* is elastic') but a properly causal one.[1]

8. The incentive to use such theory formation as a philosophical model came from noticing two suggestive parallels between non-Rylean mental episodes and theoretical entities. In the first place, the episodes in question are described in terms which show strong analogy to the ways in which we describe certain public phenomena; in the case of conceptual episodes, overt speech; in the case of sense-impressions and sensations, the perceptible attributes of physical things and bodily states. These analogies did not appear to be matters of practical convenience but rather essential features of the concepts involved. Correspondingly, the entities postulated by a theory are, typically, conceived by analogy with perceptible counterparts, and stipulated to conform to principles which parallel those to which these counterparts conform. Negative as well as positive analogies are, of course, involved in both aspects of theory formation, the building up of concepts and the laying down of principles; and there are obvious negative analogies in the case of both conceptual episodes and sense impressions.

9. In the second place, the connection of theoretical entities and processes with perceptible phenomena, like that of mental episodes with behaviour, is clearly a conceptual one, though not *a priori* in any Cartesian or Kantian sense. It is obviously not a matter of induction by observing positive instances, or corroboration by failing to observe, under test conditions, negative instances. Yet the connection is, in a broad sense, empirical, in that however subtle and suggestive a theory is as an analogical structure, it fails in its purpose unless it explains known general truths about the phenomena of which it is the theory and, hopefully, suggests new hypothesis which observation might confirm, and tests corroborate.

[1] Notice that in micro-physical explanation of, for example, the motion of a perceptible thing, one first 'identifies' this motion with a micro-physical process, and then explains the latter in terms of other micro-physical processes and the principles of the theory. In the case of the 'theory' of conceptual episodes, on the other hand, only the most promissory-note-ish reinterpretation of overt behaviour is involved in its explanation in terms of postulated conceptual episodes which are *in no sense* identical with this behaviour. The cash for this promissory note, given that conceptual episodes can be identified, in their descriptive content, with neuro-physiological episodes, is to be provided by the theoretical framework of micro-physiology.

2. Persons

10. Since it is obvious that the idea that there are mental episodes (and corresponding capacities, dispositions and propensities) did not arise as a self-conscious scientific hypothesis, and is not the sort of thing we would normally classify with 'highly confirmed theories', the use which we are making of the model of theoretical explanation is an unusual one. We have compared it to the role of contract theories in political philosophy, and seen in our programme an attempt to 'reconstruct' the conceptual framework of mental acts in such a way as to show how it might have achieved its present status, from a purely Ryleian beginning, by a series of steps none of which violates accepted standards of rationality, and none of which, in particular, involves those moves (e.g. the argument from one's own case) which have convincingly been shown to be incoherent. Success along the above lines, we have argued, would enable us to escape between the legs of 'logical behaviourism', the 'synthetic *a priori*' and the *global* 'argument from analogy'.

11. Finally, it was pointed out that any such programme must satisfy two demands:

(*a*) the demand that a form of linguistic behaviour be describable which, though rich enough to serve as a basis for the explicit introduction of a theoretical framework of non-Ryleian episodes, does not, as thus described, presuppose any reference, however implicit, to such episodes, just as we can give an Austinian description of physical objects which is genuinely free of reference to micro-physical particles;

(*b*) the demand that an account be available (in principle) of how a framework adopted as an *explanatory hypothesis* could come to serve as the vehicle of direct or non-inferential self-knowledge (apperception).

It was also pointed out, however, that this second demand is, from a philosophical point of view, the less interesting of the two, for even the logical behaviourist must postulate that we can acquire the ability to connect propensities to say, for example,

I have the propensity to say 'it is raining'

with propensities to say, for example,

It is raining

in such a way that, in frames of language-using which are candid at both the conscious and unconscious level (in the depth-psychological sense), the presence of the former propensity implies the presence of the latter. For, in the absence of some such account, the logical behaviourist is a behaviourist in the extreme sense in which Norman Malcolm uses the term[1], according to which, *even in our own case*, we must infer the existence of verbal and other behavioural propensities (e.g. propensities to pain behaviour) from overt symptoms. The bringing about of the propensity-connections described above can be taken as a Ryleian model for the bringing about of a connection between conceptual episodes of the kinds illustrated by

representing that it is raining
representing that one represents that it is raining

12. The second demand, thus, was provisionally satisfied with a *tu quoque* and will be left in this condition. The first demand, however, was given a more extended and constructive treatment.

13. A crucial step in the argument concerned the fact that the stratum of linguistic behaviour which serves as the model for non-Ryleian conceptual episodes is a non-performatory stratum. An *action* (as contrasted with *act* in the Aristotelian sense) is essentially the sort of thing which *can* be (though it *need* not be) done deliberately or on purpose. In a sense even the linguistic behaviour in our non-performatory stratum consists of actions or performances. We must note, therefore, that certain ways of classifying episodes which are, in appearance, very much like others which we would not hesitate to call actions imply that they did not occur 'on purpose' or, even in the weakest sense, 'by intention'. As (rightly) so classified, these episodes or 'acts' cannot qualify as actions.

14. If a citizen were to verbalize

I shall say: 'So, it has begun to rain'
So, it has begun to rain

---

[1] Presumably in the hope that this term of disapprobrium will not be applied to him.

the utterance would scarcely be taken to be a noticing-out-loud that it had begun to rain. Nor if he were to verbalize

I shall say: 'Therefore, we will starve'
Therefore, we will starve

would he be taken to have concluded-out-loud that the people in question would starve.

15. Of course, our Ryleian society will be held together by Austinian glue. It will be full of statings, avowals, giving arguments, tellings that, tellings to and the like. But what we are concerned with is those verbal episodes which occur when our citizens are by themselves, or when, as it were, they are overheard, rather than talking to their fellow citizens. As examples we might take: noticing-out-loud that it has begun to rain; reasoning-out-loud, 'no game came to the pool last night, so we will starve'; willing-out-loud, 'I shall put my coat on right *now*.'

16. It is important to see that the concept of locutionary non-actions make sense, because it is a framework feature of mental acts that while they can, and indeed must, at least on occasion, occur in patterns which can be characterized as mental actions—thus, deliberating about whether or not to do A, attempting to recall the time of an engagement, etc., it is also a framework feature that they occur in ways by virtue of which they are essentially non-actions—thus, perceptual takings, concludings, volitions, etc.

17. Because the thinkings-out-loud and the mental acts modelled on them with which we have been concerned are not actions, we have stressed the distinction between rules of performance and rules of criticism. Non-actions, as well as actions, are subject to rules of criticism, and the linguistic non-actions we have in mind are no exception. Linguistic rules of criticism play a key role in developing, maintaining and improving our linguistic character, thus ensuring the existence of the semantic uniformities, which are the descriptive core of meaningful speech.

18. Viewed comprehensively, linguistic activity exhibits strong positive analogies with those forms of rule-governed activity

which are called games. The preceding remarks, however, should help bring out the strong negative analogy between the stratum of language behaviour with which we are concerned and the *actions proper* which are playings of games.

III

19. Philosophical method insists of a diastole of confronting the infinite complexity of discourse with contrived models which we understand because we have made them, in the hope of seeing likenesses, and a systole of grasping at these likenesses and re-shaping our models to take their unlikenesses into account. All philosophers, however conscious of the contrast between the simplicity of philosophical formalisms and the intricacy of the forms of life which we know so well until we are asked, sooner or later exhibit this pattern. Even long Austinian periods of 'collection' are followed by attempts at 'division'.

20. The contrived model we have been collecting and dividing is a stratum in the language of a hypothetical Ryleian community. Expressions in the stratum fall tidily into such categories as *descriptive terms, logical operators, primitive expressions, defined expressions,* etc. The concept of the meaningfulness of the undefined descriptive expressions of such a language does not, we have seen, require that their correlates in semantical uniformities be 'absolute simples'. For 'simple entity' is the material mode for 'undefined descriptive term' and is relative to a linguistic framework.[1]

21. Nor is our model language a phenomenalistic one. In particular, the only colour predicates it has which are categorical rather than hypothetical pertain to material things. Our Ryleian community is at present as innocent of concepts pertaining to sense impressions (as defined in Chapter I) as it is of concepts pertaining to conceptual episodes proper.

22. On the other hand, our model language can contain such locutions as '*x* looks red to me' without violating the conditions

[1] Roughly, an entity which is simple with respect to our framework is *really* complex if its successor intension in the Peirceian framework is complex.

we have laid down for the solution of our problem. This locution must, however, be interpreted as having, roughly, the sense of 'x causes me to be disposed to think-out-loud: Lo! This is red,[1] or would cause me to have this disposition if it were not for such and such considerations.' We can also conceive it to have such related locutions (more hypothetical and impersonal) as 'x looks red from here' or 'x looks black in green light'.

23. According to our philosophical myth, a proto-scientific member of the community, Jones by name, develops the hypothesis that people's propensities to think-out-loud, now this, now that, change during periods of silence as they would have changed if they had, during the interval, been engaged in a steady stream of thinkings-out-loud of various kinds, because they are the subjects of imperceptible episodes which are:

(a) analogous to thinkings-out-loud;
(b) culminate, in candid speech, in thinkings-out-loud of the kind to which they are specifically analogous;
(c) are correlated with the verbal propensities which, when actualized, are actualized in such thinkings-out-loud; ·
(d) occur, that is, not only when one is silent but in candid speech, as the initial stage of a process which comes 'into the open', so to speak, as overt speech (or as sub-vocal speech), but which can occur without this culmination, and does so when we acquire the ability to keep our thoughts to ourselves.

24. We so construe or myth, of course, that Jones realizes that to say what a thinking-out-loud *stands for* is to classify it. In other words, he espouses our reconstruction of the language of intensions and senses, and construes, for example,

a thinking-out-loud which stands for that 2 plus 2 = 4

as

a ·2 plus 2 = 4· thinking-out-loud [2]

---

[1] I.e. '. . . disposed to visually-take-out-loud x to be red.'
[2] Utterances which are not thinkings-out-loud are classified according to how they would be classified if they were candid thinkings-out-loud; for, of course, not every utterance which has sense is a thinking-out-loud.

25. As the first step in articulating his theory Jones introduces French quotes to form sortal predicates pertaining to conceptual episodes proper, a

«2 + 2 = 4» thought episode

being the sort of thought episode which, in a thinking-out-loud frame of mind, finds its expression in a

·2 plus 2 = 4· thinking-out-loud

26. He also introduces the term 'represents' to be the analogical counterpart, in the framework of mental acts, of 'stands for' in the framework of thinking-out-loud, thus

(conceptual episode) represents the «2 plus 2 = 4»

is a statement which parallels, in the language of the theory, the Ryleian schema

(thinking-out-loud) stands for the ·2 plus 2 = 4·

27. Finally, he introduces the term 'idea' to be the analogical counterpart of 'sense', thus

(conceptual episode) represents (the idea) the «triangular»
(conceptual episode) represents (the idea) the «2 plus 2 = 4»

are statement forms which parallel, in the language of theory,

(thinking-out-loud) stands for (the sense) the ·triangular·
(thinking-out-loud) stands for (the sense) the ·2 plus 2 = 4·

28. Working as he is within the perspicuous framework which is provided by his (and our) contrived symbolism, he sees that it would be incorrect to equate

(conceptual episode) represents the «2 plus 2 = 4»

with

(conceptual episode) represents that 2 plus 2 = 4

Since he realizes, as that-clauses had been used up to his time,

that 2 plus 2 = 4

has the sense of

the ·2 plus 2 = 4·

and similarly in the case of other abstract singular terms. Thus, the statement form

—— stands for that 2 plus 2 = 4

has served heretofore to classify *overt* speech episodes as

·2 plus 2 = 4·s

Dot quote common nouns have a purely Ryleian sense. Jones sees, therefore, that it would be a category mistake to say of a conceptual episode proper that it is a ·2 plus 2 = 4· or stands for the ·2 plus 2 = 4·, and, hence, a category mistake to say that it stands for that 2 plus 2 = 4 as 'that 2 plus 2 = 4' is then used; and similarly in the case of other abstract singular terms.

29. He therefore gives an extended use to abstract singular terms, according to which it is proper to say both of a mental act that it

represents that 2 plus 2 = 4

(by virtue of being a «2 plus 2 = 4»)
and of a linguistic episode that it

stands for that 2 plus 2 = 4

(by virtue of being a ·2 plus 2 = 4·), and similarly in the case of triangularity and other intensions.

30. This new and embracing use of abstract singular terms is by no means a matter of simply interpreting them as disjunctions of expressions of the form

the ·– – –·

and the corresponding

the «– – –»

for, after all, by virtue of the analogy in function of conceptual episodes proper with the thinkings-out-loud on which they are modelled, they admit of joint classification under common nouns, the criteria for which abstract from the negative analogy between the overt and the covert. Thus, he (and we) could introduce a quoting device which permits the common nouns which it forms to apply, for example, to both

thinkings-out-loud which are ·2 plus 2 = 4·s

and

mental acts which are «2 plus 2 = 4»s

But having made this point, I shall not embark on the enterprise, for it is enough to see that it can be done, and that in a more complete account it should be done.[1]

31. That the use of abstract singular terms in the context

(mental act) represents (abstract singular term)

must be construed as an extended use is a most important point. For if it is not appreciated, the fact that abstract singular term directly classify Jonesian mental acts as, *in the extended sense*, they do will lead the unwary, of whom I count Roderick Chisholm a paradigm example, to suppose that they classify Ryleian episodes only *indirectly*. In other words, they will be led to suppose that an utterance which stands for that 2 plus 2 = 4 can be *defined* as one which in candid speech, expresses a mental act which represents that 2 plus 2 = 4. And, indeed, if one were to interpret

that 2 plus 2 = 4

as

The «2 plus 2 = 4»

utterances could be classified as «2 plus 2 = 4»s or said to stand for the «2 plus 2 = 4» only in a derivative sense. But to suppose that the abstract singular term must be given this interpretation is a mistake.

32. On the Jonesian theory it is a conceptual truth that

utterances which *stand for* that 2 plus 2 = 4 express (in candid speech) mental acts which *represent* that 2 plus 2 = 4

[1] Indeed, I have already abstracted from the fact that conceptual episodes are, in the first instance, modelled on speech episodes in specific languages. French and Japanese mental acts differ (despite Ockham) in ways which parallel the interesting and important differences between the languages in which they find expression.

But this is a logically synthetic (i.e. subject matter dependent) conceptual truth, and not, in principle, a definitional transformation of a tautology. This is why Frege's terminology is dangerous unless one watches like a hawk. For since the word 'express' is used for the causal (in a broad sense) relation between mental acts and their overt (shall we say) expression (by, alas, an expression), to use it also where we have in mind 'stand for' or 'represent' is to invite confusion, a running together of

> Utterances which express (i.e. stand for) that 2 plus 2 = 4 express (i.e. manifest) in candid speech mental acts which express (i.e. represent) that 2 plus 2 = 4

with the tautology

> Utterances which express (i.e. manifest) in candid speech mental acts which express (i.e. represent) that 2 plus 2 = 4 express (i.e. represent) that 2 plus 2 = 4

This confusion is yet more tempting if the original synthetic statement is given the formulation,

> Utterances which express (i.e. stand for) the thought (i.e. proposition) that 2 plus 2 = 4 express (manifest) in candid speech thoughts (i.e. mental acts) which express (i.e. represent) the thought (proposition) that 2 plus 2 = 4

33. On the other hand, since most conceptual episodes do not actually find overt expression, and since, from the standpoint of Jones' theory, even when thinkings-out-loud do occur they are caused (in a suitably broad sense) by mental acts, it is natural, from the standpoint of the order of being, as contrasted with the order of conceiving, to highlight mental acts, their categories and classifications, and thus concentrate attention on contexts which, from our point of view, have the form

> (Mental act) represents the «– – –»

and hence, in effect, narrow down the interpretation of abstract singular terms in the opposite direction from their 'original' or pre-Jonesian narrowness. To construe abstract singular terms as directly or in the first instance classifying mental acts and only derivatively classifying overt verbal behaviour is, by itself, no blunder. It becomes a blunder, however, if it is mistakenly supposed that they cannot also be given an interpretation according to which they directly classify overt linguistic behaviour (as did our Ryleian abstract singular terms), or a comprehensive interpretation according to which they directly classify both 'outer' and 'inner' speech episodes.

34. Thus the legitimacy of a concentration of attention on concepts and categories pertaining to mental acts, because the latter are first in the order of being, must not be misconstrued (as it has been in the Cartesian tradition) as authority to interpret these concepts and categories as first in the order of conceiving. The following parallel might be useful. It is clear, at least if we assume a realistic interpretation of micro-physical entities, that to affirm the primacy *in the order of being* of a description of objects in terms of micro-physical particles, electro-magnetic fields, and the like, is quite compatible with affirming the primacy *in the order of* conceiving of another stratum of description and explanation which is capable of standing on its own two feet. Roughly put, the priority in the order of being of micro-physical entities to Austinian entities, which means that the latter are, in a sense, difficult to define, ontologically dependent on the former, is compatible with the epistemic and methodological priority of Austinian entities to these scientific objects, which means that the latter are again, in a sense, difficult to analyse, epistemically and methodologically dependent on the former.

35. Thus, a philosophy of mind which engages in a phenomenological analysis of the *status quo*, and concentrates on priorities in the order of being without taking into account possible dimensions of epistemic priority, throwing the latter into the waste basket of 'genetic questions', is bound to resemble a realistic philosophy of nature which, like that of Paul Feyerabend in his more exuberant moments, concentrates on the world picture of theoretical science, and dismisses the careful attention rightly paid by analytic philosophers in the tradition of Moore and the later Wittgenstein to the world picture of 'common sense' and 'ordinary language' as so much conceptual archaeology. My own view is that the philosophy of mind and the philosophy of nature alike will continue to be plagued by traditional puzzles until phenomenology or, if you prefer, conceptual analysis takes possible dimensions of epistemic or conceptual priority as seriously as it does the dimension of ontological priority in the *status quo*.

2. Persons

36. The way between the Scylla of logical behaviourism and the Charybdis of Cartesianism is to be found not by construing the conceptual connection of mental acts with behaviour in static terms as synthetic *a priori* truth but by construing it as capable, in principle, of reconstruction in accordance with the logic of scientific explanation—which is, of course, just ordinary explanation writ large.

IV

37. The above quasi-historical argument, a myth in the platonic sense, can be brought to a conclusion with a brief account of why our legendary Jones has disappeared without a trace.

38. It was not long before he noticed that abstract singular terms in their explicit form as distributive singular terms, formed by the use of special quoting devices, have a subtle logic which he had not yet articulated in detail, let alone formalized or made intuitive. Thus, he saw that to do so would require an account of the derivative propositional forms in which distributive singular terms occur in subject and predicate positions, and of the derivative modes of predication which go along with these forms. It would also require an account of quantification over and into French and dot-quoted expressions, and its relation to quantification over and into the ordinary expressions which are their unquoted counterparts, involving the same designs.

39. His practical reason told him that, if possible, these subtleties should be buried beneath a surface grammar suitable for presentation in elementary to college text-books, and amenable to rules of thumb. In particular, he saw that the expressions

stands for ·– – –·
represents the «– – –»

can play the classificatory role played by the common nouns embedded within them. Thus, by using abstract singular terms in place of his perspicuous distributive singular terms, the classificatory role of statements of the form

(   ) stands for (   )
(   ) represents (   )

could be preserved. Again, rules for quantification into and over that-clauses can be sharply separated from rules for quantifying into and over contexts involving common nouns, as they would not be in a philosophically perspicuous language.

40. Again, needless to say, Jones dismissed the temptation to reconstruct the language of his community along the Tractarian lines explored in the last chapter, according to which predicates are dropped, relational predicates, for example, being replaced by the device of putting referring expressions in counterpart relations. A perspicuous language in this extreme sense would be practically impossible to use either in speech or in writing. The use of linear concatination and auxiliary predicate expressions, though unperspicuous, is immensely convenient. (And what would philosophers have done for a living if he had given us a perspicuous language?)

41. Jones, therefore, transformed, for utilitarian reasons, his perspicuous distributive singular (meta-linguistic and meta-conceptual) terms into unperspicuous abstract singular term and, by so doing, deprived 'stands for' and 'represents' of their perspicuous character as specialized forms of the copula. In these ways he covered the traces of his conceptual revolution.

42. In the new City he founds, Jones teaches his theory in its familiar unperspicuous form. In addition to teaching the younger generation to use the theory as a theory, i.e. to infer the existence of mental acts of various kinds from behavioural evidence, he trains them to connect, along lines previously discussed, the occurrence of such mental acts as, for example.

representings that 2 plus 2 = 4

with propensities to make corresponding statements of the forms

I have just represented that 2 plus 2 = 4

and, indeed, to train themselves to make such connections. This training, of course, builds on the foundation laid by the training of children in the original Ryleian community to connect the propensity to think-out-loud, for example, that 2 plus 2 = 4 with the propensity to think-out-loud

I have the propensity to think-out-loud that 2 plus 2 = 4

43. Having started the ball rolling, and given us our inheritance of a conceptual framework in which certain forms of overt behaviour are logically adequate (but, in the logistic sense, synthetic) criteria for the ascription to others of imperceptible non-Ryleian episodes, this Prometheus disappears into the mists of legendary time and leaves our profession with the task of re-tracing his steps with the guiding thread of the theory of theoretical explanation.

V

44. The framework we have been concerned to understand is that of persons as subjects of conceptual episodes proper, and before concluding this chapter with some reflections on unfinished business, it will be well to take a closer look at how these episodes relate to the persons who are, as we have put it, their subjects.

45. In the first place, representations are primarily people representing, just as waltzes are primarily people waltzing and speeches, people speaking. This is not only true of the conceptual representations on which we have recently been concentrating but also of the sense impressions, Kant's manifold of sense, for which I argued in Chapter I. Thus, to have a sense impression of a red rectangle is to be impressed (to use the familiar metaphor) not necessarily by a red, rectangular object, but impressed *in a certain manner*, to be impressed, if I may so put it, in an

of-a-red-rectangle manner

or, leaving the job of the 'of' to be performed by the inversion of the context, in an

a-red-rectangle manner

It will be remembered that, according to the account developed in that chapter, the 'of' phrase is an adjective which, when applied to the verbal noun 'impression', turns it into a verbal common noun which stands for the kind of state which is normally brought about by objects which are red and rectangular on the facing side, and which do the job which such states do according to the theory of sense impressions in terms of which they are introduced.

46. Since the phrase 'sense impression' implies that something is acting on one's senses, and since the theory tells us that sense impressions are the sort of thing which can occur in the absence of such action (as in hallucinations), it is common to use another verb which does essentially the same job without this implication, the verb 'to sense'.

47. Thus, instead of saying that a person has an impression of a red rectangle, i.e. that he has an

a-red-rectangle impression

or is

a-red-rectangle-ly impressed

we say that he has a sensation of a red rectangle, i.e. that he has an

a-red-rectangle sensation

i.e. that he

a-red-rectangle-ly senses

48. Thus it is important to see that when a 'manifold of sense philosopher' tells us that people have sensations of a red rectangle he need not be telling us that they stand in a peculiar relation to red rectangles. If he is unwary, this is how he will explicate his statement. But he need not so explicate it. For the correct view is that to have a sensation of a red rectangle is to sense a-red-rectangle-ly or, strictly speaking, because 'sense' is not a complete verb in itself, such as might take an ordinary adverb of manner, it is to a-red-rectangle-ly-sense, which alone is the complete verb.

49. Thus one can vividly a-red-rectangle-ly-sense. Indeed, since 'a-red-rectangle-ly' is here doing such a different job from ordinary adverbs of manner, *completing* rather than *modifying* the verb, we should drop the '-ly' and simply say, for example,

Smith of-a-red-rectangle-sensed

(I keep the 'of' here because there is the rhetorical inversion illustrated by

Smith a fire breathing dragon slew.)

50. My point in all this is that the only *ultimate* logical subject involved in a person's having a sense impression of a red rectangle is the person, though, of course, impressions are *derivative* logical subjects, in the sense in which smiles as logical subjects are derivative from people smiling and waltzes from people waltzing. The parallel, in this respect, between conceptual representations and the representations of sense is complete. In each case, what appears at first sight to be a relational statement involving a person and a peculiar kind of object turns out to be an act (in the Aristotelian sense) of a person, which act is of a certain sort or species, thus,

> Smith represents that snow is white

like

> Smith senses a red rectangle

has the form

> Smith V's

where 'V' is a placeholder for such verbs as

> to that-snow-is-white-represent
> to a-red-rectangle-sense

VI

51. Neither the Jonesian theory of conceptual episodes proper nor the Kantian theory of the non-conceptual representations of sense need be interpreted as introducing new sets of *basic* logical subjects, abstract entities in the one case, sense-data in the other. It is almost as misleading to speak of non-Ryleian episodes of representing as '*inner* episodes' as it is to speak of dispositions or propensities as 'in' the things or persons which have them. To speak of a representing as an 'inner episode', if it is not sheer metaphor for '(in principle) imperceptible', makes sense only as the fore-shadowing of an hypothesis to the effect that the having of representings by *persons* is to be explained by postulating that some *part* of them, e.g. the heart or the brain, has representings which cause the person to behave in those ways which originally led us to say, as we still can, that the person *as a whole* has representings. The germ of some such idea might seem to be an essential feature of those non-Ryleian frameworks. Thus, conceptual episodes

proper are episodes which (in a broad sense) cause speech episodes, and it is natural to think of at least the later stages of this process as involving bodily tissues near the organ of speech.

52. Yet the pressures of scientific theory should not be read into the essentials of the theory, and it does not seem logically necessary that what sets part of a person in motion must be a change in another part. It is not logically necessary, in particular, that in order for conceptual activity to cause a change in a part of a person the activity must be a change in another *part* of the person. As far as I can see, the conviction, characteristic of classical Aristotelianism, that no bodily part of a person is the 'organ' of conceptual thinking would not (or should not) by itself have led to the postulation of an unbodily organ of thought. Nor does it seem to have done so in the Aristotelian tradition proper. The pressure for such a conception comes from elsewhere, from religious considerations pertaining to life after death,[1] from the atomistic philosophy of nature and from bad philosophy, thus the Cartesian argument for a real distinction between mind and body.

53. It is important to bear in mind that in the Aristotelian picture of the world, persons are single logical subjects in a radical sense. They have parts only in the sense of 'virtual' parts, as the boundary between two coloured surfaces has parts only in the sense that it can be divided by another colour expanse.[2] Thus, in the Aristotelian tradition, the spatial parts of persons are derivative logical subjects in much the same way in which events as 'temporal parts' are derivative logical subjects. A hand cut off is a logical subject on its own, but a hand in name only.

VII

54. If we take the position that concepts pertaining to microphysical objects are *merely* conceptual instruments (they are, of course, at least that), then the world as we perceive it to be is unthreatened; our philosophy will be essentially Aristotelian, and we can say of the Aristotelian world of contemporary Aristotelians

[1] Though, after all, one does not need to be a dualist to believe in immortality.
[2] Of course, in a sophisticated sense it has parts in the additional sense that it can be correlated with items which have parts, thus the ideal Space of mathematical physics, and clusters of imperceptible atoms.

(such as Strawson) that it exists not only as something represented but also in itself.

55. According to our analysis, this would mean that basic singular statements in this framework depict objects in a way which is, in principle, adequate. Peirceian truths would be in Strawsonian terms. For, as we have seen, though truth does not admit of degrees, adequacy of depicting does. And if there were reason to think that basic singular statements in the language of theoretical physics[1] would depict the world and in a more adequate way, this would, of itself, be reason to characterize that language as one which, other things being equal, we should use to speak about the world, and the corresponding framework of conceptual representings to think about the world, and, in particular, to represent the objects of perception.

56. For as long as the language of theoretical physics is used primarily at the level not of singular statements but at the level of the explanation of general truths, its role as depicting localized objects and events in Space and Time (if such a role is, as I have argued, appropriate) would remain potential, and actual depicting left to singular statements in the Strawsonian framework.

VIII

57. To take a realistic stance towards scientific theories is to take seriously this role of theoretical languages as providing a method of picturing the world. This generates a familiar puzzle. It is a framework principle of the world of perceptible things that they are coloured. Colour is their primary content, that of which their perceptible structure is the structure. Again, as I have pointed out, the primary linguistic and conceptual framework pertaining to colour is that of physical objects; the occurrence of colour predicates in sense impression talk is derivative, an analogical use which is explained in terms of the use of colour predicates in discourse about physical objects. Now the physical object of the framework of common-sense cannot in any literal sense be said to have micro-physical objects as their parts. Chairs do not have

[1] By this I do not mean statements about individual micro-physical objects, for statements about wholes can be as basic, in the relevant sense, as statements about their parts.

electrons as parts in the sense in which they have legs as parts. Nor can systems of micro-physical particles be said to have colour, save in the twice removed sense that they have the power to cause sense impressions of colour.

58. In this way is generated the intriguing problem of the place of sense impressions in a metaphysics of scientific realism. It will be remembered that colour and shape predicates in the language of sense impressions are derivative from colour and shape predicates as they apply to physical things. It might be thought that if the latter are primary, then the claim that physical objects are, in the Kantian sense, phenomenal (i.e. that their esse is *concipi vel concipi posse*) must be rejected. To argue this, however, is to confuse priority in the order of conception with priority in the order of being. There is no *a priori* reason at all why it should not be derivative colour conceptions which capture the reality of colour.

59. Clearly, if scientific realism is correct, at least one more analogical transposing of colour predicates is necessary, namely that which takes us from

　　senses a red rectangle

as a predicate of Aristotelian persons, to

　　senses a red rectangle

as a predicate of a system of logical subjects. One cannot help but feel, however, for reasons on which I have touched elsewhere,[1] that this is not the last step, and that if scientific realism is correct, at the end of the road somehow the phrase

　　a red rectangle

will lose its adverbial status and, by a final transposition, will become once again a common noun for particulars, though not the particulars with which the story began.

60. The epiphenomenalist makes this point bluntly, and usually in a way which by-passes essential stages. I believe that the correct move is to say that even granted the truth of scientific realism we

---

[1] 'Reply to Aune', in *Intentionality, Minds, and Perception*, H. N. Castaneda (ed.), Detroit, 1967.

are in no position to specify in our arm-chairs the future evolution of colour concepts. Micro-neuro-physiology, which is the relevant domain of theory formation, is in its infancy. On the other hand, I find it difficult to believe that a Hobbesian epiphenomenalism will be the answer.

61. As I see it, in any case, a consistent scientific realist must hold that the world of everyday experience is a phenomenal world in the Kantian sense, existing only as the contents of actual and obtainable conceptual representings, the obtainability of which is explained not, as for Kant, by things in themselves known only to God, but by scientific objects about which, barring catastrophe, we shall know more and more as the years go by.

IX

62. But if perceptible objects are pluralities of logical subjects so are persons. And if this means that perceptible physical objects are, in the Kantian sense, phenomenal, then so, at least in their physical aspects, are persons. But what of persons as the subjects of conceptual representations? Curiously enough, it is conceptual representations, at least as we have been construing them, which seem to cause the least trouble to the scientific realist. For, as was pointed out, not only are concepts pertaining to conceptual representations analogical counterparts of concepts pertaining to verbal behaviour but, which is more important, the latter concepts are concerned with correctnesses and uniformities of linguistic configuration in relation to other linguistic configurations, extra-linguistic objects and non-linguistic behaviour. As for the 'qualitative content' of these configurations, it must, we have said, be such as to be capable of taking part in these configurations.

63. But this seems to leave the door wide open, for, as was pointed out, almost anything can be used to play the game of chess. Thus, we might be inclined to say that almost anything could be the material cause or 'matter' (in the Aristotelian sense) of the configurations which are conceptual representations. Yet things are not quite so simple. For though we have been emphasizing that the candid thinkings-out-loud which are the models for mental acts are not *actions*, and that the mental acts for which they

are the models are not *actions* but rather acts in the Aristotelian sense, nevertheless, though we have not been emphasizing the point, there *are* mental actions. And, indeed, if there were no *actions* pertaining to thinking, whether thinkings-out-loud, as in our Ryleian community, or the thinkings-not-out-loud which Jones enabled us to conceive, there would be no thinking—not even thinking-out-loud—but at best processes which, however sophisticated, would be simulations of thought.

64. Thus we must add to the requirements which must be met by the material cause of mental acts, that relevant sequences of configurations of this 'matter' can constitute *actions*, that is, be the sort of thing which can be brought about 'on purpose'. This, it might be thought, rules out the possibility that neuro-physiological excitations could be the 'matter' of conceptual episodes. The conclusion, however, is not obvious, for just as we might deliberately bring about, by telegraphing 'castle' to Texas, a castling of a Rolls-Royce king and a Bentley queen on two adjoining counties, although we did not know that the game was on such a scale and, wisely, conceived of the move merely in terms of whatever might be the material aspects of Texas chess, so we might deliberately bring about a mental action of which the material cause was such and such a sequence of neural configurations, by a representing (itself a configuration of neural activity) which, as an

I shall multiply 12 by 12

volition, conceives its aim not *sub specie* sequence of neural configurations but *sub specie* sequence of whatever it is that little thoughts are made of.

VII

OBJECTIVITY, INTERSUBJECTIVITY
AND THE MORAL POINT OF VIEW

1. Practical reasoning, in a broad sense, brings particular matters of fact, empirical generalizations, scientific laws and logical principles to bear on our values. Even the most casual attempt to botanize values confronts one with the fact that they can be classified in many ways: with respect to their material content, their logical form, their factual presuppositions, their place in various hierarchies, their status as derivative or not derivative, the distinction between values pertaining to objects, values pertaining to thoughts about objects, to thoughts about thoughts about objects, etc., etc. A full theory of practical reasoning would bring out, for example, its involvement in scientific reasoning, where the values involved are epistemic. It would also recognize the inseparability, yet distinguishability, of theoretical and practical reason in all dimensions of human life.

2. Theoretical reason is, I have argued in Chapter V, a structure of many levels. Each level has, as its basic skeleton, the statement forms and sequences of statement forms of truth functional and quantificational logic; yet, as I have indicated, these structures exist in an ambience of rules of criticism, which themselves belong to the domain of practical reason, *qua* concerned with epistemic values. A critique of pure practical reason must obviously concern itself with the way in which it contains the skeletal forms of deductive logic and by an interesting symmetry, which robs such slogans as 'the priority of practical reason' and 'the priority of theoretical reason' of unconditional truth, a critique of pure theoretical reason must concern itself with the essential involvement of practical reason in theoretical reason. As

175

usual, there are different dimensions of priority. The philosophical landscape is not only not a desert, it is not even a flat-land.

3. But my aim in this chapter is not to botanize values, nor to explore the epistemic values which are the rationale of the scientific enterprise. It is rather to explore the fundamental principles of a metaphysics of practice, with particular reference to the values in terms of which we lead not just one compartment of our lives but our lives *sans phrase*. I have said enough, however, to indicate that in my opinion the metaphysics of morals is but a fragment of a broader critique of practical reason. A philosophical interpretation of 'ought to be' and 'ought to do' with respect to everyday living must ultimately cohere with an account of theoretical reason which makes intelligible the truth and inter-subjectivity of epistemic evaluation.

4. And, indeed, a theory of practical reasoning in morals which denies the *in principle* intersubjectivity and truth of the ought-to-be's and ought-to-do's of everyday life must face the challenge of the ought-to-be's and ought-to-do's of theoretical reason. This challenge has largely been ignored. But though I think, with Charles Sanders Peirce, that the facing of this challenge is the culmination of the philosophical enterprise, I shall say nothing more about it; for my task concerns the foundations, and the keystone is nowhere at hand. Yet if the outcome of my argument is to make intelligible the intersubjectivity and truth of moral *oughts*, the argument will be in the spirit, at least, of this more embracing enterprise.

II

5. Practical reasoning is often many times removed from practice. Yet without a conceptual tie to practice, however indirect, it would not be practical reasoning. The parallel with reasoning in the empirical sciences is obvious. The latter is often many times removed from singular descriptive statements and, in particular, from those singular descriptive statements which formulate observations. Yet without its conceptual tie to such singular descriptive statements it would not be empirical science.

6. Thus, first in the order of business must be a provisional

account of the coming together of practical reasoning and practice.[1] This coming together is found in volition which, as I have put it, is the point at which the conceptual order evokes its image in the real order, as, in observation and self-knowledge, the real order evokes its image in the conceptual order.

7. Volitions are conceptual episodes which we conceive on the analogy of such candid thinkings-out-loud as

I shall *now* do *a*

Thus in one sense of 'manifest' a volition is the sort of episode which is manifested in candid overt speech by saying

I shall *now* do A (e.g. raise my hand)

In another sense, however, a volition is the sort of episode which is manifested, *ceteris paribus* (thus in the absence of paralysis and in the presence of favourable circumstances), by a doing of A, e.g. a raising of the hand.

8. We could put this by saying that, *ceteris paribus*, volitions cause actions of the kinds involved in the description of these volitions —in a broad sense of cause which must not be confused with the idea that volitions cause us, in the ordinary sense of cause, to do the action. In action 'of one's own free will' one is not caused to do what one does, and when one is caused to do something the cause is not a volition but, for example, a threat or a promise on the part of someone who, if one complies, can subsequently be said to have caused one to do what he did.

9. A child who has not acquired the propensity, for example, to raise his hand on saying

Now I shall raise my hand

has not learned 'shall'-talk, and until he has acquired this propensity he cannot be said to understand the full meaning of any practical term, for all practical terms owe their connection with action to the conceptually necessary tie between

Now I shall (action)

[1] For an elaboration of the framework sketched below the reader is referred to my 'Thought and Action', in *Freedom and Determinism*, Keith Lehrer (ed.), New York, 1966, pp. 104–39.

in the first place, as candid willings-out-loud, and, in the second place, as the conceptual representings which find overt expression in willings-out-loud, and performances (*ceteris paribus*) of the actions willed.

10. I have emphasized that volitions are not *actions* but acts in the Aristotelian sense of actualities. It does not make sense to speak of willing to will to do A, anymore than it makes sense to speak of willing to feel sympathy for someone. (In each case, however, there is such a thing as willing to do something which one conceives likely to influence one's mental propensities in the desired direction.) Nor are volitions *tryings*. Trying to do A is, roughly, doing one or more things which one thinks likely in the circumstances to grow into a doing of A. Nor are volitions *choosings*. One may will to do A without choosing to do A rather than B, even where B is refraining from doing A. Nor are volitions *decisions*. A volition need not be the culmination of a process of deliberation or practical reasoning.

11. Since my purpose in this chapter is to explore the conceptual framework of practice, I shall no longer highlight the problem of the status of mental acts and their relation to propensities and dispositions pertaining to candid overt speech. I shall speak of practical 'statements' or 'assertions' in the non-performatory sense in which these terms are used in logic; and of practical 'reasonings',[1] leaving open the question as to the exact status of these practical episodes.

12. The simplest connection of an intention with a volition is illustrated by the example of Smith, who has formed the intention of raising his hand in ten minutes. He *thinks*

I shall raise my hand in ten minutes

and, if we suppose that the intention continues as an occurrent, rather than lapsing into dispositional status, which, however, would leave the example untouched in relevant respects, and if

---

[1] The term 'argument' is perhaps too fraught with performatory overtones (as something which one 'gives' to one's public) to be completely satisfactory as a term in logical theory, in that narrower sense in which it can be contrasted with 'dialectics', the theory of rational discussion.

we suppose that nothing leads him to consider an alternative course of action, we may picture him as thinking

I shall raise my hand in ten minutes

$$\vdots$$

I shall raise my hand in six minutes

$$\vdots$$

I shall raise my hand *now*

the last of which, if Smith is not paralysed nor, unbeknownst to him, in a strait-jacket, becomes a raising of his hand. That one's 'place' in time is constantly and systematically changing is an essential feature of our conceptual framework, one which is reflected in and, indeed, constituted by, a systematic change in the content of thought with respect to tense, temporal connectives and the like.

13. In addition to the 'chronologic', which transforms intentions of an appropriate form into volitions, there are other logical features of intention which find expression in the culminating stages of practical reasoning proper. These can, in the first instance, be summed up by the general principle:

'It is the case that-P' implies $\longleftrightarrow$ 'It shall be the case that-
'it is the case that-Q'   P' implies 'it shall be the
                                  case that-Q'

14. The following comments bring out the force and significance of this principle:

(*a*) I am reconstructing English usage pertaining to 'shall' in such a way that, in candid speech, it always expresses an intention on the part of the speaker with respect to a certain state of affairs. In other words, I shall use 'shall' and 'will' in such a way that 'shall' always expresses an intention, whereas 'will' is always a simple future.

(*b*) I am so using 'implies' that '"*p*" implies "*q*"' is equivalent to '"*q*" may be inferred from "*p*"'. Implication statements, for our purposes, can be regarded as meta-linguistic in a sense which is unincumbered by the refinements introduced in our discussion of abstract singular terms. Thus,

> that-p implies that-q

will be construed as

> 'p' implies 'q'

It must not be confused with 'if p then q' which is, at heart, the '$p \rightarrow q$' of truth functional logic.

(c) I shall reconstruct 'shall' to be an operator which turns indicative statements into statements of intention. Thus,

> I shall do A

becomes

> Shall [I will do A]

(d) All basic practical reasoning pertaining to intentions can be reconstructed as a sequence of shall-statements, each of which follows from that which precedes it in accordance with the above principle or, more accurately, since this principle belongs to the third level of practical discourse, in accordance with a second-level principle which accords with it. Thus, according to this principle,

> 'Shall [P and Q]' implies 'shall [P]'

follows from

> 'P and Q' implies 'P'

and hence the following piece of first-level practical reasoning

> Shall [P and Q]
> Therefore, shall [P]

is valid.

(e) For the purposes of my argument it will be useful to construe empirical laws as implications or principles of inference. Thus, one state of affairs will be said to imply physically or causally another state of affairs, where others might prefer to say that the former logically implies the latter on the assumption of a true general premise. This interpretation of law-like statements as principles of inference, which, in any case, I think to be the true one, will make more intuitive the relation of causal implications to moral principles. I shall use 'implies' without qualification to mean causally or physically implies, where the context makes it clear that this is what is involved.

(*f*) A careful distinction must be drawn between 'shall' as an operator which operates on action verbs and 'shall' in the sense, roughly, of 'shall be the case' which operates on statements. The context will make it clear, in particular cases, which is involved. I mention the point, however, because many careful distinctions are necessary here to avoid the paradoxes which are familiar in deontic logic, but which also arise, unless care is taken, in the logic of practical discourse generally.[1]

(*g*) I shall reconstruct

> If it is raining, then I shall come in

as

> Shall [if it is raining, I will come in]

Here the action verb governed by 'shall' is 'will come in'· I shall call intentions of this form 'conditional intentions'. The 'if . . ., then – – –' is not 'implies' but the '→' of truth functional logic.

(*h*) Consider the practical syllogism

> Shall [if it is raining, I will come in]
> It is raining
> Therefore, Shall [I will come in]

Introducing the concept of 'implication relative to an hypothesis or assumption', we can say that

> 'If it is raining, then I will come in'

implies

> 'I will come in'

relatively to the assumption 'it is raining'. Thus, relatively to the hypothesis that it is raining,

> 'Shall [if it is raining, I will come in]'

[1] For an exploration of the logic of action discourse which articulates these distinctions see my 'Reflections on Contrary-to-Duty Imperatives', *Nous*, 4, 1967.

implies

'Shall [I will come in]'

Since it makes use of this dependent implication, the reasoning

Shall [if it is raining, I will come in]
Therefore, shall [I will come in]

can be said to be dependently valid. I shall make constant use of dependent implication. The context will make it clear on what hypothesis the implication depends.

(*i*) The preceding example is a further illustration of the point that all of the implications involved in practical reasoning can be established in the first instances as implications pertaining to matters of fact. There is, therefore, no need for a special 'logic of intentions' other than that formulated by the third-level principle on which I am commenting together with certain conceptual truths about the function of 'shall'. Having made this point, I shall not hesitate to use mixed practical syllogism, thus

Shall [if *p*, then I will do A]
p
Therefore, shall [I will do A]

(*j*) Finally, the conditional intentions with which we will be concerned are those in which the antecedent can be construed as a 'circumstance of action', and can, therefore, be represented by the schema

Shall [if I am in C, I will do A]

III

15. Intentions imply intentions just as beliefs imply beliefs. This point must be carefully made. We must distinguish between intentions as *states of intending* and intentions as *what is intended,* just as we distinguish between *states of believing* and *what is believed,* the so-called 'content' of the believing. In the latter case we distinguish between the implications of the *content* of a belief and the implications of the state of having a belief with that content. Thus the belief which would be expressed by the conjunction of Peano's

postulates (P) implies the belief which would be expressed by any arithmetical theorem (T), however recondite, in the sense that the one belief content implies the other. Yet, obviously, the existence of *this* implication does not carry with it the idea that

Jones believes P implies Jones believes T

16. Corresponding distinctions obtain in the case of intentions. Thus, when I speak, as I shall, of one intention I_1 implying another intention I_2, I shall be speaking about an implication between two intention-*contents*. That in *this* sense an intention I_1 implies an intention I_2 does not carry with it the idea that

Jones intends I_1 implies Jones intends I_2

An ideally rational being would intend the implications of his intentions, just as he would believe the implications of his beliefs.[1]

17. Philosophers analyse the logical relations of belief-contents by determining the logical relations of the factual statements which express them. In this chapter I shall explore the logical relations of intention-contents by exploring the implications of the practical statements which express them.

18. If 'P' implies 'Q', then it is *unreasonable* to believe that P is the case without believing that Q is the case. (Though, as noted above, in point of fact one may well believe the former without believing the latter.) Similarly if

'It shall be the case that P' implies 'It shall be the case that Q'

It is *unreasonable* to intend that P be the case without intending that Q be the case. (Though, again, in point of fact one may very well intend the former without intending the latter and may even intend that the latter *not* be the case.)

IV

19. Intentions are not limited to intentions *to do*, whether now, or later, or on the condition that a certain circumstance obtains.

---

[1] It is, however, familiar fact that when we become aware of the implications of our beliefs we often change our mind. It is equally true that when we become aware of the implications of our intentions we often, shall I say, change our heart.

There are also intentions *that something be the case*. The latter, however, are *intentions*, practical commitments, only by virtue of their conceptual tie with intentions *to do*. Roughly

It shall be the case that-*p*

has the sense, when made explicit, of

(*Ceteris paribus*) I shall do that which is necessary to make it the case that-*p*.

20. It is important to see that I can not only intend to do something myself, I can also intend that someone else do something, i.e. that it be the case that he does it. Intentions pertaining to the actions of others are not 'intentions to do' in the primary sense in which

I shall do A

is an intention to do. Thus, in spite of their superficial similarity,

Tom shall do A

and

I shall do A

do not have the same conceptual structure. The former has the form

(*Ceteris paribus*) I shall do that which is necessary to make it the case that Tom does A

whereas the latter cannot, without the absurdity of an infinite regress, be supposed to have the form

(*Ceteris paribus*) I shall do that which is necessary to make it the case that I do A[1]

21. These considerations highlight the fact that the intention expressed by a 'shall' statement is invariably the speaker's intention. Thus,

Tom shall do A

---

[1] This is not to say, however, that

It shall be the case that Tom does A

has no first person parallel which would be subsumable with it under common practical principles. It is merely to emphasize the conceptual primacy of intentions to do even in the case of intentions that someone do.

expresses the speaker's intention that Tom do A. This 'first person' feature of intentions consists in part in their relation to the

I shall do

which can become the commitment to do something *here* and *now* which is volition.

22. Now it is clearly important to distinguish between the *expression* of an intention and the *ascription* of an intention. Thus,

Shall [I will do A]

expresses, in candid speech, an intention to do A. On the other hand,

S intends to do A

ascribes to S an intention which he would express by using the former sentence.

23. In the case of autobiographical self-ascriptions, thus

I intend to do A

one ascribes to oneself an intention to do A and 'implies' the shall-statement

Shall [I will do A]

as made by the speaker, in much the same sense of 'implies' as the autobiographical belief ascription

I believe that it is raining

'implies' the statement

It is raining

as made by the speaker.

24. This familiar point enables me to highlight the first logical challenge to the idea that practical reasoning is reasoning in a proper or full-blooded sense of the term. For whereas ascriptions of intention have proper negations, shall-statements do not.[1]

---

[1] For an exploration of the place of negation in practical statements see my 'Imperatives, Intentions and the Logic of "Ought"', *Methods*, 8, 1956 [reprinted with substantial alterations in *Morality and the Language of Conduct*, edited by H. N. Castaneda and George Nakhnikian, Detroit, 1963].

Thus, in the case of ascriptions of intention, there are the four forms

> S intends to do A
> It is not the case that S intends to do A
> S intends not to do A
> It is not the case that S intends not to do A

But at the level of the corresponding shall-statements, there are only the statements

> Shall [I will do A]
> Shall [I will not do A]

25. Of course, a person need not commit himself to either of these statements, just as a person need not commit himself to either 'It is raining' or 'It is not raining'. And we must recognize the interrogative

> Shall I do A? = Shall [I will do A]?

just as we recognize the interrogative

> Is it raining?

26. The absence of what I shall call external negation in the case of shall-statements is in sharp contrast not only with its presence in the case of ascriptions of intention but, also, and with this we begin to touch directly on the issues I wish to discuss, its presence in the case of obligation statements. Thus, statements of all of the following forms seem to be appropriate:

> Jones ought to do A
> It is not the case that Jones ought to do A
> Jones ought not to do A
> It is not the case that Jones ought not to do A

27. This radical difference between 'shall' and 'ought', together with the fact that ought-to-do's seem to be as legitimately the subject matter of practical reasoning as shall-do's, presents us with our initial problem. What is the relation of 'ought' to 'shall'?

V

28. It might be thought that 'ought' differs from 'shall' in that 'ought' is used to tell someone to do something. This is a mistake. We can think and, if I am right, think truly and even know, that we ought to do a certain action. There need be no performance of telling anyone—even ourselves—to do anything. We can, and do on occasion, tell ourselves to do something, but deciding what to do is no more telling ourselves what to do than deciding what is the case is telling ourselves what is the case.

29. Of course, moral obligations rest on states of affairs, many of which are actions or the results of actions. Interesting cases are provided by promises, demands, legislation, verdicts, sentences, etc., etc. But these grounds of *prima facie* obligation must be distinguished from the practical premises and reasonings which take them into account, and the latter is essentially non-performatory and can, without changing its character, go on *in foro interno*.

30. The actions we and others have performed (including illocutionary acts) are relevant to our practical reasoning as part of the circumstances in which we must act, and even deliberating *in foro interno* about what to do is a course of action which can itself be deliberately undertaken. But neither 'shall' thoughts nor 'ought' thoughts are themselves actions, and when practical reasoning is done out loud it is, as such, the sort of thing which is *overheard*—which means that we are abstracting from the rights and duties which might arise from the fact that it is heard.

31. Moreover, the idea that the job of 'ought' statements is to tell someone to do something would not, by itself, throw any light on the fact that 'ought' statements, unlike 'shall' statements, have an external negation. For we can also use 'shall' statements to tell people to do something.

32. For all these reasons it can be doubted that the contrast between mere thinking-out-loud and illocutionary performance throws any light on the difference between 'shall' and 'ought'.

VI

33. 'Shall' statements are, as such, neither true nor false (which indicates, again, that an extended use is being made of the term 'statement'), though the descriptive statements embedded in them are either true or false. Furthermore, it follows from the absence of an external negation that *no one* can contradict a 'shall' statement, not even the person who makes it. This raises the question of the intersubjectivity of 'shall' statements. In what sense can two people have the same intention?

(1) There is the sense of 'same intention' which parallels that in which two people in different places say the same thing if they say 'the book is *here*'. In this sense two people who intend to visit the Taj Mahal can be said to have the same intention.

(2) Yet two people can have the same intention in a tougher sense, thus that a certain state of affairs obtain—e.g. that a certain child be happy. Of course, the derivative intentions to do that which might bring this happiness about are no longer in the tough sense the same.

(3) I can intend that someone else do A (intend him to do A), and he can intend to do A, and the verbal expression of the two intentions may be similar, thus,

> He shall do A
> I will do A

and even more similar if 'shall' is used in our technical sense. There is, nevertheless, an asymmetry. For, obviously, only *his* intention can grow directly into *his* volition and *his* action. My intention with respect to his action can grow into a volition only if practical reasoning draws a conclusion from it concerning some influence I can bring to bear.

34. This latter consideration highlights the obvious fact that even where the descriptive content of two people's intentions is in the strongest sense the same not only are the intendings numerically different, which is true even in the case of belief, but the total content of the intendings involves a special mode of egocentricity (expressed by the word 'shall') which is, in practical discourse, the

counterpart of the egocentricity of demonstratives. The latter is the egocentricity involved in the impact of the world on discourse, the former is the egocentricity involved in the impact of discourse on the world in volition.

35. If, therefore, we distinguish between the descriptive element in the content of an intending, and that element which is expressed by the operator 'shall', we can say that where the descriptive content is, in a tough sense, the same—as in the case of the child's happiness—the two intentions are 'parallel'. Traditional emotivism would speak here of an 'agreement in attitude'.

36. The egocentricity (in the practical mode) of 'shall', and the absence of an external negation, pose the problem of the relevance of the concepts of intersubjectivity and truth to practical discourse.

VII

37. From these initial considerations concerning the conceptual grammar of 'shall' let us turn our attention to 'ought'. We have emphasized that 'ought' has an external as well as internal negation. This fact gives rise to a strong feeling that there is truth and falsity with respect to 'ought', for it seems absurd (and in the last analysis is absurd) to admit the form

$$\sim Op$$

as well as

$$O \sim p$$

without accepting

It is true that Op
It is false that Op

Indeed, to read

$$\sim Op$$

as

It is not the case that Op

is tantamount to admitting that there is truth and falsity with respect to obligation, for

It is not the case that O*p*

has the same sense as

It is false that O*p*

Of course, we can pitchfork Nature out of the door by insisting on reading

∼O*p*

as

Not O*p*

refusing to use the locution

It is not the case that O*p*

but it may well return by the window.

38. However it may be with truth, there remains the question of intersubjectivity. In how tough a sense of 'same' can two people make the same ought statement?

39. Let me begin with a simple and familiar model, the story of one Smith who moves through the world accompanied by a team of ideal scientists. Among them are physicists, geologists, historians, neuro-physiologists, logicians, even students of the gods. They are masters of what have been called the 'positive' sciences. Yet we shall grant them knowledge (in whatever sense it *is* knowledge) of the ought-to-do's and ought-to-be's pertaining to epistemic activities—without staying to analyse the authority of epistemic norms. Let us refer to this team as the Academy.

40. Smith is near a heavy object (O), a long steel rod (R) and a stone (S). The members of the Academy consult among themselves and agree that

The necessary and sufficient condition of Smith's raising the heavy object is his using the rod as a lever and the stone as a fulcrum

They rephrase this as

Smith raises O implies and is implied by Smith using R as lever on O with S as fulcrum

So far, so good. Then we find them saying

If Jones wants to raise O, he ought[1] to etc.

At this point they hear Smith say

I shall raise O

and, since he seems to be speaking candidly and not deceiving himself, they conclude that Smith intends—or, for our present purposes, wants—to raise O. We might expect them to continue by reasoning as follows,

If Smith wants to raise O, he ought to use R, etc.
Smith wants to raise O
Therefore, Smith ought to use R, etc.

Yet, particularly when we reflect on other examples, we are perplexed by the idea that the 'ought' statement can be derived by *modus ponens*. To use a familiar type of example, suppose they see Smith's aunt coming and hear him say

I shall poison my aunt this afternoon

After surveying the environs and finding that a small packet of prussic acid is the only poison available, they agree that

A necessary and sufficient condition of Smith's poisoning his aunt this afternoon is his administering this packet of prussic acid

They even say

If Smith wants to poison his aunt, then he ought to administer, etc.

Can they proceed by *modus ponens* to infer

Smith *ought* to administer, etc.?

41. It does not seem so, and it is essential to see *exactly* why. Hare[2] has given us the beginning of the thread, yet it remains to

---

[1] Cf. 'If Jones is going to raise O, he must use R, etc.'
[2] R. M. Hare, *The Language of Morals*, Oxford, 1952, pp. 33 ff.

follow it to the end of the labyrinth. Put in our terms, separated, that is, from the 'logic' of imperative performances in which it is embedded, his point is that the schema

If S wants to bring about X, he ought to do Y

which is the schema of what are technically (but misleadingly) called hypothetical imperatives, has the sense of

'Shall [S brings about X]' implies 'Shall [S does Y]'

which implication concerning shall-statements is grounded in the implication

'S brings about X' implies 'S does Y'

in accordance with our third-level principle discussed above.

42. To appreciate the soundness of this analysis of the hypothetical imperative and its importance for our problem, it is enough to see that

'S wants to bring about X'

has the sense of

'S intends to bring about X'

Since to say that a person intends to bring about X is to ascribe to him a propensity to represent 'I shall bring about X', the fact that the reconstruction offered above mentions the relevant shall-statement counts in its favour. And since the hypothetical imperative is clearly grounded on the causal implication

'S brings about X' implies 'S does Y'

the overall form of the reconstruction seems appropriate.

43. If, now, returning to the original example, we take into account the fact that the intending in question is Smith's intending we notice that to capture the sense of the hypothetical imperative, the implication has the peculiar feature that *only one person, i.e Smith, can draw an inference in accordance with this implication*. To make this fact explicit, let us reformulate the implication as

'Shall [I poison, etc.]' implies (*quoad* Smith) 'shall [I administer, etc.]'

44. Thus, Smith, but no one else, is authorized by *this* implication to reason

Shall [I poison my aunt]
Therefore, shall [I administer, etc.]

45. Of course, if Roberts and his aunt come on to the scene the Academy could have arrived at the conclusion

If Roberts wants, etc., he ought, etc.

which would mean

'Shall [I poison, etc.]' implies (*quoad* Roberts) 'shall [I administer, etc.]'

But this implication authorizes no one but Roberts to reason in the parallel way.

46. Even if our scientists saw pairs of men and their aunts galore approaching, and accepted as relevant the general theoretical implication

For all values of '*s*' '*s* poisons his aunt here this afternoon' implies '*s* administers, etc.'

which transposes into the general practical implication

For all *s*, 'shall [I poison, etc.]' implies (*quoad s*) 'shall [I administer, etc.]'

47. Notice that the second implication involves a double use of quantification, for it is equivalent to

For all values of 'I' and for all *s*, 'Shall [I will poison my aunt, etc.]' implies (*quoad s*) 'shall [I will administer, etc.]'

The fact that the range of values of 'I' coincides with the range of values of '*s*' should not obscure this important difference. The modification of 'I' by '(*quoad s*)' is required by what we have called the special egocentricity of 'shall'.

48. Thus the general practical implication becomes an implication proper which governs possible inference only when specified with respect to particular values of '*s*', thus,

'Shall [I will poison my aunt, etc.]' implies (*quoad* Tom) 'shall [I will administer, etc.]'

which authorizes Tom to reason

Shall [I will cause my aunt, etc.]
So, shall [I will administer, etc.]

VIII

49. Hypothetical imperatives typically rest on causal connections, and, like most singular causal statements in everyday life, they are rarely if ever the direct application of a general causal law. Thus,

If Jones wants a drink, he ought to go to the next corner

is not the application of a supposed general law to the effect that

If anyone is to get a drink, he must go to the next corner

50. We have already noted that hypothetical imperatives typically presuppose that the person in question is in a certain circumstance. This point must now be elaborated. The first step is to bring this presupposition into the content of the imperatives, thus,

(Since S is in C)
If S wants to bring about E, he ought to do A

becomes

If S wants to bring about E, he ought to do A, if he is in C *and* S is in C

Let us focus our attention on the complex if statement, and neglect the conjoined assertion.

51. There are many ways in which general law-like statements can be idealized. Thus it is often required that a 'genuine' law-like statement contain no reference to particular objects, times or places. Whether or not ideal science would give us such, it's clear that we often have to settle for less. Now the nomologicals with which we are concerned are those which can generate general hypothetical imperatives. These nomologicals concern the causally

necessary conditions for bringing about a certain kind of state of affairs in a certain kind of circumstance.[1] They have the form

Doing A_i if C_j is causally necessary to the realization of E_k

Or, putting it in terms of causal implication, we have the family of implications

'x brings about E_k' implies 'x does A_i if in C_j'

These implications, which for obvious reasons can be called 'instrumental implications', are 'binding on all rational beings' in the sense that as empirical generalizations their inductive soundness is independent of the desires and inclinations or cultural ties of specific individuals or groups. Transposed into practical discourse as a general hypothetical imperative, they become

'I shall bring about E_k' implies 'I shall do A_i, if in C_j'

Even after this transposition the implications remain binding on all rational being. Any restriction belongs in the circumstance clause. Thus to restrict it to WASPs is to include the characteristic of being a WASP in C_j. For if being a WASP is irrelevant to bringing about E_k by doing A_i in C_j, then there is no point in including it anywhere; while if it is relevant, the relevance is a causal one and belongs in the content of the implication and not as a limitation on those for whom it holds.

52. Thus a limitation of the general hypothetical imperative to WASPs will not take the form

'I shall bring about E_k' implies (for all WASPs) 'I shall do A_i in C_j'

but

'I shall bring about E_k' implies 'I shall do A_i if in $C_{j\diamond}$'

where '$C_{j\diamond}$' differs from 'C_j' by including the additional characteristic of being a WASP. In this sense general hypothetical imperatives can be said to hold 'for all rational beings'. They are simply

[1] The complexity of the instrumental nomologicals which are relevant to the bringing about in social contexts of any but the most trivial ends must constantly be borne in mind. The simplicity of the schematic letters 'A', 'C' and 'E' should not blind us to this fact. We must take into account the effects of our action on the actions of others as well as the effect of the actions of others on the outcomes of our own.

the transposition into practical discourse of empirical instrumental generalizations.

53. Notice, however, that although general hypothetical imperatives hold for all rational beings, there is an important sense in which each such imperative formulates not one single implication but a family of implications, one for each rational being. This complication reflects the fact that 'I' is a systematically ambiguous term. A general hypothetical imperative asserts that each rational being can *validly* argue

> I (Tom) shall being about E_k
> So I (Tom) shall do A_i if in C_j
>
> I (Dick) shall bring about E_k
> So I (Dick) shall do A_i if in C_j
>
> etc.

54. There is an obvious temptation to use *modus ponens* to detach the *ought* from the hypothetical imperative, thus,

> If S wants to bring about X, he ought to do Y
> S wants to bring about X
> So, S ought to do Y

On the above analysis the premises become, respectively,

> 'I shall bring about X' implies (*quoad* S) 'I shall do Y'

and

> S accepts 'I shall bring about X'

From these premises the only thing of any interest that we can infer seems to be

> 'I shall do Y' is implied (*quoad* S) by an intention S accepts

55. This *suggests* an analysis of

> S ought to do Y

as

> 'I shall do Y' is implied (*quoad* S) by an intention S accepts

Such an analysis, however, clearly won't do as it stands. For even in the first person there is something odd about the reasoning

If I want to poison my aunt, I ought to administer, etc.
I want to poison my aunt
Therefore, I ought to administer, etc.

and hence about the idea that it is equivalent, as the analysis claims, to the reasoning

'Shall [I will bring about X]' implies (*quoad* me) 'shall [I will do Y]'
I accept 'shall [I will bring about X]'
Therefore, 'shall [I will do Y]' is implied by an intention I have

56. Notice that in the case of purely theoretical reasoning an implication statement generates a corresponding pair of reasonings, thus,

'*p*' implies '*q*'

governs the inference

p
Therefore, *q*

and serves as a premise in the inference

'*p*' implies '*q*'
I accept *p*
Therefore, '*q*' is implied by a proposition I accept

57. Even more important, for future reference, is the fact that

'*p*' implies '*q*'

presupposes the truth of '*p*' and must be distinguished from

'*p*' (if true) would imply '*q*'

Thus the following is, in an important sense, complete:

'*p*' implies '*q*'
Therefore, '*q*' is implied by a true proposition

If, therefore, there were a concept pertaining to intentions paralleling that of truth (call it, perhaps, 'validity') then

'Shall [p]' implies 'shall [q]'

as opposed to

'Shall [p]' (if valid) would imply 'shall [q]'

would presuppose the *validity* of the antecedent.

58. For the moment, however, we have only the concept of an intention which one *has* or *accepts* to hold the place of this concept of validity.

59. It is clearly one thing to reason

Shall [I will bring about X]
Therefore, shall [I will do Y]

where the major premise may be an impulse, or where the principle in accordance with which it is made is not itself explicitly considered, and quite another to be at the reflective level of the hypothetical imperative. Thus, if

I ought to do Y

did have the sense of

'I shall do Y' is implied by an intention I have

it would be because of some special feature of this level of practical reasoning.

IX

60. But is the first person use of *modus ponens* to get

I ought to do Y

so absurd? Surely, it might be said, the fact that this reasoning occurs at the second level of discourse about intentions enables it to have the force of

'Shall [I will do Y]' is implied (*quoad* me) by an intention which I have *all things considered*

61. The phrase 'all things considered' is scarcely sufficient, in and of itself, to render the suggestion plausible. The best it can do is to make possible a willing suspension of disbelief during which further exploration can take place. The first attempt to be considered is almost as old as philosophy itself. It rests on the concept of 'informed' or 'enlightened' self-interest. It conceives of 'intentions' as generated by reasoning in which factual premises are combined with valuational premises which, though not themselves intentions, are the sort of thing which when combined with factual information about what a person is or will be in a position to, lead to conclusions which are intentions.

62. We have been using 'shall' as our intention operator. Let us use 'would' as our valuation operator.[1] The pattern I have in mind for generating 'shall's out of 'would's goes somewhat as follows:

Would that-*p* were the case
'That-*p* is the case' implies and is implied by '*s* does A'
It is possible for *s* to do A

Shall be the case [that-*p*]
Shall [*s* does A]

Needless to say, this schema requires a commentary in which it is pointed out that when a person considers only the state of affairs that-*p* he may be prepared to say

Would it were the case that-*p*

but, when he considers it along with the state of affairs that-*q*, be prepared to say, rather,

Would it were not the case that-$(p \cdot q)$

More generally, in addition to the above schema, an account of valuational preference is required. I shall assume that such an account is available, for the special problems it raises are not at issue.

[1] It is common to use it n connection with that-clauses, thus

Would that such and such were the case

But it is important to see that it can—and must, if our analysis is correct—occur in first level discourse, thus

Would he were here

as contrasted with

Would it were the case that he was here

63. Now the classical theory I have in mind postulates a ground floor of dispositions and propensities to have thoughts of the form

Would that-*p*

(where that-*p* may be relatively simple or very complex), which need not remain the same and which, indeed, may well differ from person to person. These specific valuings are shaped in many ways and can be shaped by self-training. Yet it is also true to say that they arise out of the individual's bodily, mental and social needs, and are initially shaped by a social training which, of course, continues to play a more or less subtle and more or less dominant role.

64. These specific valuings need not be ego-centred. Only the crudest form of the theory takes the valuing expressed by

Would that he not be suffering

is really the valuing candidly expressed by

Would that I not be in his shoes

65. But whatever the character of these ground-floor valuings, the theory holds that they are dominated by an over-arching ego-directed valuing expressed, in our terminology, by

Would that I led a satisfying life

To the extent that a person is logical, this valuing, combined with beliefs about the world, about the propensities of his fellow man, about the character of his ground-floor valuings and about available sources of satisfaction, generates a life-plan valuing which organizes ground-floor valuings into a coherent system. As circumstances develop, the application of this plan generates intentions which are carried out in action. Most people lead blurred and fluctuating lives because of their doubts, their ignorance and the faltering grip of logic and the breaking in of impulse.

X

66. Let us reintroduce Smith, who is a budding genius, and the Academy. After studying him they consult among themselves and agree

If Smith wants to lead a satisfying life, he ought to lead a life of kind L

They go to him and tell him this. When he challenges this, they persuade him, after a little Socratic deflation, to come to the Academy as a Junior Fellow. After several years of study he cries 'I see!' and proceeds to think along the following lines

If I want to lead a satisfying life, I ought to lead a life of kind L

Ex hypothesi he has built into him the over-arching valuing

Would I led a satisfying life

In accordance with the previous analysis, he concludes

'Would that I led a life of kind L' is implied (*quoad* me) by a value which, all things considered, I accept

[Perhaps, on the egoistic assumption, he is entitled even to say

'Would that I led a life of kind L' is implied (*quoad* me) by a *valid* value, indeed, the primarily valid value]

However this may be, according to the theory, the above is equivalent to

I ought to lead a life of kind L

67. Drawing on additional knowledge of scientific principles, laws, empirical generalizations, the probable outcomes of actions of various kinds in various kinds of circumstance described with a subtlety of a casuist, he continues

If I want to lead a life of kind L, I ought to do such and such actions (A_i) in such and such kinds of circumstance (C_i)

where these policies take into account all the subtle ways in which circumstances may vary and yet seem, on casual inspection, to be the same. These policies, therefore, are not to be interpreted as rules of thumb. Smith has available all the general knowledge which is even *in principle* relevant to his conduct. His policies are general in the logical sense in which a fantastically complex law-like statement is general, even though it happens to apply to but one instance. *Indeed, his policies are the practical counterparts of just such law-like statements.*

68. Assuming the premise of possibility necessary to turn 'would's into 'shall's, he draws two families of conclusions

(*a*) Shall [I will do A_i on any occasion in which the circumstances are C_i]

(*b*) 'Shall [I will do A_i whenever the circumstances are C_i]' is implied (*quoad* me) by an intention which, all things considered, I accept (or, perhaps, by a valid intention)

69. The latter is considered by the theory to be equivalent to

(For any t) I ought to do A_i at t, if I am in C_i at t

The theory thus claims that a categorical ought statement asserts that one is committed to a general intention of the form

(For any t) shall [if I am in C_i at t, I will do A_i at t]

by virtue of its being implied by the life-plan valuing. Roughly, categorical imperatives are *derivative general conditional intentions*.

70. Confronted by a particular circumstance, Smith surveys his scheme of classification, classifies the circumstance as C_i, sees that the relevant action is of kind A_i and infers

'Shall [I will do A_i]' is implied (*quoad* me) by my life plan intention

which, according to the theory, has the sense of

I ought to do A_i

In harmony with all this machinery he draws the first-level practical conclusion

Shall [I will do A_i]

which, if the relevant time is *now*, is a volition. In the absence of paralysis, not to mention overwhelming intellectual fatigue, this volition grows into a doing of A_i.

71. The core of the above practical reasoning, given the factual information, can be telescoped as follows:

Shall [I will lead a satisfying life]
Therefore, shall [I will do A_i at t]

At the second level we have

'Shall [I will lead a satisfying life]' implies (*quoad* me) 'shall [I will do A_i at t]'

which is regarded by the theory as equivalent to

If I want to lead a satisfying life, I ought to do A_i at t

interpreted as

'Shall [I will do A_i at t]' is implied by my life-plan intention

which, according to the theory, authorizes

I ought to do A_i at t

XI

72. Is this view plausible? It is, as Prichard[1] saw, one strand in Plato's thought. The latter develops, in a number of dialogues, the concept of an art of living which he conceives of as the art of achieving, in so far as possible, a satisfying life. Assuming that a shoemaker values, for whatever reason, the making of shoes, and that no other values become relevant during shoemaking hours, that he knows what the various stages of making a shoe require him to do to the leather, and how to do it, then he will turn to and make the shoe—within the limits of his material. So, too, a man in possession of the art of living will turn to and create a satisfying life within the limits of his opportunities.

73. 'But,' the question naturally arises, as Plato saw, 'what guarantees that Smith, however meticuously he plans his life and carries out his policies, will behave in the ways we think of as moral?' In other words, what guarantees that the intricate policies of his art of living coincide in content with the content of moral principles? Might not his policies include such items as

(At any time t) shall [if I have a ring which makes me invisible at t, I will wear it at t and take all available loose cash to buy research equipment with]

not to mention more exotic policies?

[1] See his Inaugural Lecture, *Duty and Interest*, Oxford, 1928.

74. Plato, of course, offers a lengthy argument to prove that the policies of the art of living, i.e. of achieving a satisfying life, coincide with sound moral principles; and there is more than a little to his argument. Yet, as Prichard points out, even if Plato had been successful in establishing this *coincidence*, he would not have succeeded in establishing the conceptual identity of moral reasoning with the reasoning we have been illustrating; nor that the 'ought' of

> If I want to lead a satisfying life, I ought to do A_i

can yield, by *modus ponens*, given the over-arching aim of leading a satisfying life, the unqualified assertion

> I ought to do A_i

There seems to be no conceptual absurdity in either

> Doing A_i would be conducive to a satisfying life, but I ought not to do A_i

or

> Doing B would not be conducive to a satisfying life, but I ought to do B

XII

75. It might be thought that the trouble is easy to locate. It consists, it might be said, in the fact that the 'all things considered' of our story is ego-centred. Well, let us postulate, then, that Smith is a benevolent man not only at the level of specific valuations but that, in addition to valuing his own happiness for its own sake, he values the welfare of people generally (including himself) for its own sake.

76. He returns to the Academy and further study convinces him that

> In the case of anyone, if he wants to promote the general welfare, he ought to do A_j whenever the circumstances are C_j

where, as before, his classificatory framework for actions and circumstances is ideally fine-grained, yet the reference to actions and circumstances is logically general. He applies this general hypothetical imperative to himself, thus,

If I want to promote the general welfare, I ought to do Λ_j whenever C_j

77. On the other hand, he still has available the hypothetical imperatives pertaining to the art of achieving a satisfying life for himself which were explored in the previous sections. And are there not available such hypothetical imperatives as

In the case of anyone, if he wants to promote the welfare of hummingbirds, he ought to do A_k whenever C_k

which he can also apply to himself?

78. It begins to look as though with the abandonment of psychological egoism the general approach we have been considering conceptually permits the use of *modus ponens*, given relevant information, to conclude

I ought to do Λ_i

or

I ought not to do A_i

depending on what one wants, *all things considered*, whether it is one's own happiness, the welfare of people generally or the welfare of hummingbirds. Yet we feel that the moral ought is, *in principle*, unequivocal, i.e. that if, like Smith, we had ideal knowledge, what we ought to do would be uniquely determined.

79. It will have been noticed that I have just introduced the phrase 'the moral ought'. This, it might be thought, gives us the answer. The moral ought is to be *defined* in terms of the schema

I morally ought to do A $\longleftrightarrow$ 'Would [I will do A]' is implied by a valuation I accept all things *pertaining to the general welfare* considered

80. But this is too easy. It still leaves us with the puzzling idea that *unqualified* 'ought' is a matter of what we *want*, all things considered.

XIII

81. Yet what is the alternative? Perhaps the whole attempt to construe 'ought' in terms of the hypothetical imperative is a mistake. Perhaps we should concentrate on the clue that it is a conceptual truth that, to put it roughly, what *one* person ought to do in a situation of a given description, *anyone* ought to do in a situation thus described.[1] Yet it is notoriously difficult to supplement this formal consideration with material content, and to do so in a way which has an equally clear conceptual tie with the concept of obligation. I know of no successful theory along these lines, though interesting attempts, in different directions, have been made by Marcus Singer and R. M. Hare.

82. Singer's attempt involves, as I see it, a failure to grasp the significance of the distinction between 'ought to be' and 'ought to do'. In other words, it fails fully to take into account the difference between

It ought to be the case that everyone, if in C, *does* A

and

In the case of everyone, he ought, if in C, *to do* A

and, by so doing, fails to appreciate a logic of the concept of a 'circumstance' in a principle of action.[2] It is the latter of the above statement forms which expresses principle concerning what people ought to do.

83. Singer's argument, when spelled out, looks as follows:

(1) Ought-to-be (not-[(x) x is in C $\rightarrow$ x *does* A])
(2) Ought-to-be ((Ex) x is in C $\cdot$ x *does* not-A)
(3) (Ex) ought-to-be (x is in C $\cdot$ x *does* not-A)
(4) (Ex) ought-to-be (x is in C $\rightarrow$ x *does* not-A)
(5) (Ex) ought (x is in C $\rightarrow$ x *to do* A)
(6) (*Ceteris paribus*): (x) ought (x is in C $\rightarrow$ x *to do* not-A)

Unfortunately, the *ceteris paribus* move from 'somebody ought to

---

[1] This conceptual truth, it will be noticed, is embodied, *in a certain sense*, in the accounts we have been considering, whatever their shortcomings.

[2] For an exploration of this concept see my 'Reflections on Contrary-to-duty Imperatives', *Nous*, 4, 1967.

do' (5) to 'everybody ought to do' (6), which appeals to the 'generalization principle'—roughly, what's right for one is right for all, *in the same circumstances*—cannot discount the fact that the 'circumstances' referred to in (1) are, from the standpoint of the relevant principle of action, an incomplete description, for from the latter point of view the circumstances proper include *everybody else doing* A.

84. When formulated in such a way as to bring this out, the argument becomes

(1) Ought-to-be (not-[(x) x is in C $\rightarrow$ x *does* A])

(2') (y) ought (y is in $\{C \cdot (z) z \neq y \cdot z$ is in C $\rightarrow z$ *does* A$\} \rightarrow y$ *to do* not-A)

and the relation between (2') and

(6') (*Ceteris paribus*): (y) ought (y is in C $\rightarrow y$ *to do* not-A)

becomes either trivial (i.e. 'ceteris paribus' amounts to 'provided that everybody else in a circumstance which includes C, *does* A') or a *non-sequitur*, since the relevance of the other circumstance factors must be empirically determined on their own merits.

85. Moral principles are not to be derived from considerations pertaining to the consequences of *everybody* behaving in a certain way in a certain kind of circumstance, whether it be a matter of the consequences being undesirable (as in negative utilitarianism) or desirable (as in traditional utilitarianism). Moral principles primarily concern the consequences of *anybody* acting in a certain way in a certain kind of circumstance, and it is only because of the subtle involvement of what others do in the relevant description of an agent's circumstances that it is a conceptual truth that if the consequences of *anyone* doing A in a certain fine-grained kind of circumstance are good, the consequences of *everyone* doing A in *precisely that kind of circumstance* must also be good. With these careful qualifications, the move is simply that from 'any' to 'all'.

XIV

86. The point of view of benevolence described above is not the moral point of view, though, as Kant saw, it is easily confused

with it. Even generalized and embracing benevolence is, so to speak, an external point of view. If I were to say, in all candour,

> Would that language-using featherless bipeds generally led satisfying lives

I would be expressing a friendly sentiment, which might be very strong indeed, with respect to language-using featherless bipeds. What, then, is the moral point of view? If anyone has captured its essence it is surely Kant. And in the following argument I shall lean heavily on his views, though I shall not hesitate to restructure them, where necessary, to bring them into touch with the current state of the problem.

87. The central theme of Kant's ethical theory is, in our terminology, the *reasonableness* of intentions. In what sense or senses, if any, can *intentions* be said to be reasonable, i.e. have a *claim* on the assent of a rational being? Kant clearly construes this task as parallel to the task of defining in what sense or senses, if any, *beliefs* can be said to be reasonable, i.e. have a *claim* on the assent of a rational being. As in his epistemology, Kant sides with the rationalists against both the empiricist and the sceptic—but gives rationalism that twist which makes all the difference. In both areas his insights were so revolutionary that they are even now just beginning to be absorbed.

88. The primary distinction Kant draws, with respect to the reasonableness of intentions, is that between 'hypothetical' (or, as I prefer to put it, 'relative') and 'categorical' reasonableness. The simplest examples of intentions whose reasonableness is purely 'relative are provided by what Kant calls 'hypothetical imperatives'.

89. In the terminology suggested above, the hypothetical imperative asserts that (since S is in C) the intention which he would express by saying

> I shall do A

is reasonable *relative to* the intention which he would express by saying

> I shall bring about E

90. One merit of using the term 'relative' to characterize the reasonableness of the above intention is that it enables us to avoid confusing the reasonableness (for S) of the intention to do A relative to the intention to bring about E, with a supposed reasonableness (for S) of the intention to do A *on the hypothesis that he intends to bring about E*.[1] This confusion generates the mistaken idea that the hypothetical imperative authorizes S (since he is in C) to reason

I intend to bring about E
So, I shall do A[2]

whereas the hypothetical imperative actually says that (given that S is in C) a reasoning on his part to the effect that

I shall bring about E
So, I shall do A

would be valid, in that the premise does (given that S is in C) imply the conclusion.

91. Thus the reasonableness invoked by a hypothetical imperative is the reasonableness of a conclusion intention relative to the premise intention in a (possible) piece of practical reasoning. It does not commit itself concerning the reasonableness of either the premise intention or the conclusion intention *per se*.

92. Let me prepare the way for the next stage of the argument by reminding you of the distinction between the *validity* and the *goodness* of arguments in the domain of theoretical reasoning. An argument can be valid, but fail to be good, by having a false premise. To say that it is *valid* is, in our terminology, to say that its conclusion is reasonable *relative to* its premise. To say that it is *good* is to add that its premise is reasonable—for, I shall assume,

---

[1] This mistake is a consequence of the failure to bear in mind the distinction between what is implied by an intention-content and what is implied by the state of having an intention with that content.

[2] This argument clearly presupposes, for its validity, the principle that it is reasonable to do whatever is implied by the content of an intention we happen to have. Explicitly formulated, this principle would read

If x has an intention of content I, and I implies (for x) 'I shall do A', then x ought to do A

and this can be readily seen to be a false categorical imperative.

truth is a special case of reasonableness. A true proposition is one which has a certain claim to be assented to by a rational being. Just how this claim is to be analysed is the problem of truth, which was explored, if not resolved in Chapters IV and V.

93. One would expect, then, that a good practical argument is one in which the conclusion intention is not only implied by the premise intention, so that it is reasonable *relative to* the premise, as in the case of arguments authorized by hypothetical imperatives, but also one in which the premise intention is reasonable *per se*. And, indeed, Kant is clearly looking for a property of intentions which corresponds to *truth*. In short, he is attempting to discover what might make practical arguments *good* as opposed to merely *valid*. My purpose in this chapter is to show that he took us to the very threshold of success.

94. Let us now make a preliminary attempt to understand what it might mean to say of an intention that it is 'categorically reasonable' or 'categorically valid'.

95. Let us suppose that in the circumstance in which I now find myself I ought to do a certain kind of action A. The following *categorical* ought statement we shall suppose is true.

I ought to do A

Standing behind this categorical statement, however, is a condition of the form *since* (or *because*) I am in 'C', we are thus led to the *conditional* ought statement

If I am in C, I ought to do A

This in turn points in the direction of

Anybody ought to do A, if he is in C

but before attempting to understand the logical status of the reference to *anybody*, let us dwell for a moment on the first person conditional.

96. The first point to be made is that the antecedent of this conditional refers to a circumstance, rather than, as in the case of

If I want to bring about E, I ought to do A

to an intention. Thus, if the ought statement tells us that the intention to do A is reasonable, it does not tell us, at least explicitly, that it is reasonable relative to *another intention*. Its explicit message is that the intention to do A is reasonable relative to *the condition of being in C*. On the other hand, if we accept, as we have, the principle that intentions can only be derived from other intentions, this reasonableness points to the argument

> I shall do A, if I am in C
> I am in C
> So, I shall do A

in other words, *implicitly* the reasonableness of 'I shall do A' is relative not only to the circumstance but, also to the *conditional* intention

> I shall do A, if I am in C

It is, therefore, *this* intention which must be categorically reasonable, if the original ought statement is to express a categorical imperative.

97. We are thus led to the idea that

> I ought to do A, if I am in C

is equivalent to

> 'I shall do A, if I am in C' is categorically reasonable

Note that in this statement categorical reasonableness is predicated of a *conditional* intention. 'Categorical' in the sense which applies to reasonableness must not be confused with 'categorical' as a classification of propositional forms.

98. But what are we to make of the idea that an intention of the form

> I shall do A, if I am in C

can be categorically reasonable? Obviously the reasonableness does not consist in the logical form of the intention. Intentions of this form do not show themselves to be sound, for example, by unpacking into tautological intentions such as

> I shall stay or go, if I am threatened

or unsound by unpacking into contradictory intentions such as

I shall stay and go, if I am threatened.

99. But how can the specific subject matter of an intention be involved in its reasonableness without turning the latter into a disguised form of the relative reasonableness asserted by a hypothetical imperative? Curiously enough, the key to the answer is found by seeing how close we can come to capturing the distinctively *categorical* reasonableness of morally sound intentions by construing it as a special case of the relative reasonableness ascribed to intentions by hypothetical imperatives.

100. Now the hypothetical imperative which comes closest to capturing the moral point of view is that of impartial benevolence. Granted that it fails, how is this failure to be understood? One is tempted to say that the actions it prescribes coincide with the prescriptions of morality. If this is indeed the case, then it is difficult to see how the hypothetical imperatives of impartial benevolence and the categorical imperatives of morality could be as radically different in form as they are commonly taken to be. Granted that their difference is one of conceptual form rather than content, are there not other dimensions of conceptual form than the superficial ones which meet the eye?

101. Thus notice that the hypothetical imperative

If S wants to maximize the general welfare (GW), S ought to do A_i if S is in C_i

combines the two modes of conditionality, expressed, respectively, by 'if S wants' and 'if S is in C'. According to our analysis, this hypothetical imperative tells us that

'I shall maximize GW' implies (for S) 'I shall do A if I am in C'

The implication is, as we have seen, one of our special kind we have called 'instrumental'. And if the implication holds for S it holds for any rational being, for we are supposing, as before, that the hypothetical imperative is simply the transposition into practical discourse of an inductively established empirical generalization.

102. This complex hypothetical imperative *as such* asserts the reasonableness of the conditional intention

I shall do A, if I am in C

relative to the intention

I shall maximize GW

We can now point out that *if* the antecedent intention was itself *categorically* reasonable, and *if*, as we have been assuming, categorical reasonableness is the practical counterpart of truth, *it would follow that the consequent intention was itself categorically reasonable.*

103. It has been easy to assume that relative and categorical reasonableness are incompatible: that an intention can have one or the other, but not both.[1] This assumption is simply false.

104. To bring out the implications of this point, remember that a good theoretical argument is one in which (*a*) the conclusion is reasonable relative to the premise, and (*b*) the premise itself is categorically reasonable, i.e. true. Implication preserves truth in theoretical arguments. We should explore the possibility that it preserves categorical reasonableness in practical arguments. If so, then, an intention can be categorically reasonable, and yet *derivative* from another intention—provided, of course, that the latter in turn is categorically reasonable.

105. *Categorical* reasonableness must not be confused with *intrinsic* reasonableness. The confusion between these two has been even more damaging to Kant exegesis than the tendency to suppose that a categorically reasonable intention cannot be conditional in its logical form. On the other hand, even if categorical reasonableness is not the same as intrinsic reasonableness, we are faced with the fact that if there are to be *derivative* categorically reasonable intentions there must be one or more intentions whose categorically reasonableness is non-derivative or intrinsic. Are any to be found?

---

[1] Of course, if an intention is *merely* relatively or hypothetically reasonable it cannot be categorically reasonable as well.

106. What of the antecedent of the above complex hypothetical imperative

I shall maximize the GW?

It is a worthy intention, one that we should encourage people to have—though not, as Kant emphasizes, at the expense of the sense of duty. Yet it does not seem to have any feature which calls for the predicate 'intrinsically and categorically reasonable'.

XV

107. Let us continue to beat about in the neighbouring bushes. The first thing to note is that the instrumental nomologicals on which the above complex hypothetical imperatives rest generate not only hypothetical imperatives but other practical implications which, though closely related, are not in the strict Kantian sense hypothetical imperatives. For not all statements to the effect that one intention implies another can be put in the form of a hypothetical imperative, at least if we tie this term to Kant's paradigms.

108. To develop this point, we must remember that not all intentions are intentions *to do*. There are also intentions *that something be the case*. And if the existence of one state of affairs causally implies the existence of another, then the intention that the one obtain causally implies the intention that the other obtain.

109. Thus the instrumental nomologicals which generate the general hypothetical imperatives

'I shall maximize GW' implies (for each rational being) 'I shall do A_i, if I am in C_i'

also generates, for example,

'It shall be the case that Tom (Dick, Harry) maximize GW' implies (for each rational being) 'It shall be the case that Tom (Dick, Harry) does A_i, if he is in C_i'

and, indeed, the doubly general practical implication

For all values of 'x', 'it shall be the case that x maximize GW' implies (*for each rational being*) 'it shall be the case that x does A_i if x is in C_i'[1]

110. Here the 'shall's are 'shall be the case's and though the egocentric 'I' has *apparently* dropped out, it is still present by virtue of the conceptual relationships between 'it shall be the case . . .' and 'I shall do . . .'

111. The difference between the general hypothetical imperatives and the general practical implications schematized in § 109 lies in the fact that whereas the former authorize *each* person to reason *about himself*, thus,

> I shall maximize GW
> So, I shall do A_i if in C_i

the latter authorize *each* person to reason about *anybody*, including, of course, himself. It authorizes Tom to reason about himself, thus,

> It shall be the case that Tom maximizes GW
> So it shall be the case that Tom does A_i, if in C_i

and also about Dick, thus,

> It shall be the case that Dick maximize GW
> So, it shall be the case that Dick does A_i, if in C_i

XVI

112. We are now ready for the thirty-two-dollar question. We have been grooming categorical reasonableness to be the practical counterpart of truth. But in theoretical reasoning truth, and hence the *goodness* of arguments, is *intersubjective*.

---

[1] The implications which are formulated in ordinary language as hypothetical imperatives are formulated as 'ought to do's because the consequent intentions are intentions to do

If one wants . . ., then one ought to do . . .

On the other hand, the implications with which we are now concerned are intentions that something be the case. They appear in the material mode of speech as hypothetical 'ought to be's, thus,

If one wants X to be the case, Y ought to be the case

e.g.

If one wants a good crop, the soil ought to be moist

113. Consider the argument offered by Tom,

> There was lightning at t p
> So, there was thunder at $t + \Delta\, t$ so, q

This is, we shall assume, not only *valid* given the familiar law of nature but *good*, i.e. it is true that there was lightning at t.

114. If so, then Dick's argument

> There was no thunder at $t + \Delta\, t$ $\sim q$
> So, there was no lightning at t so, $\sim p$

though equally valid, can't also be *good*. This is because Tom and Dick are contradicting one another, when Tom says 'p' and Dick says '$\sim p$'.

115. Tom's practical reasoning,

> It shall be the case that Dick maximizes GW
> So, it shall be the case that Dick does A_i if in C_i

although it is *valid*, as being in accordance with an implication which is binding on each rational being, it is essentially *private*. In spite of the fact that Tom is reasoning validly about Dick, and that he would be reasoning with equal validity if he reasoned in the same way about *anybody*, including himself, his argument does not have the *intersubjective* status which would make possible a logical clash of his argument with Dick's equally valid argument

> It shall *not* be the case that Dick does A_i if in C_i
> So, it shall *not* be the case that Dick maximizes GW.

Dick's

> It shall not be the case that Dick maximizes GW

does not stand to Tom's

> It shall be the case that Dick maximizes GW

as Dick's

> It is not the case that there was lightning at t

stands to Tom's

> It is the case that there was lightning at t

116. Two people can affirm the same proposition in a strong sense of 'same'. But as far as the intentions we have so far considered are concerned, intentions can at best be parallel. They are irreducibly egocentric, even when this egocentricity is latent as in

Tom: it shall be the case that the war ends
Dick: it shall be the case that the war ends

This dialogue provides an excellent example of 'agreement in attitude'. But if the depth form of these statements is

Tom: (*Ceteris paribus*) I (Tom) shall do what I can to end the war
Dick: (*Ceteris paribus*) I (Dick) shall do what I can to end the war

the agreement in attitude is not an identity of intention.[1]

117. What of

Tom: *we* shall do what we can to end the war
Dick: *we* shall do what we can to end the war

These statements in the first person *plural* have the interesting properties that (*a*) they express the speakers' intention, yet (*b*) the intentions expressed are in the strongest sense the same. Put in terms of the distinctions I drew in my opening remarks, the *intendings* are two in number, but the *content* of these intendings is the *same*, in as strong a sense as the content of the two believings expressed by

Tom: There was lightning at *t*
Dick: There was lightning at *t*

is the same. I shall put this by saying that the *intendings* expressed by

We shall do . . .

have an intersubjective form.

---

[1] It might be thought that since two people can use egocentric referring expressions and yet 'make the same statement', the same might be true in the case of intentions. But egocentric referring expressions can be counterparts and hence used by different people to make the same statement (e.g. 'Jones is here by me': 'Jones is there by you'), because they gear in with an intersubjective framework of relative location. If there were intersubjective intentions . . ., but then this is exactly the problem.

118. This intersubjective form stands out when it is a matter of intendings to do. When, however, it is a matter of intendings that something be the case, the distinction is likely to be lost, unless we index the 'shall' to indicate the form of the intending *to do* which the intendings imply.[1] Thus the intersubjective intention expressed by

It shall$_{we}$ be the case that the war end

would contrast in form, for example, with the personal intention

It shall$_I$ be the case that the roses be planted

XVII

119. We have answered the thirty-two-dollar question by finding the necessary dimension of intersubjectivity. There remains, however, the sixty-four-dollar question of categorical reasonableness. Some paragraphs back, when we were beating about in the neighbouring bushes, I asked if the antecedent of a certain complex hypothetical imperative could be construed as categorically reasonably valid, pointing out that if so, its categorical reasonableness would be transmitted to that which it instrumentally implied. Since that time we have (*a*) taken into account intentions that something be the case, and (*b*) brought into the picture intentions which have intersubjective form. Have these additional resources brought us closer to our goal? I believe they have.

120. Cerid the intersubjective intention

It shall$_{we}$ be the case that our welfare is maximized

If this intention were intrinsically categorically reasonable, or valid, then, by virtue of the relation of 'shall be the case' to 'I shall do', so also would

We shall each of us so act as to maximize our welfare

---

[1] In the case of wishes as contrasted with intentions we have the locution

We would that . . .

to contrast with

I would that . . .

Here the 'we' and 'I' express the form of the wish. In the case of intentions, however, it is only intentions to do which exhibit this distinction. The functions of the indices is performed in ordinary language by the contrast between 'from a personal point of view' and 'from the point of view of the group' or, of more interest, 'from a moral point of view'.

121. We now take into account the vast number of complicated instrumental nomologicals which we suppose to have been established (in principle) by the physical and behavioural sciences, and are represented by the schema

'x so acts as to maximize GW' implies 'x does A_i if in C_i'

Given these implications, the categorical validity of the above intention entails the categorical validity of the family of inter-subjective intentions

It shall$_{we}$ be the case that each of us does A_i in C_i

which, on our analysis, is equivalent to the family of ought statements

If any of us is in C_i he ought to do A_i

122. Notice that although the validity which these ought statements ascribe to the intersubjective intentions with respect to any of us that he do A_i in C_i is a *derivative* validity, it is nevertheless a *categorical* validity. The 'ought' itself can properly be characterized as categorical, and contrasted with the 'relative' ought of the hypothetical imperative.

XVIII

123. We ascribe a valuing to Smith by saying

Smith values . . .

In the argument to date, we have taken the appropriate sentence which Smith might use to express his valuing to be

Would that . . .

Now when the valuing is, as I put it, from a personal point of view, let us suppose that it is properly expressed by the sentence

I would that . . .

e.g.

I would that I were in England
I would that Tom was well

Corresponding to these, there would be ascriptive sentences having the form

Smith values, from a personal point of view, . . .

124. What are we to contrast with this? What is to be the expressive counterpart of the ascription

Smith values, *from a moral point of view*, . . .

The answer suggests itself

We would that . . .

Roughly, to value from a moral point of view is to value *as a member of the relevant community*, which as far as the present argument is concerned, I shall assume to be mankind generally.[1]

125. Notice that the above sentence, which *expresses* a valuing, must not be confused with the plural value *ascription*

We value . . .

It is still an individual who is valuing, but he is valuing in terms of *we*. Let us suppose that Smith and ourselves belong to the same community (as on the above assumption we do), then the corresponding value ascription would be

Smith values as *one of us* . . .

126. Valuing, in other words, has a *subjective form* as well as a *content*. The subjective form we have hereto taken into account is the 'personal point of view'. Moral philosophers have emphasized the universality of the *content* of a moral evaluation, thus,

Would that anyone in C_i did A_i

I wish to emphasize the universality of the subjective form of moral evaluation

We would that anyone in C_i did A_i

127. Let me emphasize that from the fact that Smith values something, X, as one of us, it doesn't follow that

We value X

---

[1] Thus, interesting points remain to be made about the tribocentricity of moral judgments in the not too remote past, and on what it would be to change from speaking of a being as 'it' to speaking of it as one of 'them' in a sense which radically contrasts with 'one of us', and from there to speaking of the being as a member of the encompassing community within which we draw relative distinctions between 'we' and 'they'. Perhaps the most interesting point is that to discuss with another person what ought to be done *presupposes* (shall I say dialectically?) that you and he are members of one community.

We may well—indeed, often do—differ in what we value as members of the community. Yet *in principle* there could be agreement. 'We would that . . .' lacks the logical privacy of 'I would that . . .'

128. Let me give a parallel from our earlier exploration of classical theories. Our ego-centred Smith might well value things differently at different times, as his beliefs about himself and the world change. Thus at noon he might say

I shall not cross the Rubicon tomorrow

and at evening

I shall cross the Rubicon tomorrow

But although his 'shall' is egocentric, it is *abidingly* egocentric. He is, in a tough sense, asking the *same* question when he asks at different times

Shall I cross the Rubicon on such and such a date?

129. Furthermore, given his over-arching aim of a satisfying life, he would be, *in principle*, at all times in agreement with himself about his values; that is to say, if he had at all times the knowledge available in his ideal Academy he would have agreed with himself at all times about the values implied by this over-arching aim. There would be, *in principle*, agreement between, so to speak, Smith-at-t_1, Smith-at-t_2, etc. His categorical oughts at one time can contradict those of another time. Yet these contradictions are, in principle, resolvable.

130. The parallel logical point holds with respect to the members of our community, in so far as they value the general welfare not from a personal point of view—external benevolence—but *as one of us*.

131. I pointed out above that if the intersubjective intention

It shall$_{we}$ be the case that our welfare is maximized

were intrinsically categorically reasonable, the family of intersubjective intentions

It shall$_{we}$ be the case that each of us does A_i in C_i

would also be categorically reasonable, though derivatively so.

132. Let us now remove the 'if', for the intention

It shall$_{we}$ be the case that our welfare is maximized

does seem to have an authority which is more than a mere matter of its being generally accepted. It is a conceptual fact that people constitute a community, a *we*, by virtue of thinking of each other as *one of us*, and by willing the common good *not* under the species of benevolence—but by willing it as one of us, or from a moral point of view. Thus, the autobiographical

An intention which I accept

is replaced by '. . . is an intersubjectively valid intention'.

XIX

133. If my argument is correct, the valuings which are expressed by ethical statements are universal in *three* dimensions.

(*a*) in their content
   . . . if any of us is in C_i he do A_i
(*b*) in their subjective form (their logical intersubjectivity)
   We would that . . .
(*c*) in their objectivity (in that there is, in principle, a decision procedure with respect to specific ethical statements)

I see no reason why this objectivity should not be said to legitimate the use of the concepts of truth and falsity with respect to ethical discourse.

134. These considerations pertaining to the conceptual structure of the moral point of view amount to a thoroughly Kantian metaphysic of morals. Thus, they amount to:

(*a*) The conception of a moral polity—Kant's Kingdom of Ends

(It is this conceptual feature of the moral point of view which implies the Kantian principle that everyone shall be treated as an end in itself and not as a means only. For to treat someone as a means only is, in effect, to consider his place with respect to our conduct not from the point of view

We would that . . .

but from a point of view which singles him out, by virtue of some special relation to ourselves, as an exception. It is to consider him from the point of view

I would that . . .

or, at least, from the point of view of a sub-community to which I belong.)

(*b*) the conception of moral principles as universalized maxims—we would that *anyone* in C_i do A_i

(*c*) by virtue of the logical relation of 'any' to 'all', the conception of moral principles as implying

We would that *all persons always did* A_i in C_i
(Kant's 'law of nature' formulation)

(*d*) the conception that there is a common epistemic obligation to accept categorical imperatives

(For categorical imperatives are simply the transposition into the moral framework of scientific truths of the form

(s) (t) 's promotes the common good at t'
implies 'if s is in C_i at t, s does A_i at t)

135. Alas, the ideal knowledge of our philosophical fiction is not even close at hand. Thus, the ideal 'consensus' of those who share the moral point of view is only 'in principle' there, and reasoning from the moral point of view proceeds in a context of ignorance and diversity of opinion. But, then, the same is true of consensus on matters of fact, scientific laws and theoretical principles. There, as here, the philosophical task must be to exhibit the conceptual structure within which this ignorance and this difference of opinion exist, and which, by making rational inquiry possible, provides the means by which (in principle, alas!) they can be overcome.

XX

136. Kant believed himself to have established that the 'we' of the moral point of view is *rational beings generally*. At first sight, however, this seems to be a mistake, a confusion between the class of those for whom instrumental *implications* are binding, which

does, indeed, consist of rational beings generally, and the class of those for whom categorically valid intersubjective *intentions* are binding.

137. The distinction involved can best be made by returning to the general hypothetical imperatives of benevolence

'I shall maximize the GW' implies 'I shall do A_i, if in C_i'

We pointed out that the scope of the 'I' consists of rational beings generally, since the implications are simply the transposition into practical discourse of inductively established nomologicals. We failed, however, to emphasize that the welfare to be maximized is the welfare *of a group to which a particular 'I' belongs*, thus,

'I shall maximize the GW of my group' implies (for each rational being) 'I shall do A_i if in C_i'

And if we ask which group is that, we see that it by no means follows from the above that the answer must be 'rational beings generally'. We must draw at least a conceptual distinction between the class of those on whom the implications are binding, and the class of those the promotion of whose welfare is the object of the benevolent intention of a particular 'I'.

138. The distinction remains when we transpose the instrumental implication into the realm of intersubjective intentions.

'It shall$_{we}$ be the case that each of us so acts as to maximize our welfare' implies 'It shall$_{we}$ be the case that each of us does A_i if in C_i'

As before, the 'implies' can be glossed with 'for each rational being'. But, as before, it by no means follows that the group whose welfare is 'our' welfare consists of rational beings generally.

139. It might, however, be argued that only if the 'we' of 'our welfare' is the 'we' of 'we rational beings generally' is an intersubjective intention of this form categorically valid. This *might*, as we shall see, be true if the welfare in question is what might be called epistemic welfare, but not if we take into account, as we must, needs and desires generally.

140. Now, we saw that the categorical validity of an intersubjective intention of the form

It shall$_{we}$ be the case that our welfare is maximized

would seem to consist in the fact that it is by virtue of such an intention that a group or community *is* a group or community. Roughly, a community consists of individuals who intend *sub specie* such an intention, the scope of 'we' being the members of the community.

141. This is not to say, of course, that there will be agreement as to just what is instrumentally implied by this intention, or that on particular occasions the implications a person believes it to have will prevail against an alternative arrived at by practical reasoning 'from a personal point of view'.

142. Can we say that rational beings generally constitute a community? They would do so if they shared the intersubjective intention

It shall$_{we}$ be the case that each of us rational beings so acts as to promote our welfare

143. Now, since an individual can have an intention of intersubjective form even if no one else in point of fact shares it, an individual rational being could have an intention of the above form even though few, if any, other rational beings had such an intention. To have this intention is to *think* of oneself as a member of a community consisting of all rational being. It is possible, therefore, for a rational being to think of himself as a member of such community, even though this community does not actually exist.

144. If, however, the following two premises were established, this community could be shown to be a reality:

(*a*) To think of oneself as rational being is (implicitly) to think of oneself as subject to epistemic oughts binding on rational beings generally

(*b*) The intersubjective intention to promote *epistemic* welfare implies the intersubjective intention to promote welfare *sans phrase*

These premises would entail that the concept of oneself as a rational being implies the concept of oneself as a member of an ethical community consisting of all rational being. To be sure, this implication need not be recognized. Indeed, it would take all the dialectical skill of a Socrates, a Hegel or a Peirce to bring it to the surface. Yet if the above premises were true, all rational beings would 'implicitly' think of themselves as members of an ethical community consisting of all rational beings. But since a community exists if the relevant individuals think of themselves as its members, the ethical community of rational being would have an 'implicit' existence.

145. The first of the above premises is not implausible. If we accept it we can conclude that 'implicitly' all rational being constitute an *epistemic* community. The second premise, despite Peirce's valiant efforts, remains problematic, and without it the argument for the reality of an *ethical* community consisting of all rational beings, the major premise of which is the 'fact of reason', remains incomplete.

XXI

146. I shall conclude by drawing the implications of the above analysis for certain traditional puzzles pertaining to Kant's ethical theory. For this purpose the most significant feature of this analysis is the point that the categorical validity of an intention can be derivative.

147. It is this fact which enables us to see how 'teleological' and 'deontological' themes are harmonized in Kant's ethics. Thus specific moral principles are categorical oughts, but the categorical validity of the intersubjective intentions, that any rational being in a certain kind of circumstance do a certain kind of action,[1] is derivative from the categorical validity of the intersubjective intentions that our welfare be maximized. Thus, when Kant speaks in the *Metaphysical Elements of Ethics* of the happiness of others as a categorical end[2], what he says is in no way in-

---

[1] "... this 'I ought' (*Sollen*) is properly an 'I would' (*Wollen*) valid for every rational being, provided only that reason determined his actions without any hindrance" (Abbott, p. 68).

[2] Abbott, p. 303.

consistent with his claim that the ought of moral principles is categorical rather than the hypothetical ought which pertains to the relation of means to ends.

148. Again, when Kant stresses intentions, he is not disregarding consequences. It is because doing A_i in C_i maximizes the general welfare that the intention to do A_i in C_i is categorically valid. Of course we may be, and often are, mistaken about what kind of action in what kind of circumstance will promote the general welfare, but what we ought to do hinges on what would actually happen. On the other hand, the moral character of our motive is a function of what we *think* will happen as a result of our action, though not of this alone.

149. When Kant insists that we ought to act from a sense of duty he is not making the absurd mistakes which have often been attributed to him.[1] He is simply repeating the point with which he opens the argument of the *Fundamental Principles of the Metaphysics of Morals*, that the only unconditional good is a good will. By this he means that the only state of a person which is unconditionally good from a moral point of view is the disposition to act from a sense of duty. He has two points in mind: (*a*) Whereas action from *any* motive can have bad results, the sense of duty alone is such that only *by virtue of ignorance* does it have bad results. Action from other motives even where ignorance is absent can lead to bad results. Thus the sense of duty is the only motive which has a direct conceptual tie to the categorically valid end of moral conduct. In this sense a good will is a categorical ought-to-be. (*b*) Although the general welfare is also an end in itself, a categorical ought-to-be, the ought-to-be of the happiness of any *given* individual is, Kant believes, conditional on his having a good will.

150. As Broad has pointed out, Kant is not always clear about the respective status of specific categorical imperatives (categorically valid maxims) and higher order principles about what distinguishes categorically valid maxims from those which are not. Thus, when he writes in *The Critique of Practical Reason*,

---

[1] E.g. by Sir David Ross in *The Right and the Good*, p. 5.

'The principle of happiness may, indeed furnish maxims, but never such as would be competent to be laws of the will even if *universal* happiness were made the object. For since the knowledge of this rests on mere empirical data . . . it can supply only *general* rules, not *universal*.'[1]

he confuses the *sound* point that the intersubjective *validity* of the intention to maximize universal happiness cannot be explicated in terms of benevolence, with the *unsound* idea that empirical data are not relevant to determining the validity of specific categorical imperatives (general conditional intentions or maxims). The meta-ethical principle that those intentions of the form

We would that anyone did A_i if in C_i

are categorically valid, which would be the legislation of an organized community of ideally rational beings *qua* motivated by the categorically valid intention to maximize the common good, does not absolve us from the necessity to use empirical data in our attempt to determine what ought to be done in particular kinds of circumstance. *Any* legislator, motivated by the common good, must ask questions of the form: What kind of action in this kind of circumstance would promote the common good? Only an omniscient legislator would not have to hedge his answers with 'probably' and 'for the most part'.

151. Kant is insisting that the principles in terms of which the concept of a categorically valid intention is to be explicated are not empirical principles. They are *a priori*, and can, in principle, be known by a 'mere analysis of the conceptions of morality'.[2] The fallibility of moral philosophy is not the fallibility of empirical induction.

152. The various so-called formulations of 'the categorical imperative' are meta-ethical principles which locate categorical imperatives (in the sense of specific categorically valid maxims) in the total structure of categorically valid intentions to which they belong. Thus the formulation in terms of legislation appropriate to a 'Kingdom of Ends', though it comes last, actually points to the derivability of categorically valid maxims from the intrinsically categorical intention that 'all ends [be] combined in a

---

[1] Abbott, p. 125.   [2] ibid., p. 59.

systematic whole (including both rational beings as ends in themselves, and also the special ends which each may propose to himself).'[1]

153. The formulation: 'act on maxims which can at the same time have for their objects themselves as univeral laws of Nature'[2] reflects the logical relation between *any* and *all*. The intention—from the moral point of view or, as Kant would say, from the point of view of a rational being as such—with respect to *anybody* that he do A_i in C_i doesn't entail the *intention* that *everybody* do A_i in C_i (for we don't intend the impossible). Thus, a state of affairs in which everybody conforms to categorically valid maxims is itself a categorical ought-to-be, and the wish that it be the case a categorically valid wish.

154. Finally, the principle that '. . . each [rational being] must treat itself and all others never merely as means, but in every case at the same time as ends in themselves'[3] reflects the fact that the intrinsically valid intention which is the prime mover of the domain of categorically valid intentions is the intersubjectively valid intention that each of us rational beings promote our common good. This state of affairs is an end-in-itself in which particular individuals appear symmetrically as *agents* and *patients* in an ethical community.

[1] Abbott, p. 51.   [2] Abbott, p. 56.   [3] Abbott, p. 52

APPENDIX: INNER SENSE

I

1. We saw[1] that in the case of the non-conceptual representations of spatial configurations, Renatus adopted the principles

> a non-conceptual representation of (a K_1 R a K_2)
> = (a non-conceptual representation of a K_1) R* (a non-conceptual representation of a K_2)
> = (a K_1* non-conceptual representation) R* (a K_2* non-conceptual representation)

The fact that the non-conceptual representations are, respectively, K_1* and K_2* and are related by R* guides the understanding, *ceteris paribus*, to form the conceptual representation that—to make the point in first approximation—a K_1 physical object is R to a K_2 physical object.

2. In the case of Time a careful Renatus would distinguish between

> a conceptual representation of a bang following a whiz

and

> a conceptual representation of a bang following a conceptual representation of a whiz

In particular he would distinguish between

> a memory of a bang following a whiz

and

> a memory of a bang following a memory of a whiz

3. A Renatus who has pondered the way in which our con-

[1] Chapter I, §§ 59 ff., above.

ceptual representations of the spatial structure of physical states of affairs are guided by 'counterpart' features of our sense impressions will be led to speculate concerning what it is about our non-conceptual representings which guides the understanding in its representation of temporal relations.

4. He may be tempted to think that since sensory representings *can* stand in temporal relations, there is no need to introduce counterpart characteristics. Thus, in perception, the understanding would be guided in its representation of temporal relations by temporal features of these sensory representations, whereas in its representation of spatial relations it would, as we have seen, be guided by counterparts of spatial characteristics. Renatus might claim, for example, that, *ceteris paribus*, we represent that a bang follows a whiz because an impression of a whiz has been followed by an impression of a bang; and that, *ceteris paribus*, we (ostensibly) remember that a bang followed a whiz, because an image of a whiz was followed by an image of a bang.

5. If he makes this move he claims that there is an asymmetry between the cases of Space and Time. Is there any reason for holding that the two cases are on a par, i.e. that counterpart characteristics are also involved in the experience of temporally related events?

6. There seems, at least, to be no absurdity in the idea that the features of sensory representings by virtue of which they guide the understanding in its conceptual representation of temporal relations between perceived events is not *directly* the temporal relations of the impressions but rather counterpart relations within a *co-existent* structure of sensory representations. Thus, Renatus might claim that when an impression of a whiz is followed by an impression of a bang the impression of the whiz persists and, in addition to the simultaneity of its later stages with the initial stages of an impression of a bang, takes on an additional relation to the latter which is a counterpart of the relation of temporal succession.

7. The suggestion might be diagrammed as follows:

Diagram I:

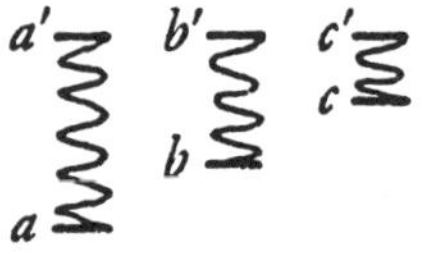

$$a' \quad b' \quad c' \qquad a \text{ precedes } b; \; P^* \; (a', b')$$
$$\qquad\qquad c \qquad b \text{ precedes } c \; ; \; P^* \; (b', c')$$
$$\qquad b \qquad\qquad a \text{ precedes } c; \; P^* \; (a', c')$$
$$a$$

where P^* is the counterpart of (temporally) *precedes*.

8. We could then claim that it is $P^*(a^*, b^*)$ rather than the *precedes* (a, b) in which it is grounded which guides the understanding in representing that a whiz is followed by a bang. Thus, from the standpoint of transcendental philosophy, that which makes sensory states *representative* of temporal order would be the counterpart relation P' rather than the properly temporal relation of precedence. We would be confronted once again by the schema

an impression of (a K_1 R a = (an impression of a K_1) R^*
    K_2)   (an impression of a K_2)

specifically,

an impression of (a whiz pre- = (an impression of a whiz) R^*
    ceding a bang)   (an impression of a bang)

9. He might then go on to argue that the concept of such a counterpart reconstructs that puzzling feature of experience which is called the specious present, which, as traditionally conceived, is an incoherent combination of literal simultaneity and literal successiveness.

10. This concept of a counterpart dimension in which sensory representings, literally simultaneous, can stand in relations which represent successiveness gains additional support from reflection on the perception of motion.

11. Consider, for example, the perception of the raising of a hand. Obviously we must distinguish, to begin with, the perception of a sequence from a mere sequence of perceptions. It is the former with which we are concerned. Thus, our aim is to under-

stand the structure of a series of non-conceptual and conceptual representings, of which an intermediate member might be diagrammed as follows as far as its conceptual component is concerned:

Diagram II:

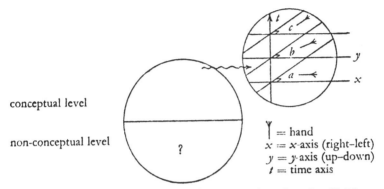

conceptual level

non-conceptual level

?

Υ = hand
x = x-axis (right–left)
y = y-axis (up–down)
t = time axis

12. What of the non-conceptual representings involved? If we make use of the notion of 'persistence' *without mobilizing that of a counterpart dimension which represent temporal order* we get Diagram III:

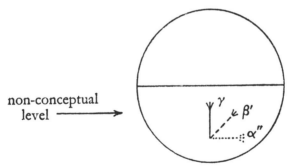

non-conceptual level $\longrightarrow$

where the impression α, of which the current state is α'', began before β, of which the current stage is β', while γ is the initial stage of a still later impression.

13. Notice that with respect to the dimension of counterpart spatial characteristics these sensory states have a common origin, and do not differ, in principle, from a complex sensory representing such as might be involved in the perception of a

Hindu god the arms of which were differently illuminated, thus
Diagram IV:

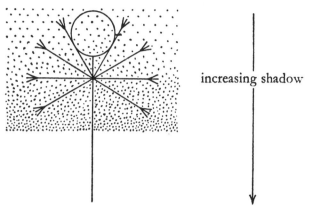

increasing shadow

14. If, however, we introduce a counterpart dimension, τ, which represents temporal succession, and modify the diagram accordingly, we get
Diagram V:

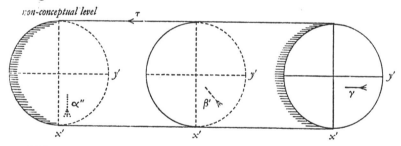

which preserves the common origin as far as counterpart spatial dimensions are concerned, though the sensory representings α'', β', γ, are serially ordered in the τ-dimension, and thus can guide the understanding in the conceptual representation of the successive positions of a hand in physical space, as in Diagram II.

15. I submit that the concept of a τ-dimension of sensory representings is closely related to, though it does not coincide with, Kant's concept of 'the form of inner sense'. The discrepancies are grounded in Kant's failure to distinguish clearly between Time as a form of intuition and such a τ-dimension of the manifold of sense.

16. Since a form of the manifold of sense is a form of represent-*ings*, a confusion of the τ-dimension with Time as a form of intuition leads to the idea that the intuit*eds* of which Time is the form are intuitively represented represent*ings*. Time thus becomes the form of inner intuition.

17. The idea that everything which is *intuitively* represented as in Time is a represent*ing*, i.e. a state of the empirical self, coheres with the 'subjectivistic' ('phenomenalistic' in the Berkeleyian sense) aspects of Kant's thought which were finally overcome in the second edition refutation of idealism.

18. If Kant had clearly drawn the relevant distinctions, the way would have been open for him to argue that the fact that τ-characteristics are characteristics of represent*ings* doesn't require that the intuitive represent*ings* which are synthesized by the understanding in response to them be representings of represent*ings*. For in the case of Space, in spite of the fact that the σ-characteristics (we may call them), which are the counterpart of spatial characteristics, are also characteristics of represent*ings*, the corresponding intuitive representings are representings of *non-representings*, i.e. spatial structures. Thus, that a form of sense is a form of (unrepresented) represent*ings* does not require that the corresponding form of intuition be a form of (represented) represent*ings*.

19. The more clearly Kant saw that what is intuited in Space is not 'sensations' (sensory representings) but physical structures, in spite of the fact that in some sense Space is a form of sensibility, the more clearly he should have seen that what is intuited in Time can also be physical in spite of the fact that in some sense Time is a form of sensibility.

20. Notice that the concept of Time as the form of inner intuition gives aid and comfort to the confusions involved in the distinction between primary and secondary qualities. The temptation is to think of colour, for example, as, in the first instance, a feature of inner intuit*eds* (colour sensations), and only in the Lockean sense, and then discursively, a feature of physical things.

21. Once the confusion between the τ-dimension of sensory states and Time as a form of intuition is overcome, there is no reason whatsoever to deny that an intuited can, as such, be both spatial and temporal, and, indeed, as the second edition refutation of idealism shows, every reason to affirm that the intuitive core of perceptual experience is the representation of items which are as directly temporal (and, for that matter, as directly coloured) as they are spatial.

22. The sharp division between intuiteds which are spatial but not temporal and intuiteds which are temporal but not spatial, which was aided and abetted by Kant's failure to draw these distinctions, did, however, serve a useful purpose. For it enabled Kant to argue that all representings of spatial structures as located in Time are discursive rather than intuitive, and hence a function of the understanding. That from our point of view, according to which the intuitive representing of *this-suches* is itself a function of the understanding, this trip is unnecessary, should not blind us to the fact that it played an important, if not indispensible, role in the development of the Critical Philosophy.

II

23. To round out this excursus on inner sense, it should be pointed out that the domain of the τ-dimension need not be restricted to 'persisting' sense impressions. Two extensions can be conceived:

   (*a*) Images, which have already been construed as sharing with impressions the counterparts of spatial characteristics proper, could be taken to share τ-characteristics as well.

   (*b*) The domain of τ-characteristics can be extended to include conceptual representings.

24. The first of these extensions would enable us to take account of those features of ostensible memory and imagination which correspond to the 'specious present' of perception. Remembered motion, though not present, is as 'specious' as perceived motion, as is imagined motion. This extension seems quite unproblematic.

25. The second extension calls for additional comment. What is

to be accounted for is the fact that we conceptually represent our conceptual representings as having location in Time. What guides the understanding, for example, when we conceptually represent that we have just conceptually represented that 2 plus 2 = 4?

26. The obvious answer, 'the fact that you have just represented that 2 plus 2 = 4', is not compelling. I shall not pause to evaluate the argument from the possibility of error in ostensible recall, but shall turn instead to the moves Renatus might make in extending the theory of the τ-dimension to conceptual representings.

27. He begins by suggesting that, as in the case of perception, the original representing, this time a conceptual representing that 2 plus 2 = 4, 'persists' and acquires a relation to subsequent representings which 'represent' that it began to take place before they did.

Diagram VI:

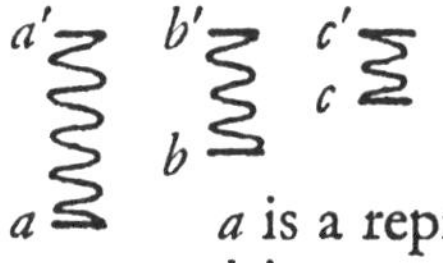

a is a representing that 2 plus 2 = 4
b is a representing of a red rectangle
c is a representing of a whiz

Thus, we would have

a precedes b, b precedes c, a precedes c.
P* (a', b'); P* (b', c'), P* (a', c')

28. The claim would be that the understanding conceptually represents that I conceptually represented that 2 plus 2 = 4 a moment ago, because, in part, I am now representing that 2 plus 2 = 4 in a way which puts this representing in the P* relation to other representings which are now going on.

29. This account requires, of course, that I now be representing both that 2 plus 2 = 4 and that I have just been representing that 2 plus 2 = 4. It is, however, possible, in the light of the considerations advanced in Chapters III and VI, that what persists of the representing that 2 plus 2 = 4 is something less than a full-

fledged representing that 2 plus 2 = 4. Thus our account of inner conceptual episodes diverged from the Cartesian, among other respects, in that according to it an episode's being a representing that 2 plus 2 = 4 is not simply a matter of it having a certain 'purely occurrent' character. It essentially involves dispositions and propensities pertaining to the occurrence of other conceptual episodes, not to mention overt behaviour.

30. On the other hand, it does *involve* that the representing have a 'purely occurrent' character, for these dispositions and propensities are bound up with something which we conceive of as doing a job analogous to that which is done, in overt candid speech, by the sign design '2 plus 2 = 4'. Let us refer to this something as a 'conceptual sign design'. Might it not be the conceptual sign design episode shorn of the powers and propensities which made it in the full sense a representing that 2 plus 2 = 4, which persists and takes its place in the τ-series?

INDEX

Abstract entities, 106, 110
  as changing, 130
  eliminability of statements about, 107, 107 n.
  sub-set of distributive objects, 106
Abstract singular terms, 81, 95 ff., 137
  analogy with chess pieces, 128
  and distributive singular terms, 95, 96, 165 f.
  as classifying linguistic and conceptual episodes, 128, 163 f.
  modifiers of—contrasted with differentia of ordinary specification, 128–31
Accidents
  as dependent particulars, 41
Action, 177 ff.
Acts
  constituting, 36
  diaphanous, 34, 63
  epistemic, 37
  of synthesis, 40
  Cf. Mental Acts
Analogical Concepts
  and methodological dependence, 21
  and the postulation of sense impressions, 18–26
  and the postulation of thoughts, 154
  in theoterical science, 18, 21, 49
  Cf. Counterpart Characteristics, Functional Classification
Appearance
  and the conceptual representations of individuals, 39–42
  as existing primarily as representable, 41 f.
  as existing primarily as represented, 41 f.
  as not existing *simpliciter*, 41 f.

Apperception, 72, 156, 166
  and sense impressions, 10 ff.
Archimedes, 52
Aristotle, 15, 18, 61
  his views on continuity, 148
  Cf. Descartes, Kant
Austin, 140

Behaviourism, 12
  logical, 68, 71, 97, 155, 156
Bergson, 37–8
Berkeley, 28, 39 n., 41, 138
Black, 17 n.
Broad, 227

Cantor, 148
Carnap, 76, 82, 99, 101, 112, 136, 143
Categorical Imperative, 202, 223, 228
Categorical Reasonableness, 211 ff.
  intersubjectivity of, 215
  preservation of in practical reasoning, 213
Chisholm, 17 n., 162
Colour
  as a power to cause sense impressions of colour, 171 ff.
  as primary content of physical objects, 171 ff.
  irrelevance of to mechanics, 45 f.
  primarily applied to physical things, 171 f.
Complex Common Nouns, 24
Complex Object Statements
  contrasted with relational statements, 25
'Concept'
  Kant's use of, 2–3
Concept Empiricism, 55
Concept Formation
  abstractive theory of, 19 ff., 27 f.

Index

Index

PROP, 133
Propositions
    atomic, 29, 119–21
    molecular, 119–21
    Cf. intensions
Psychological Egoism, 205

Qualities
    primary *vs.* secondary, 45, 235
    Cf. Colour
Quine, 77

Reality
    formal *vs.* objective, 48
Reasonableness
    categorical, 211
    compatibility of categorical and
        relative, 213
    intrinsic and derivative, 213
    of intentions, 208
    related to truth, 210
    relative to intentions, 209 f.
Receptivity
    and intuition, 2 ff.
    and guidedness, 16, 30
    and secondness, 15
    and the productive imagination, 7
Referring expressions, 194
    definite descriptions, 122 f.
    demonstrative, 125
    non-demonstrative, 125
    the open texture of their criteria,
        124 f.
Reichenbach, 96
Representations
    general, 6
    of a manifold, 8 f.
    of a manifold as a manifold, 8 f.
    of individuals, 6
    of sensibility, 17
    of the understanding, 9
    of thises, 4 f., 7
    of this-suches, 5ff., 40
    manifold of, 8 f.
    Cf. Conceptual Representations,
        Non-conceptual Representa-
        tions
Representings
    as representations *qua* acts, 32
    contents of, 60
    existence 'in', 33, 60
Representings-in-themselves
    as not in time, 36
    Cf. Appearance

Riemannian Geometry, 128
Ross, 227
Rule-governed Activity
    its analogy to games, 107, 157 f.
Rules
    for criticizing (ought-to-be's), 75–
        7, 157, 175
    for linguistic performance
        (ought-to-do's), 75–7, 157
    semantical, 101 ff., 114, 125 f.
Russell, 63, 79, 122
Ryle, Chapter VI, *passim*

S–assertability, 101 ff.
Scientific Realism, 56 n., 146, 171 ff.
    and finitism, 147 f.
    and Instrumentalism, 143 ff.
Semantic uniformities, 77 f., 80, 114,
        125, 137
Senses, 65 ff.
    esse is *concipi*, 65
    Fregeian, 65, 82
    intensions as sub-class of, 65 n.,
        93
    intersubjectivity of, 65
Sense Impressions
    and apperception, 10–11
    as conceptual, 13
    as explaining conceptual represen-
        tations, 17 ff.
    as inner episodes, 10
    as non-conceptual, 10 ff.
    as particulars, 168, 172 ff.
    as sensory states of persons, 18,
        167 ff.
    as 'states of consciousness', 9 f.
    classical treatment of, 9 ff.
    confusion with minimal concep-
        tual representations, 13–15, 23
    postulation of, 9, 11
    their role in perceptual activity,
        16 ff.
Sensibility, Chapter I, *passim*
    as a faculty of representation, 2
    Cf. Intuition, Receptivity
'Shall'
    as an operator, 180 f.
Shall-statements
    and negations, 185
    as expressions of intention, 179 f.,
        193
    distinguished from 'ought' state-
        ments, 186, 188
    in practical reasoning, 180

Index